YOUR BOAT BELOWDECKS

YOUR BOAT BELOWDECKS

THOMAS REALE
and
MICHAEL JOHNSON

HEARST MARINE BOOKS
New York

The Publisher and the Author do not take responsibility for any of the ideas presented here. Boat owners are encouraged to use common sense when applying any techniques suggested in these pages.

Copyright © 1990 by Thomas Reale and Michael Johnson

Recognizing the importance of preserving what has been written, it is the policy of William Morrow and Company, Inc. and its imprints and affiliates to have the books it publishes printed on acid-free paper, and we exert our best efforts to that end.

Library of Congress Cataloging-in-Publication Data

Reale, Thomas.
    Your boat belowdecks / Thomas Reale and Michael Johnson.
      p. cm.
    Includes bibliographical references.
    ISBN 0-688-08338-2
    1. Boats and boating—Maintenance and repair. I. Johnson,
Michael (Michael Ross) II. Title.
VM322.R43 1990
623.8'223'0288—dc20

Printed in the United States of America

First Edition

1 2 3 4 5 6 7 8 9 10

BOOK DESIGN BY PAUL CHEVANNES

I'd like to dedicate my half of the project to my amazing wife, Elaine, whose support, encouragement, and tactful criticism were absolutely essential.

Thomas Reale

ACKNOWLEDGMENTS

In Seattle we'd like to thank the helpful people at Fremont Electric Company; Doc Freeman's, Inc.; Fisheries Supply Company; Field Marine Company; Dunato & Sons Boatyard; Seacraft Yacht Sales.

In Anchorage: Alaska Yacht World; David Denig-Chakroff and Eric Marchegiani.

CONTENTS

INTRODUCTION

In the writing of this book, we drew upon our combined thirty-five years' worth of knowledge and experience, both in boatyards and at sea, to provide a guide that the average boat owner can use either alone or with an owner's manual in order to perform common repairs and maintenance on a pleasure craft.

In our numerous experiences with the boating business, we've run across a very limited range of useful reference materials. At one end of the spectrum, there are the shop manuals for engines and transmissions. These are written primarily for the professional mechanic and tend to take a certain level of expertise for granted. At the opposite end of the spectrum, books written for the general boating public are not nearly technical enough. Too many books and magazines give little more than a very broad treatment of a boat's mechanical needs and provide none of the details actually needed to perform a job. With these thoughts in mind, we decided to write a book that would fill a major gap in the boating reference market.

What we will cover are the sorts of day-to-day maintenance chores, upkeep procedures, and troubleshooting guidelines that an average person can take care of with a minimal familiarity with tools and mechanical objects.

It's silly to pay someone else thirty to fifty dollars an hour to perform uncomplicated jobs that you can do yourself. Performing these jobs helps you get to know your boat and keeps you in tune with its condition, and that makes you a better, safer skipper. Doing the simple repair jobs can prevent more expensive repairs later on, and can help you avoid the inconvenience and danger of breakdowns when you're on the water far from help.

An important point to remember is that this book does not contain everything you need to know, even on the subjects that we cover in detail. The enormous variety of boats on the market and the ever-increasing supply of equipment and accessories from manufacturers all over the world make it impossible to include all the details about every possible job.

Therefore, we'll usually recommend that you refer to your owner's manuals for additional specific information. If you don't currently have owner's manuals for all the mechanical units on board your boat, make it a point to get them. You should have manuals for the engine, the transmission, all the pumps on board, the head, the hydraulic steering, the battery charger, the stove, the heater, and all the electronics.

If you buy a new boat, make sure that the dealer supplies you with the manuals. The dealer should have them available, or can certainly get them from the supplier or builder. A boat is not fully equipped without them, so make sure you start out right.

If you've bought a used boat, and the original owner doesn't have the manuals, all is not lost. You can usually obtain copies from the manufacturers, at little or no cost. Get the model name and/or number of the item and write to the manufacturers. Supply as much information as possible to make sure that you receive the proper manuals. To obtain the names and addresses of accessory manufacturers, talk to local boat and accessory dealers, or get a copy of one of the buyer's guides, as mentioned in "Sources of Information."

Once you've got a complete set of manuals, don't keep them at home. When you've got a problem on the boat, a complete set of manuals in your living room isn't going to do you much good. If you're concerned about losing or damaging them, make copies for the boat.

You should also have copies of the shop manuals for your engines. You can buy these from engine dealers and distributors, and even if most of the information is beyond your mechanical abilities, there will always be some material that you can use, and as your mechanical skills increase, more and more of these books will make sense to you. The manuals will also be helpful if you have someone else perform work on the engine. Most mechanics don't own every manual in existence, so you might save time and money even if you're not doing the work yourself. If a manual's price seems a bit steep, sometimes in the fifty- to seventy-five-dollar range, keep the rates at your local boatyard or engine shop in mind. If the manual saves you one hour's worth of work, it will probably have paid for itself.

Make sure when ordering manuals, or any engine parts, that you exactly which engine you have. Somewhere on the engine block is a metal tag with all the information you need: the builder's name, the engine model number, and the serial number. Copy all of this data and keep it handy. Some engine builders made several different engines that are similar in size and configuration, but that differ significantly in detail. There are also periodic model changes, so you need to know exactly which one you own.

INFORMATION SOURCES

When you're looking around for dependable information, word of mouth can be quite valuable. In some cases, a knowledgeable boat owner who has experience with certain aspects of maintenance and repair can help you to make intelligent decisions about your purchases, and about which people on the local scene are dependable and helpful.

However, having owned boats for a number of years doesn't automatically qualify anyone as an expert. For example, we had one customer who had owned a traditional Scandinavian double-ended sailboat for years. One quirk about its rig was that it didn't have a backstay. His friends convinced him that it was normal practice to have a backstay and he'd better get one installed soon, before his mast came crashing down. They also told him that his practice of running an extension cord aboard through a porthole was foolish, and that he'd eat up his zincs in no time.

Neither of these practices really needed to be changed, and adding a backstay could have been dangerous. A sailing rig is a carefully designed, fairly sophisticated piece of engineering, and you don't change it without expert advice and a good deal of thought. And the setup he used for providing AC power was crude but effective for his needs, and certainly didn't contribute to the galvanic corrosion of his underwater metals. It is generally good practice not to take as gospel the advice of anyone just because he has owned boats for years.

BENEFITS OF DOING IT YOURSELF

Performing your own maintenance work can be drudgery, it can be enjoyable, or it can fall somewhere in between. And with rare exceptions you will almost always save money.

You'll gradually acquire a feel for what's working well on your boat, what's going to need attention soon, and what's broken beyond repair. You might be surprised at the number of boat owners who haven't a clue as to when things are working properly and when they aren't. While boat maintenance and repair take a certain amount of skill and knowledge, it's not exactly brain surgery. As you begin to care for your boat and its equipment, you'll learn how to diagnose what's wrong when things start to act up, and you'll learn how to recognize what's fixable by you and what needs to be referred to professionals. You'll also be better able to evaluate the work done by others. You'll be able to ask intelligent questions about repair procedures, and be better able to recognize the difference between legitimate charges for complicated jobs and flagrant bill padding.

When you're having work done on your boat, make sure that you and the mechanic know exactly what's to be done, and at what point you wish to be consulted before incurring additional expense. Don't drop the boat off with vague instructions to fix it, and then complain afterward that someone took advantage of you. Get an estimate beforehand, and get a detailed description of what's going to be done and how much it's likely to cost.

While dishonest repair people do exist, the problem isn't nearly as pervasive as some boaters would have you believe. Most often, disputes arise because of faulty communication and unwarranted assumptions on both sides of the transaction.

It's also been our observation that the people who complain the most about repair costs are the people who understand the least about things mechanical. Someone who pays a mechanic to change light bulbs in cabin lamps and doesn't know how a circuit breaker works is the one who's going to complain the loudest when the bill comes in.

If you have any questions about repair procedures, or if you want to learn how to do them yourself, your mechanic or rigger should be willing to show you. A confident mechanic isn't threatened by an owner who wants to learn how to do some of the repair and maintenance tasks himself, and a smart mechanic will encourage it. A boat owner who has spent a few weekends getting dirty and fighting the perennial access problems inherent in boat work is a boat owner who can appreciate the work performed, and with whom it's much easier to communicate. And, not infrequently, once a boat owner finds out what's involved in some of these ''simple'' jobs, he's more than willing to let the mechanic do it after all.

In either case, the owner and mechanic find that they are communicating better, and that misunderstandings decrease as the relationship develops.

Learning the ins and outs of maintenance will also help you to plan your boat's down time. Waiting for catastrophic failure is not only unwise, it's also dangerous. If you can plan to have your routine work and your major repairs done at the convenience of your boatyard and yourself, everyone benefits.

For example, if you closely monitor your engine's condition, and have periodic oil analysis performed, you can schedule valve work, overhauls, and other work to be done in the off-season. That way, your boat is out of service at a time that's convenient to you, you don't have to deal with a spoiled vacation, and frequently shop rates are lower.

Too many people are in the habit of using a boat hard all summer, and when it's put up for the winter, it's a case of out of sight, out of mind. Then, when spring rolls around, everybody makes the same discovery—the boat didn't fix itself over the winter. Then everybody calls the yard on the same weekend, and can't understand why it's going to take so long to have the work done.

PURCHASE AND MAINTENANCE COSTS

Another consideration in buying and maintaining a boat is cost. This is important when you're making your buying decision, and it's important when taking care of maintenance and repair.

When buying a boat, whether it's new or used, consider carefully how it's going to be used. The boating market isn't divided into good and bad boats. Every boat is a compromise among performance characteristics, construction quality, cost, and the demands of the market. While one builder might emphasize offshore, heavy-weather performance and hull integrity, another might lean more toward high-speed performance and creature comforts. If the boat suits its intended use and gives adequate value for the money spent, it's a good boat.

And when it comes to purchasing a boat, it's hard to avoid the cliché "You get what you pay for." There are bargains and good deals, as well as the occasional rip-off, but for the most part, a 30-foot sailboat that costs $45,000 and a 30-foot boat that costs $75,000 are not the same boat with different price tags. Some boats are built with more emphasis on quality of construction, while others are built as well as can be managed within a certain price ceiling. The latter are usually referred to as "price boats," as well as other, less flattering terms.

Much of the difference in quality isn't apparent to the casual observer, but there *is* a difference. Construction materials, attention to design and construction details, cost of installed accessories, and standard sail-away equipment all enter into a selling price. This is not to say that every buyer wants, needs, or will necessarily be happy with the "better" boat. Just as it would be foolish to take a price boat across the Pacific, it also doesn't make sense to pay for an oceangoing yacht for day sailing on an inland lake.

Keep in mind that more money generally translates into a more durable boat, but, given everyone's financial limits, compromises are inevitable. Don't kid yourself, or let a salesperson kid you, into believing that you're saving $30,000 because you're a smart buyer. Go in with your eyes open and keep your expectations reasonable.

When you're looking at boats to buy, learn to look past the obvious and to go below the surface, both figuratively and literally. Check things like service access, headliner details, and the brand names on accessories. Be a little leery of the latest and, according to the advertising copy, greatest new equipment, whether it's an engine or a light bulb. You might want to let other folks be the guinea pigs for new items.

The more complex one of these innovations is, the greater the probability of breakdown. For something as complex as an engine, the time needed to set up and operate a parts and service network can be considerable. Some outfits never do get up to speed, and go out of business, leaving customers holding the bag with expensive equipment that they can't repair or maintain.

When buying equipment and parts, you can save money in some areas by buying supplies from nonmarine sources, such as automotive supply houses, discount stores, and RV shops.

However, don't assume that just because similar items are sold by marine and nonmarine stores at different prices that the marine item is always a rip-off. There are quite a few legitimate reasons for charging more money for supplies that are made especially for marine use, some of them involving serious safety considerations. Where it's feasible in this book, we'll point out and recommend less expensive sources for parts and supplies, but don't automatically buy cheaper items. In many cases, it can be a false economy. It is often in your long-term interest to pay more for a good item that will last, rather than a marginal one that won't.

This is often the case when replacing items that came as original equipment on the boat. Some people have the notion that if the boat builder saw fit to install something, it must be pretty good unit. If your boat is a well-known brand, the original equipment is probably at least adequate for more uses. However, often the items installed by the factory, especially on price boats, are marginal for long-term use, and not necessarily suited to your needs.

When replacing an item of this type, ask yourself how well it has performed and, if it was adequate, why you are replacing it now. If it has served you long and well, go ahead and get another one. If it died before its time, consider a better-quality upgrade.

MARINE SURVEYORS

Before you buy a used boat, most lending institutions, as well as the prospective insurance company, will require a professional survey. Customarily, the buyer pays for the survey, so you should insist on being able to pick the person for the job. It's also not a bad idea to hire a surveyor to look over a new boat before buying it. The survey can point out construction shortcuts and potential service-access problems, and can identify any failures on the part of the builder to conform to industry standards or practices. It can be a good bargaining tool, as well as provide an objective, unemotional look at things that new-boat lust may have hidden from your view.

The problem is that, for the most part, anyone can call himself or herself a marine surveyor. There is a national association of surveyors that has some fairly stringent membership requirements, but belonging to the association doesn't guarantee that a surveyor is either good or honest, nor does lack of membership mean that someone is not. Ask around at local banks and insurance companies that deal with boat loans and insurance policies, and ask for recommendations. Ask the folks at the local boatyards as well. The surveyor you want is painstaking, fussy, and downright picky about details. The surveyor you don't want is the one that all the local dealers love. We know of at least one surveyor who was never wanting for work from the dealers. We referred to his outfit as ''See No Evil Marine Surveys.'' Some of the boats we worked on after he had surveyed them had faults that a chimp could have found but were never mentioned on any survey forms. He was either horribly incompetent or horribly crooked.

In sum, you should be careful when buying a boat, whether new or used, and obtain as much information as possible about maintenance of the accessories on board, and about repair and upkeep procedures. Many of the petty annoyances that result from equipment neglect will fade away, and you'll become a happier, more confident boat owner. Your cruises and vacations will have fewer interruptions, and you and your passengers will be safer as well.

1
TOOLS

HERE'S THE single most important thing to keep in mind when buying tools for your boat: *Don't buy junk tools!* Whether your boat is worth $1,000 or $100,000, whether you plan on having nothing more than a basic emergency kit or a complete set suitable for long offshore passages, you should carve this in stone—*Don't buy junk tools!*

Stick to name brands like Snap-On, Sears Craftsman, Proto, or Mac. Not only will they fit better and last longer, but some are unconditionally guaranteed, meaning that any time you break a tool, they replace it free of charge. You probably won't break many tools, but the guarantee is a good indication of quality.

The perfect tool kit for your boat includes the proper tool for every job, contains no tools that you never use, and takes up no more space than a spare seat cushion or two. The tools never rust or break, they return themselves automatically to their assigned homes in the box, and they never, ever fall overboard or into the dark recesses of your bilge. While the ideal is obviously impossible, this chapter can get you pretty close.

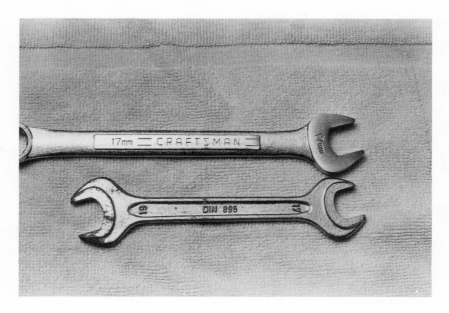

Fig. 1.1.   *Good versus not-so-good wrenches.*

If you're only going to have a basic set of emergency tools or board, think about the word "emergency" for a minute. When your engine swallows an air bubble and quits, there's no wind, and the tide is carrying you toward the rocks, do you *really* want to rely on tools whose only virtue is that you could get a great big box of them really cheap?

Inexpensive tools do not make any more sense for day-to-day repair and maintenance chores. There are reasons why cheap tools are cheap. Inexpensive screwdriver blades have an annoying tendency to snap off or mangle screw heads beyond recognition. Bargain-basement wrenches frequently don't fit fastener heads very well, and they usually derive their strength from bulk rather than from high-quality metal and efficient design. When working in the very tight spaces that are so maddeningly common in boats, bulky, oversized tools can make simple jobs difficult and difficult jobs impossible. (See Figure 1.1.)

Cheap tools also grow rust like Iowa grows corn. First-class tools are usually nickel-chrome-plated, an advantage for life in a hostile environment. Tools without a rust-resistant finish, especially those with moving parts, can turn into solid chunks of useless brown metal on board a boat.

Don't fall into the trap of buying a cheap set of tools "temporarily," until you can afford good ones. Once the cheap tools are on board, you'll either convince yourself that they're not all that bad (even if they are) and you have to live with them, or you'll wind up buying good ones eventually anyway, resulting in two sets of tools. Not an economical move. If you can't afford a decent set of basic hand tools, you spent too much money on your boat!

Buying preassembled "boater's" tool kits is another mistake. You're paying someone else to assemble a bunch of tools, most of them of dubious quality, that might or might not coincide with your needs. And the odds of that coincidence occurring, given the large number of variables involved, is pretty slim.

Many engine manufacturers will include a few tools with the motor. Almost without exception, they're junk. You'd be hard-pressed to find anything in a discount store that's of such low quality, so lose them. You'll want to examine them first, though, to see what sizes of wrenches, sockets, and screwdrivers, you'll need, and to see if there are any oddball tools peculiar to your engine.

The best way to get a kit that's right for you, your boat, and your kind of boating is to start with a set of basic, high-quality, universally useful tools, and build from there. You add and subtract tools as your accessories change and your skills increase, and eventually you build an efficient, tailor-made set of tools, spare parts, and supplies that's as nearly perfect for you and your boat as possible.

Keep in mind that all of this information is subject to modification to your situation. If you've got an unlimited budget for tools and enough room aboard for a complete machine shop, what the hell. Go on out and get yourself a couple of tons of tools and shipboard machinery, and hire someone to take care of it all for you.

However, given the fact that you're reading this book, it's probably safe to assume that your circumstances are a bit more modest. You'll never be able to carry enough tools to cover every possible problem, but with careful selection of some basics, and occasional attention to updating and trimming your kit, you can be prepared for the vast majority of situations.

As you're doing your routine maintenance and repair jobs, any gaps in your tool collection become obvious. You have to loosen a Phillips-head screw, you don't have a Phillips screwdriver, you've found a gap. Make a note of it, and buy what you need ASAP.

As you build your tool kit, you may find that you begin to accumulate unnecessary duplications. Take inventory occasionally and cull out the redundancies. Do you really need a pair of pliers, a small pair of water-pump pliers, *and* a set of Vise Grips®? Do you regularly use *all* of those deep sockets, or just two or three of the more common sizes? If you use them, then keep them aboard. If not, send them home. Every tool that you carry should have to earn its way into the box.

Whenever you install new equipment, check to see if you have the tools necessary to maintain and repair it. For instance, are you going to need Allen wrenches to open the back of that new depth-sounder to replace the fuse? Metric or Society of Automotive Engineers (SAE) sizes? Allen, or hex key, wrenches fall into that category of tools that you don't use often, but when you need them, there's just no substitute. However, if you don't have any Allen-head fasteners anywhere on board (unlikely, but possible), there's no sense in carrying a set of the wrenches around.

THE BASIC TOOL KIT

So, what are these basic tools that form the foundation for the perfect tool kit? Try this set on for size, and adapt as needed:

You'll need both box-end and open-end wrenches in all the common (and a few uncommon) sizes. While some jobs allow you to use either type, many others will require either one or the other.

The best way to deal with that problem is to use combination wrenches. Quite often, you'll know the size of the fastener, but you won't know which type of wrench will work best until you try it on for size. Having both types in one wrench avoids swapping back and forth and searching through the kit. (See Figure 1.2.)

A set of wrenches from ⅜ inch to ¾ inch in ¹⁄₁₆-inch increments will cover the vast majority of fasteners. A set of ignition wrenches will take care of the fasteners smaller than ⅜ inch.

For larger wrenches, it's usually best to figure out which ones you'll need and buy them individually. Sets of big wrenches are expensive, and will almost certainly include several that you'll never use.

Many engines use metric fasteners. Sizes 10- through 17-millimeter, a set of metric ignition wrenches, and a few individually purchased wrenches in the larger sizes should suffice.

If you're thinking that buying all those wrenches is a waste of money, since you've already got a perfectly good "Crescent" wrench that fits all those different-sized nuts and bolts, forget it. Adjustable wrenches (Crescent Wrench is a trademark of the Crescent Tool and

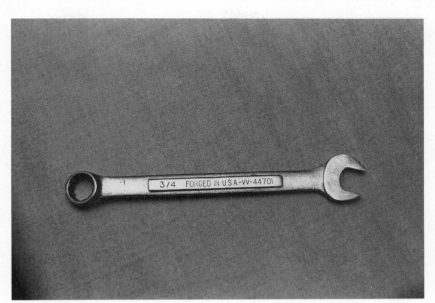

Fig. 1.2.   *Combination wrench, box and open ends.*

Machine Company) are heavy, awkward, and usually impossible to maneuver into tight spots. They also have a tendency to round off the heads of stubborn bolts or nuts because of their imperfect grip on the fastener. They're useful in some situations, and you should include one in your kit, but they aren't meant to serve as replacements for a complete set of combination wrenches.

A set of socket wrenches is just about indispensable. On some jobs, socket wrenches are the most convenient tools to use, while on other jobs, they are the only *possible* tools to use. A ratchet wrench, sockets, and a few accessories, such as drive extensions, universal joints, and deep sockets, make up a subset of tools that no self-respecting mechanic would be without. (See Figure 1.3.)

Socket wrenches are grouped according to drive sizes. The drive size is the dimension of the square protrusion that turns, or drives, the socket. The most common drive sizes are ¼ inch, ⅜ inch, and ½ inch, with ⅜ inch being the most widely useful. If you have a ⅜-inch socket set, you can use drive adapters to convert to other drive sizes. Since socket wrench sets have more accessories and possible add-ons than some makes of automobile, it might be a good idea to look through a tool catalog to familiarize yourself with what's available.

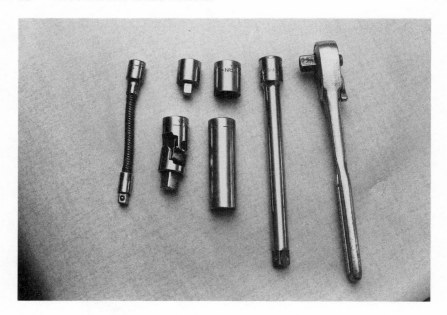

Fig. 1.3.   *Ratchet or socket wrench and accessories.*

Sizes of socket wrenches should closely follow the sizes of your combination wrenches, both in SAE and metric sets. One area where you can save a few dollars is in ratchet wrenches and drive accessories. Both SAE and metric sockets use the same ¼-inch, ⅜-inch, and ½-inch drive sizes.

Accumulating screwdrivers can get out of hand. What with different blade widths and lengths for slotted screwdrivers, different-sized Phillips screwdrivers, stubby screwdrivers, offset screwdrivers, jeweler's screwdrivers, Reed and Prince screwdrivers, and Torx® screwdrivers; screwdriver bits for your socket set, your drill motor, and your impact wrench, screw-holding screwdrivers, and magnetic screwdrivers, you can fill a good-sized toolbox with screwdrivers alone. Obviously, some restraint is called for here.

Start with slotted drivers with blades of ⅛ inch, ¼ inch, and 5/16 inch in standard lengths. Add number 0 and number 2 Phillips drivers and an offset screwdriver, and you'll be pretty well covered.

A good flashlight and a hand mirror are inexpensive but valuable additions to your kit, and while they're often used together, the criteria for getting the most for your money are quite different.

With flashlights, even more so than with many other tools, it really pays to spend a few extra dollars for a good one. The ones that you find at the check-out counter at the grocery store, between the razor blades and the "Space Aliens Ate My Baby" tabloids, are best left right there. Electrical contacts are very susceptible to corrosion, and, aboard boats, cheap electrical contacts have a life span that's measured in hours.

Buy a solid, industrial-type flashlight, and if you can find the kind that has rubber armoring, so much the better. Put fresh alkaline batteries in it, buy a set of spare batteries and a couple of extra bulbs, and you should be set for quite some time.

Hand mirrors are great for looking behind, under, and around things, and they're frequently the only way you *can* see into some places. But here, forget everything we said before about buying high-quality, precision equipment. The mirrors with ball-joint swivels, extendible handles, etc., are fine for use in a garage, but after you've broken a couple of them, you'll see the wisdom in going to a five-and-ten and buying a sixty-nine-cent pocket mirror. For once, cheaper is better!

A hammer will be very useful for driving punches and chisels, adjusting packing glands, tenderizing meat, and so on. The most frequent use, though, will be in loosening rusted or corroded fasteners. Since you won't be using the hammer for driving or pulling nails (let's hope), you should have a mechanic's ball peen hammer, rather than a carpenter's claw hammer.

You want a hammer that has a head big enough to have some authority when dealing with stubborn fasteners, but not so big that it takes two men and a small boy to carry it around. Twelve to 24 ounces is a good neighborhood, somewhere in between a tack hammer and a sledgehammer.

Get a hammer with a wood handle. Wood is light, strong, won't corrode, and you can adjust the length to suit your needs. Sawing an inch or two off the handle will make it easier to use in tight spaces.

A tape measure will come in handy from time to time, mostly for measuring things. You probably won't have much use for a tape over ten or twelve feet long, and it's good to have one that's divided into both American and metric graduations.

The advantage isn't so much that you'll be able to speak metric to impress your European friends, but if you're mounting a piece of equipment and need to find the center of a line or panel, it's a lot easier to find the midpoint of 860 millimeters than of 33⅞ inches.

In the pliers department, a pair of slip-joint pliers, a pair of needle-

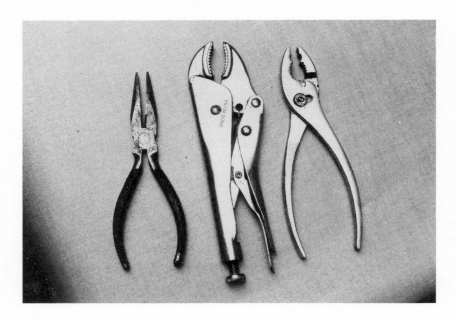

Fig. 1.4. *Needle nose, locking, and standard slip-joint pliers.*

nose pliers (with wire cutter), and a pair of water-pump pliers such as Channellocks brand should do for starters. You might want to pick up a pair of locking pliers eventually (Vise Grips® brand are by far the best), but they probably aren't essential in a starter set. (See Figures 1.4 and 1.5.)

For maintaining your batteries, you should have a hydrometer for testing battery fluid, and a terminal cleaner for ensuring good contact between your battery and cables.

Unless you've got a large boat with loads of extra storage space, a mechanic's metal toolbox will probably be too large and ungainly for you. Options include small plastic tackle boxes, canvas tool bags or pouches, and various miscellaneous containers, preferably nonmetallic.

If you decide to use a plastic box, make sure to buy one that has a good clasp. While dumping your toolbox out on deck provides a good opportunity for taking inventory, it's usually more convenient to do that at your leisure, rather than by mistake. If you choose a metal box, you can avoid damage to your decks and woodwork by covering the bottom of the box with carpeting. Outdoor carpet works well and won't absorb moisture.

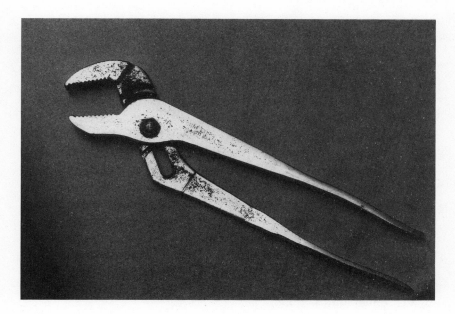

Fig. 1.5. *Water-pump pliers.*

So far, the tools mentioned would cost you a little over $200, and that's paying full retail prices out of the Sears catalog. With a little judicious shopping, watching for sales, and buying the right sets, you could easily knock a third off that total. And, if you really want to economize, you could try to find name-brand tools at flea markets and garage sales and save a lot more.

ADDITIONAL TOOLS

Once you've got your set of basics established, you'll probably want to keep adding tools from time to time, as you feel the need. Following are some ideas on "second-string" tools, important but not quite as essential as those already mentioned.

Get a hacksaw with a rigid, tubular frame. While the flat, adjustable frames can use blades of different lengths, they tend to wobble and distort under hard use. Saw blades come in different numbers of teeth, or points, per inch, with eighteen and twenty-four being the most common. Get both.

To align your engine and to adjust valves, you'll need a set of feeler gauges, also known as thickness gauges. They're nothing more than a set of thin metal leaves in graduated thicknesses used to measure gaps. Get a set that goes down to at least 0.002 inch.

For electrical work, get a good crimping tool to secure solderless crimp terminals to wire. A good combination tool will crimp terminals, cut and strip wire, and might have a small bolt-cutting tool included. It should have a strong joint and padded handles. (See Figure 1.6.)

A multitester, also known as a VOM (volt-ohm-milliammeter) is used for testing electrical circuits, checking wiring and batteries, and testing ground wires and connections. (See Figure 1.7.) (See the ''AC and DC Electrics'' chapter for more information on crimp-on fittings and meters.)

Sooner or later you'll have to deal with a fastener that just won't come loose. There are a few specialized tools that are worth their weight in gold in those circumstances.

A nut splitter works very well, as long as there's room for it over the top of the corroded fastener. You place it over the frozen nut and tighten down until it splits.

An impact driver can be used on stubborn nuts, bolts, and screws. You attach the appropriate bit or socket, apply pressure, and bash it with your trusty ball peen hammer. If an impact driver won't loosen it, sell the boat!

Cold chisels can be used to split or hack off frozen fasteners, too. Just be sure to wear eye protection when using them.

Files are useful for smoothing off irregular metal edges, knocking off metal burrs, etc. If your supply will be limited, get a ''four-in-hand'' file (four types in one) and maybe a round (''rat tail'') file for good measure.

While there are some uses for a pipe wrench aboard, they are rather few and far between. Strap wrenches are more compact, cheaper, and incapable of the damage that an incorrectly used pipe wrench can inflict.

If you find yourself in need of a drill motor, give some thought to buying one of the cordless, rechargeable types. The better ones will drill through just about anything that a 120-volt model will, and you don't have to worry about finding a working AC outlet (a real problem in some marinas), stringing extension cord, or getting a shock when things are wet. They're especially nice for working aloft. If you don't plan on drilling lots of holes in metal, one of the less expensive models should do just fine.

If you do use 120-volt drill motors, or any other 120-volt tools, you should also use a ground fault circuit interrupter. Some AC outlets on

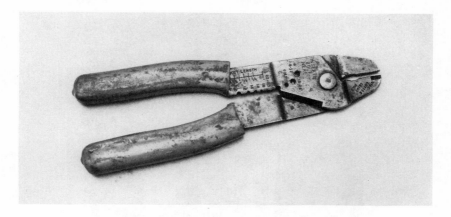

Fig. 1.6. *Electrical connector crimping tool.*

boats are equipped with GFCIs, or you can buy portable models. They're not expensive, and could save your life.

If you plan on doing most of your own engine work, such as valve adjustments, you'll need a torque wrench. The click types are best, although pretty pricey for occasional use. A twenty-dollar beam-type wrench will probably work just fine for you.

ODDS AND ENDS

Miscellaneous tools to consider as the need arises would be: tubing cutter for copper tube; gasket scraper; tin snips; a magnetic pickup tool for tools that love to dive into inaccessible hiding places; razor knife, ½-inch or ¾-inch wood chisel for plugs; and large sockets (especially for keel bolts).

A complete tool kit includes more than just tools. Other items you'll need include electrician's tape, duct tape, Teflon® tape, seizing wire (stainless steel *only*), sealants, a stock of spare fasteners and electrical connectors, thread lock, jumper wires, lubricants, wire ties, disposable gloves, hand cleaner, safety glasses, particle masks, sandpapers (wet or dry), a stock of spare fasteners and electrical connectors, coat hangers, through-hull plugs, cotter pins, and various other bits and pieces.

MISCELLANEOUS HINTS AND LEFTOVERS

Too many boat owners, in an attempt to save space, weight, and money, rely on multipurpose gadgets like screwdrivers with blades

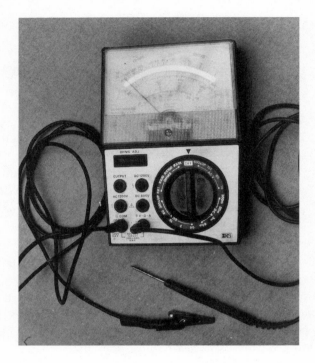

Fig. 1.7. *Analog-type multitester, with alligator clip attached to negative probe.*

that can be stored in the handle, hammers with screwdrivers that screw into the handle base, wrenches that fit "all sizes" of fasteners, etc. Beware of any tools that are advertised on TV after midnight.

Having good tools doesn't mean that you never have to take care of them. Don't put tools away wet, and spray around some moisture-displacing lubricant such as WD-40® or LPS 1® from time to time, especially on moving parts like plier joints and ratchet-wrench innards.

Assembling a practical, efficient, and affordable tool kit for your boat and your kind of boating can be an interesting and satisfying experience. Having and using the right tools for maintaining and repairing your on-board equipment will make your maintenance chores easier, and the easier a job is to perform, the more likely it is to get done regularly.

Tool List: the Basics

- Combination wrenches, ⅜ inch to ¾ inch in ¹⁄₁₆-inch increments
- Metric combination wrenches, 10 to 17 millimeter

- Metric and SAE ignition wrench sets
- 8-inch adjustable (Crescent-type) wrench
- ⅜-inch socket wrench, with SAE and metric sockets closely matching the combination wrench sizes. Throw in a universal joint and a 6-inch drive extension, too.
- Screwdrivers with blades of ⅛ inch, ¼ inch, and 5/16 inch in standard lengths
- Number 0 and number 2 Phillips drivers and an offset screwdriver
- 12- to 24-ounce ball peen hammer, with wood handle
- 12-foot tape measure, with English and metric markings
- Slip-joint pliers, needle-nose pliers, water-pump pliers, and Vise Grips®
- Battery terminal cleaner and hydrometer
- Flashlight and hand mirror
- Toolbox

Additional Tools:

Hacksaw and blades
Feeler gauge
Electrician's crimping tool
Multitester
Impact driver
Punch and cold chisel set
Files—four-in-hand and rat tail
Strap wrench
Cordless drill motor and drill bits
Torque wrench
Miscellaneous tools:
    Tubing cutter for copper tube
    Gasket scraper
    Tin snips
    Magnetic pickup tool
    Razor knife
    Wood chisel
    Large sockets (especially for keel bolts)
    Plug-in AC circuit tester

2
FASTENERS AND CLAMPS

USING THE right fasteners is as important to getting a job done correctly as using the right tools. Replacing a faulty pump with the correct part and proper tools is time wasted if you use screws where bolts are needed. Knowing where and how to use the appropriate fasteners will often make the difference between a repair or installation that will last and one that will only cause problems later on.

Marine-grade fasteners—including screws, bolts, nails, rivets, staples, etc.—are most often made of stainless steel, bronze, silicon-bronze, brass, Monel®, or aluminum. Of these, the most common material is stainless steel. It's strong, corrosion resistant, and easy to find in marine stores. It is more expensive than the garden-variety stuff you'll find in your local hardware store, and with good reason. The plated steel fasteners they sell down at the hardware store have a very limited life expectancy aboard boats, especially boats exposed to salt water.

Stainless fasteners won't corrode except under extreme conditions, and they won't discolor the way steel fasteners will. We've seen plenty of cases where owners have tried to save money by not using stainless

Fig. 2.1. *Bolts,* left to right—*round, hex, flat, and oval heads.*

steel, with dismal results. The steel fasteners corrode to the point where they either disintegrate completely, or, in the case of larger nuts and bolts, they rust and fuse together. In either case, they leave unsightly rust marks, usually in very visible locations.

Brass or bronze screws are sometimes used in interior woodwork. These materials aren't as strong as stainless steel, but in many applications, they're more than adequate. Also, the warmer colors of the fasteners blend in better with interior wood.

Bolts come in a variety of configurations and sizes. The most common types used in boat work are hex, flat, oval, and round head. (See Figure 2.1.)

Screw types and configurations include flat, oval, round, and pan heads; wood; sheet metal (also called self-tapping screws); and lag screws. (See Figure 2.2.) Some builders use screws that are driven with a square-drive tool. The head contains a square hole, and tools are available with interchangeable drive bits to match the different sizes.

Screw sizes are usually given in numbered sizes, with a number 2 being very small, and a number 14 very large. Most of the fastening done with screws aboard boats is done with number 6, 8, and 10 screws. Bolt numbered sizes go from 2 through 12, with larger sizes starting at ¼ inch, and going up from there in ¹⁄₁₆-inch increments.

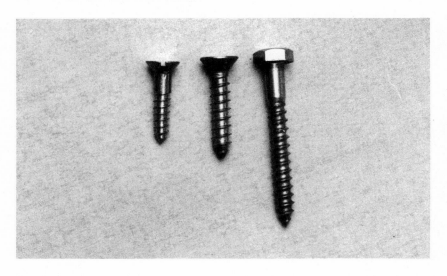

Fig. 2.2. *Screws,* left to right—flat-head wood screw, flat-head sheet-metal screw, lag screw.

Probably 80 percent of the bolts used on a boat, at least in the areas we're concerned with, are between number 8 and ⁵⁄₁₆ inch.

When buying fasteners for repair and maintenance work, *always* buy extras. For one thing, if you need four 1½ inch by number 10 machine screws, four washers, and four nuts, and that's all you buy, you can almost count on dropping one or more of them overboard or into the bilge.

The other point is that buying and accumulating excess parts and fasteners is the best way to build an inventory of spares. If you use mostly number 8 and number 10 wood screws, buying extras will guarantee a stockpile of useful fasteners.

The fastener kits preassembled for the typical boat owner include a pretty even distribution of fastener types, sizes, and lengths, but no one uses fastener types, sizes, and lengths evenly. You're likely to find yourself running out of your favorite sizes in a hurry, and left with some oddball leftovers that you'll have to invent projects for.

All that being said, some of the kits are good buys, often including a convenient parts box for storage. The expense of leftover items can be tolerated, especially if your local supplier only sells stainless fasteners in prepackaged blister packs rather than individually.

The blister packs are convenient for the seller, but tend to be expensive and inconvenient for the buyer. You usually can't buy the exact quantity you want, nor can you buy extra nuts and washers without buying more bolts. And you're frequently paying as much for the packaging as you are for the fasteners.

The most common thread types for fasteners in the United States are Unified National Coarse and Unified National Fine, commonly known as coarse and fine threads. In stainless fasteners, the vast majority of threaded fasteners are coarse thread. This simplifies inventory keeping, since coarse thread bolts will only accept coarse thread nuts, and vice versa.

Washers also come in a variety of types, including flat, fender, spring (lock), and finish washers. (See Figure 2.3.) Lock nuts are commonly used and are available in stainless steel, the most common type having a nylon insert that grips and holds the bolt, preventing the nut from backing off. They're a bit more expensive than a standard nut and lock washer, but provide a more positive locking action. One drawback is that they can be difficult to install, especially over a long bolt in a hard-to-reach location.

When installing equipment with through-bolts and nuts, you should use flat washers whenever possible and you should always use them with lock washers. The washer gives the nut a flat surface to tighten against, and provides additional bearing surface for the nut.

When bolting up heavy loads, especially when installing equipment on thin wood or fiberglass panels, fender washers should be used to distribute the load over a larger area. The extra bearing surface of the extra-wide washers provides an additional margin of safety. For extreme cases, such as the installation of sheet winches on a sailboat or anchor winches on any boat, backing plates should be installed. (See Figure 2.4.) These are essentially large, one-piece washers made of metal such as marine-grade aluminum or stainless steel that are drilled to accept the fasteners attaching the equipment to the boat. They distribute the load over a very wide area, ideally preventing the winch from being pulled off the deck.

Installing equipment involves making some judgment calls, including choosing the equipment, selecting fasteners, and deciding about the unit's function and placement. These judgment calls are products of experience, but some general points about the decision-making process can be made.

When deciding what kind and size of fastener to use for a project, there are several factors that should be taken into account. For example,

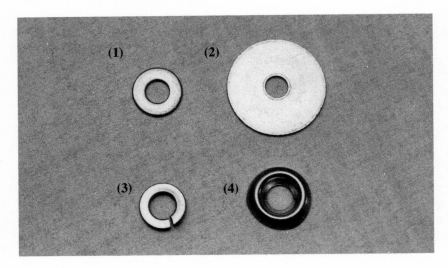

Fig. 2.3.   *Washers—(1) flat washer, (2) fender washer, (3) spring-type lock washer, (4) finish washer.*

what kinds of loads will be placed on the item and fasteners? How large should the fasteners be? What material will be best? Is there access to the back of the panel? Is there likely to be a compatibility problem between metals—will the fasteners be a source of galvanic corrosion?

The type of load or stress placed on a fastener can be either a compression, tension, or shear load. Compression stress is caused by forces that push materials together. Tension stress is caused by forces pulling materials apart. Shear stress is caused by forces trying to slide one object past another.

Most equipment installation problems involve either tension or shear stress, and frequently a combination of the two. For example, when supporting a barometer, the fasteners are subject to the shear stress of the weight of the unit trying to slide down the bulkhead, as well as the tension stress of it trying to pull the fasteners out.

In any installation involving tension and shear forces, the best and safest bet is to use the largest practical through-bolt, backed up by a flat washer and a lock washer and nut or lock nut. However, such an arrangement isn't always possible. In many instances, the back of the panel just isn't accessible. In those cases, through-bolting isn't an option, and you'll usually use screws.

Fig. 2.4. *Backing plate.*

Beware of using pop rivets in instances where through-bolting isn't possible. Pop rivets are used in some production situations because they're fast and cheap, but you shouldn't rely on them to support much weight. For ornamental trim work they're probably okay, but don't trust anything valuable to them.

Frequently, the size of the fastener is determined by the size of the mounting holes provided in the item being installed. Clocks, fuel filters, radio brackets, etc., have the mounting holes predrilled, so their size and placement isn't an option.

While it's true that you can always use smaller fasteners than required, it's seldom a good idea. If the hole will accept a ¼-inch fastener, use a ¼-inch fastener.

Always consider the weight of the item, especially when you figure in the shock loads imposed by a boat crashing through heavy seas. Just because things stay in place when you install them in the harbor is certainly no guarantee that they'll stay there at sea.

Fastener head type is important also. With through-bolts, you've got a choice of hex, round, or flat heads, and screws use flat, oval, round, and pan heads, with varying types of slots as well: straight, Phillips, square drive, or Reed and Prince being the most common options.

It's usually helpful to predrill the mounting holes when working with wood. It's essential in many cases, such as in metal or fiberglass. When drilling holes in wood, select a drill the same size or slightly smaller than the root diameter (measured without threads) of the screw.

A properly sized pilot hole provides a good start for the screw, leaving enough material around the circumference to allow the threads to grip.

If you're fastening one piece of wood to another with screws, it helps to drill the pilot hole in the piece nearer the screw head one drill size larger than the hole in the back piece. The screw then draws the two pieces together, rather than just passing through both of them.

When drilling holes in metal, it's a good idea to start the hole with a center punch to keep the drill bit in place when it starts to turn, and prevent it from skating over the surface. Use a cobalt or tungsten-carbide drill bit, especially when drilling stainless steel, and lubricate the area with cutting fluid, oil, or a spray lubricant.

When drilling large holes in metal, make a small hole first, and then progressively enlarge the hole with larger bits until you get the desired diameter. Also, be sure your bits are sharp. Trying to drill through stainless steel with a dull bit can turn into a career.

Driving screws into fiberglass is different from driving into either wood or metal, the most difficult aspect being the choice of the correct pilot drill size. With wood and metal, there's a certain amount of margin for error. With fiberglass, however, there's one size pilot hole and one size only, especially when drilling through thick panels. If the hole is $\frac{1}{64}$ inch too small, the screw will shear in two while you're driving it in. If it's $\frac{1}{64}$ inch too large, the fit is sloppy.

A good method for drilling fiberglass is to start with a pilot hole just a tad larger than the root diameter, and then try driving the screw. If it won't drive, increase the hole diameter by 64ths of an inch until you get a good, snug fit. It can help to lubricate the screws with silicone, either spray or sealant.

Wood screws won't work in fiberglass because they're tapered, and will drive in until they jam.

When working with fiberglass, use Phillips-head sheet-metal screws. They provide a more positive grip for the screwdriver, and the heads are less likely to strip under pressure than are slotted head fasteners.

When screwing directly into fiberglass, countersink the pilot hole slightly before driving the screw. This can prevent the adjacent gel coat from cracking and chipping, and also provides a good pooling spot for the sealant.

If you use staples for fastening purposes, make sure you use bronze, Monel®, or stainless-steel staples. The standard staples that come with most guns are very rustable steel, and they'll discolor and run rust stains all over creation in a hurry.

Whenever you're installing or replacing fasteners, do so with the thought in mind that you'll be the one having to remove them. This means using only marine-grade metals, lubricating the fasteners when appropriate, and not resorting to playing hide-and-seek with essential items. These precautions will save time, expense, and frustration in the long run.

REMOVING FROZEN FASTENERS

Eventually, even if you follow all the accepted practices, the time will come when you will have to remove a fastener that's intent upon remaining in place. While every situation is unique in some ways, there are some general tips on technique that might help.

The most common case you'll run into is a nut that's rusted tight to a bolt. Even stainless fasteners can corrode, given the right circumstances and enough time, and fittings on engines, transmissions, and couplings are frequently not made of stainless steel.

The first thing to try is lubrication, either with an all-purpose lube or penetrating oil. This works especially well if the corrosion isn't too severe, and if you've got plenty of time to allow it to work. Apply it liberally, and wait. Rapping the part sharply with a hammer can sometimes speed up the process. If you've got a couple of days, reapply from time to time.

An impact wrench is ideal for removing stuck fasteners, if you've got working room and the proper sockets. Impact tool makers recommend that you use only special high-strength socket wrenches with them. Fit the socket to the impact wrench, place it over the fastener, and turn it counterclockwise as far as it will go. While maintaining tension on the tool, strike the top smartly with a hammer. Repeat until the thing moves.

If this doesn't do the job, it's time to get physical. Frequently, additional leverage can work wonders. If you've been using a ¼-inch or ⅜-inch drive socket wrench, try using a ½-inch drive wrench, using drive adapters to fit wrench to socket.

A useful socket wrench accessory is a breaker bar. This is a long steel bar attached to a socket wrench drive fitting. It's rigid and durable, so you can attach it to the proper socket, fit the socket onto the troublesome nut, and beat the end of the bar with a hammer until something gives. Sometimes it works, sometimes it makes things worse, and sometimes it's just a great way to work off some steam.

If you're using a combination wrench, use the box end rather than the open end, if space permits. The box wrench contacts the fastener in more places, reducing the chances of rounding off the head. And, if you've got the option, six-point wrenches, whether box end or socket, grip more securely than do twelve-point wrenches.

The least effective tool for use on corroded nuts and bolts is an adjustable wrench. What these wrenches gain in adaptability, they give up in grip quality, making them excellent choices if you're ever in a situation where you're *trying* to round off a nut.

When a nut or bolt head is rounded off, complications set in. Your choice of tools is reduced, and chances of doing damage to both the boat and yourself increase. If the head isn't too badly rounded, you can sometimes force the next smaller size wrench, either box end or socket, over it. If you carry both SAE and metric wrenches, there's quite a variety of sizes available, and you can usually find one that's close enough that you can force it on with a hammer. Of course, it will have to be forced back out once it's removed, but that's usually not too difficult.

Adjustable locking pliers, such as Vise Grips®, can be very useful, provided you don't squeeze the head so tightly that you clamp it more firmly to the bolt.

Another option is a tool called a nut splitter. This device employs a screw-driven hardened wedge that's forced through the side of the nut, splitting it. Other options include hacksaws, cold chisels, and great big hammers, all employed with quite a bit of profanity.

Screws that are frozen in place require slightly different tools and techniques. The most common problem is a botched-up head, caused by a frozen fastener or by trying to drive the screw with the wrong-sized screwdriver. Cheap screwdrivers cause more than their share of such problems, since their points don't fit the screw slots properly.

If a stubborn screw head is still intact, try an impact wrench. They are usually supplied with an assortment of straight-slot and Phillips-head attachments, and work quite well for fasteners that are corroded in place.

If the head is too badly damaged, you can try fashioning a new slot, either with a hacksaw or a cold chisel. This is a low-percentage move, since the slot seldom conforms well to the screwdriver bit, but once in a while, you get lucky.

Another common problem occurs on Phillips-head fasteners installed with pneumatic screwdrivers and with screwdriver bits in drill motors.

Too often, the operators of these tools just run the screws in until the bit loses its grip. It churns away, rounding off the edges of the screw slots, effectively destroying the screw head.

You can sometimes reconfigure the slots by pounding a screwdriver or a screwdriver bit into the screw head, gaining enough purchase to remove it. With slot- and Phillips-head fasteners, if enough of the head is exposed, you can grab it with Vise Grips® or pliers and back it out.

If all other methods fail, the last resort is to drill a hole down the middle of the fastener and use a screw extractor. This is not a job for the faint of heart or the easily discouraged.

To use either of the two types of extractors available, you're going to have to drill a hole down the center of the fastener, drive or thread the extractor into the hole, and back everything out. Sounds easy enough, but there are a number of obstacles to be considered.

The most difficult part is drilling the hole. If the fastener head is badly damaged, and it almost always is or you wouldn't be going through this, you'll have to devise a way for the drill bit to get through the head and into the body of the fastener. You can either file the head flat, or use a cold chisel or hacksaw and remove the head entirely. If you tried to remove the thing with pliers and managed to wring off the head, this decision has already been made for you.

Once you've got a decent working surface, your next problem is drilling the hole. This is difficult enough with mild steel fasteners, and when you're working with stainless, more difficult yet. Use a center punch to give your drill bit a good starting point. Make sure that the point of the punch is *exactly* centered before you strike it, since an off-center dimple will only compound your already considerable problem.

Once you've got a starting point, it's time to drill. If you're drilling into a stainless fastener, you'll probably need a *sharp* cobalt drill bit. Check the instructions that came with your screw extractors for the correct bit size for the fastener you're removing. It also helps to have a variable-speed drill motor, since you want to proceed slowly and cautiously.

Apply some cutting fluid or lubricant to the area, and go to it. It's essential that the hole you're drilling be exactly parallel to the length of the fastener. If you start the drill off-center or drill the hole at an angle to the fastener's centerline, you may wreck your chances of removing the fastener without damaging the surrounding material.

Take your time, stopping frequently to inspect your progress and to relubricate the hole. When you've drilled deep enough to give your extractor a good hold, stop. The depth will vary, depending on the size of the fastener being removed.

There are two kinds of screw extractors available. One type, such as the Easy-Out brand, uses a set of reverse-thread extractors that are turned into the drilled hole, gripping tighter and backing out the screw as they're threaded in. The other types are rectangular or hexagonal in section, and are driven into the hole. Extractor and screw are then gripped with a wrench and backed out.

With small fasteners and extractors, there's always the potential for snapping off the extractor inside the hole in the fastener. If you thought drilling through a stainless-steel fastener was tough, just wait until you try drilling through a screw extractor.

Once you've gone through this ordeal, you'll appreciate the value of preventing the problem in the future by using the proper fastener for the job, and lubricating bolts and screws before installing them, either with grease, WD-40®, or one of the antiseizing compounds on the market.

Fig. 2.5. *Proper 180-degree orientation of hose clamps.*

CLAMPS

When buying hose clamps, make sure that you buy all-stainless clamps. The less expensive clamps have stainless bands and steel worm gears or screws. The problem with these units is that while the band lasts indefinitely, the worm gear can corrode away, either becoming difficult to remove, or removing itself as the worm gear disintegrates. If you're uncertain about the clamp's makeup, check the worm gears with a magnet. If the magnet sticks, find a different clamp.

When using a clamp, if the hose, fitting, and clamp are all the proper sizes for each other, overtightening isn't necessary to ensure against leaks. If you find that the only way to stop a leak is to tighten the clamp until hose material oozes through the holes in the band, something's wrong. In most such cases, the hose is too large for the fitting it's clamped over. Supertightening might solve the problem temporarily, but using components of the correct sizes is a better solution.

Also, when double-clamping a hose, the worm gears should be staggered 180 degrees from each other to better seal against leaks. (See Figure 2.5.)

3
SPARE PARTS

EVERY BOAT should have a set of spare parts and supplies on board for emergencies. The size and content of the kit, however, will vary tremendously, depending on the boat's size, equipment, and intended use.

On the one hand, an outboard runabout that spends all of its time in warm water and on crowded waterways, and never ventures out after dark, can probably get by with not much more than a tow rope, a bailing bucket, and a few well-chosen screwdrivers and wrenches. At the other extreme, a cruising boat that spends a lot of time offshore or in coastal cruising will need enough spare parts and supplies to be largely self-sufficient.

Since most boaters' use patterns fall somewhere in between the two extremes, the size of the ideal parts kit will vary as well. We'll include a description of a very complete set of parts, and you can delete the items you find unnecessary.

It's important to review your on-board parts kit from time to time, and to replace items that have been used up. You should also examine the kit before leaving on a vacation or extended cruise to unfamiliar waters, or to an area where the availability of parts and service is unpredictable, or different from what you're used to.

If the accumulation of an extensive parts kit seems like too large an expense, ask yourself what your vacation is worth. Does being stranded in an unfamiliar place, waiting for delivery of a five-dollar alternator belt seem like a wise use of your time? And don't think that just because your boat is new you don't have to carry any spares. Older boats are more prone to breakdowns, but new boats are by no means immune.

To decide which parts to buy before cruising to unfamiliar waters, you should investigate parts and service availability before leaving home. Cruising guides, advice from others who have been there, a look at the local yellow pages, and a talk with your engine dealer or distributor can tell you a lot.

Don't buy second-rate parts for spares, reasoning that you probably won't even need them. If you do use them, chances are that you'll be in a tight spot to begin with. And that's not the time to rely on bargain-basement parts. Buy top-quality items and rotate your stock as you go. When you need a tune-up or regular preventive maintenance, use your spares and replace those with new spares. That way, you will always be aware of the shape your spare equipment is in, and it will not end up aging away, corroded, or broken down when you need it.

ENGINE PARTS

Whether an engine failure spells catastrophe or is a mere inconvenience depends on several factors. A sailboat auxiliary that fails when the weather is pleasant and there's a good wind to get home on can present little more than a challenge in sailing skill, and perhaps a longer day on the water than anticipated. Likewise, an engine problem in a twin-engine boat can be irritating, but not necessarily life-threatening, if weather and sea conditions are mild. On the other hand, a boat—power or sail—that's far from home and help and has a broken belt or a burst hose, will need things patched together immediately to reach a safe haven.

A complete engine-parts kit includes spare belts and hoses, a voltage regulator, water-pump impellers or pump-rebuild kits, and a complete set of filters. A case or more of motor oil should be on board, depending on how much oil your engine or engines hold. Some transmission fluid and antifreeze should also be included. Engine hoses wear out from age, heat, and abrasion. They can burst almost without warning and put your motor out of commission in no time. If your motor is buried far out of sight and mind, and if you don't monitor your gauges and lights, a hose failure can do permanent damage, spoiling a lot more than just a vacation.

Check your hoses periodically, feeling each one along its length for soft spots. Purchase a couple of lengths of the proper hose size for your spare parts kit and cut them to length if any short sections fail. Most motors use one size of hose for all of the connections, but double-check this before buying.

Belts aren't so easily adapted to size. The proper length and width for each belt is critical, and a spare or two for each one is essential. When buying belts, don't automatically assume that the belt listed in your manual is the one that's on your motor. A slightly different alternator or pulley can necessitate a different belt, and if a change was made on the production line, or if the boat was previously owned or repaired by someone else, you might need a nonstandard belt. The safest bet is to get the manufacturer's name and model number directly from the belt, or take the belt with you when ordering spares. Some engines use double-belt systems, running two identical belts over a set of pulleys. If one belt in a twin-belt system fails, replace both. Twin belts are sold as matched sets and are cut from the same piece of material to ensure identical length measurements. Belts of even slightly different lengths will cause problems.

Raw-water pumps are notorious for giving up the ghost at inopportune times. As with hoses, failure to notice and repair in time can get expensive indeed. For short cruises, a spare impeller and gasket might be all you need. For longer trips, you might want to have a complete spare pump on hand. If a problem develops, especially if the weather or sea conditions are bad, it's easy to remove the entire pump and slap the new one in, after first making sure that no loose impeller blades have entered the engine (see page 66). You can then rebuild the old one at a more convenient time. This is especially handy if the problem is more severe than a mere failed impeller.

For gasoline engines, you will need to stock a complete set of tune-up parts, including spare points, plugs, condenser, rotor, and distributor cap. A set of plug wires, a coil, and a fuel pump should be carried on long trips.

A diesel spare parts kit should include a set of injectors and a lift pump, or for shorter cruises, a single spare injector, with washers. Most diesel builders sell complete, prepackaged spare parts kits, calling them "cruising kits" or something similar, but they tend to be expensive and include everything but a spare engine block. You can usually assemble your own kit for less money and tailor it to your needs.

Some of the new, smaller diesels require more frequent valve adjustment than others. If your motor demands this, or if there's a chance that you might need a valve adjustment, carry a set of valve cover gaskets.

Oil coolers, on both gas and diesel engines, use circulating raw water, so an entire spare unit should be carried.

If you have a generator set on board, make sure that all of the above-mentioned engine parts and supplies are available for it, and include an AC voltage regulator as well. A smooth-running generator isn't going to do much good if it can't put out any juice.

ELECTRICAL SUPPLIES

Of course, an ample supply of every type of fuse on board is essential. Check your electronics manuals to see if there are any internal fuses you might need to know about, and buy spares. Although circuit breakers seldom fail, a spare of each size could come in very handy.

A complete set of crimp terminals, electrical tape, some spare wire in various sizes, light bulbs, flashlight batteries and bulbs, and the appropriate tools should be on board. Solenoid switches, similar to the units used on engine starter motors, are sometimes used to minimize long runs of large wire, and are relatively fragile items. Consult your local parts store for spares, and have them aboard, especially on long trips. Engine starter, anchor winch, and head are likely locations for solenoids.

Disassemble your running lights and check the bulbs and terminals for corrosion. Bulbs for running and navigation lights must meet federal specifications for brightness and visibility, so make sure that you have the correct replacement bulbs on board for all of your navigation lights. Substituting bulbs not meeting these specs is not recommended, and besides being illegal, could reduce your visibility to other boats. Running lights are infamous for corroding and failing when you least expect it.

Go through your boat inside and out, disassembling all the light fixtures and noting all bulb part numbers. There are many different kinds of light bulbs that are not interchangeable, and a midsize cruising boat can easily require a dozen different types.

MISCELLANEOUS PARTS

Spare parts and/or rebuild kits should be on board for every pump your boat uses, including bilge pumps, pressure water pump, shower sump pump, washdown pump, etc. Also in-line filters should have replacement elements handy.

Some filters, especially for freshwater systems, will accept replacement elements of differing types. For example, you might find elements for your filter at a discount or department store that are considerably cheaper than the ones you normally buy. Before buying them, check the specifications to be sure that the same filtering ability is present. If the size of the holes in the element, usually measured in microns, is larger, the element will be cheaper, but won't filter as well.

A toilet repair kit should definitely be on board. See the "Marine Heads" chapter for details.

If you carry an outboard engine for your dinghy, include tune-up parts, shear pins, a spare prop, and a spare rope for the recoil starter. An inflatable dinghy should carry a repair kit, in case of punctures or tears in the fabric.

Include a spare propeller shaft and matched coupling, as well as a spare prop (two if you've got a twin-screw boat), prop nuts, cotter keys, and keys for the prop and coupling keyways.

Spare shaft packing should be carried. Check for the proper size packing material the next time your stern gland is repacked, and include extra when you travel. You can even precut the material to the proper length, using an exposed section of prop shaft for measurement. If you do so, don't just throw the packing rings into the toolbox. Rough treatment can batter the material out of shape, so store it in a small plastic box or compartment.

A spare burner for your stove should also be included. Fuel from an unfamiliar or unreliable source can cause unexpected problems. If your heater uses glow plugs or wicks, get extras.

If you've got any unusual or hard-to-find equipment on board, carry more than the usual amount of spares. Oddball pumps, stoves, refrigerators, etc., will always choose a time when you're farthest away from help to break down.

Finally, things like spare ignition and door keys, hose washers, anchor winch handles, air horn, switches, and deck fitting keys should be on board and handy for that one time in a thousand when you drop their counterparts overboard.

All of the parts mentioned above won't do you any good if you store them carelessly and allow them to deteriorate. Dry, secure homes should be found for everything, and an inventory list should be kept on board and up-to-date.

A complete set of spare parts and equipment can instill a well-deserved feeling of security when you're far from home, when the weather turns unexpectedly nasty, or you're caught in a tough situation. Keep your inventory current and tailor your supplies to your boat and its uses, and your boating adventures should be more pleasant than death-defying.

BUYING PARTS

Finding and buying repair and replacement parts can be the most perplexing and frustrating problem a boat owner can have. While the opportunities for time wasting, misunderstanding, and frustration are almost unlimited, some knowledge about the process can reduce the difficulties to a manageable level.

The most important thing for people who have some experience in buying car parts to recognize is that the manufacturing processes in the boating world and the automotive world are very different. The system for finding and acquiring repair and replacement parts for boats is not nearly as sophisticated or efficient as the system in use in the auto industry. Boat builders for the most part build only the hulls, decks, superstructures, and some of the interior accommodations. All of the mechanical items, from engines and transmissions to pumps, cables, and switches, are built by other, independent manufacturers.

For example, take your brand-new Seaslug 38, with twin engines, a flying bridge, and more or less typical accommodations. The folks at the Seaslug factory have designed and built the hull and deck, and the boat's interior fittings, including bulkheads, berths, and shower stalls, at their factory. They then purchased the mechanical and electrical accessories from different manufacturers. They assemble all of the parts into any one of a number of configurations, all coming under the name Seaslug 38.

There are usually several engine options, often including a combination of two or more gas-powered inboards, a couple of diesel engines, and maybe a stern-drive or two. Each engine option will demand a unique combination of gauges and control cables, since different engines have varying sending units and throttle and shift control locations. Wiring harnesses will be peculiar to each combination, and other items such as bilge pumps and steering assemblies, will differ from package to package because of space or mechanical considerations.

Also, the builder may offer that particular boat with the flying bridge and the second helm station as an option. Other options can include freshwater cooling for the motors, generator sets, and so on.

With all of the possible combinations, you've got the potential for quite a few different boats, all known as Seaslug 38. So, you can see how easily problems can arise when you go into your local parts store and say, "I need a shift cable for my 1984 Seaslug 38."

Unfortunately, many boat owners expect the parts to be standardized as they are in cars and when the person at the parts counter indicates that more information is needed, the boat owner storms off, mumbling about the degeneration of society in general and the incompetence of service people in particular. If you tell the parts person that you need an eighteen-foot Morse 33C cable, however, you're in business. You'll be surprised at how much smarter your parts people are when you give them sufficient information.

When you're buying engine parts, knowing the engine builder isn't always enough, either, especially with gas engines. A marinizer such as Crusader or OMC will buy motors from Ford or General Motors, and offer differing combinations of carburetors, distributors, and alternators, according to different engine applications and specifications.

For details on engine gauges and sending units, see the "Diesel Engines" chapter. Additional help in identifying parts for gas engines is in the "Gasoline Engines" chapter.

There are several places to go for repair and replacement parts. The local dealer for your brand of boat is usually a good source of information, and if you're lucky, his parts and service crew will be familiar with your boat and accessories, and be able to advise you on your purchases.

In most localities where pleasure boating is a popular activity, there are parts and supply houses that specialize in the more common accessories and repair parts. However, even for a well-equipped parts store selling mostly name-brand equipment, the sheer number of spare parts and supplies available is daunting. Finding a well-stocked dealer that employs knowledgeable help can save time and money. The large variety of parts and equipment also reinforces the idea that you stick with name brands whenever possible. Tracking down parts from some outfit that operates out of a post office box in East Tree Stump can be a trial.

If there's a piece of equipment installed on your boat that you can't identify, or if you can't locate a local dealer or distributor for the item, there are a couple of things you can do. Get in touch with the boat builder, and ask for a list of suppliers of equipment for your boat's year and model.

If that doesn't work, try *Boating Industry* magazine's *Marine Buyer's Guide,* published every year, listing names and addresses of nearly every builder, supplier, and distributor of boats, accessories, and parts in the country. Some of the boating magazines also publish annual lists of the names of boat builders and accessory manufacturers, but the *Boating Industry* lists are much more extensive, and categorized in several different ways, making searches easy. For ordering information, see the Sources of Information section, page 254.

When buying parts locally, especially if you live in an area where there's a lot of boating activity, you'll find that your suppliers fall into two categories—retail parts suppliers and marine discount houses. You should be aware of the differences between the two before you go shopping for parts.

Marine retail stores tend to have higher prices, but you'll generally find that the level of service and reliable information is greater than in the discount houses. They frequently have repair facilities and personnel available, and their help can be valuable when you're unsure about technical specs or installation information.

Shopping at marine discount houses is similar to shopping mail order. The stores usually don't have technical people on the staff, so any problem that you might have with installation or operation is between you and the manufacturer. If you know what you want, and how to install and use it, however, discount stores can be great places to save money. Also, for things that don't require installation or operation assistance, like fenders, life jackets, and dishes, savings can be significant.

Mail-order houses can be money savers, since they buy in large quantities and can afford to sell items at a comparatively small markup. However, there are several disadvantages. One of the more obvious ones is the lack of local dealer support. If you're buying something high-tech like a Loran or radar set, you'll probably save a significant amount of money by buying through the mail. What you give up in this situation is the technical assistance of a local dealer and technicians. It costs money to maintain a shop and to employ and train technicians, and that's part of the purchase price you pay when you buy locally. What you receive in return is advice and expertise in installing and maintaining complex equipment.

However, if you know *exactly* what you want, and are experienced in installing it or know someone who will install it for you, it might pay off to buy through the mail. Bear in mind, though, that if you have problems with the unit or with the installation, your local dealer isn't going to drop everything to rush to your aid. As a matter of fact, if you call up and tell him that you're having trouble installing or operating something that you bought through the mail, he's liable to get downright sarcastic with you.

Another aspect of mail order that's often overlooked is the price of shipping. The price listed in the catalog can look very attractive, but when you add shipping and handling charges, you might find yourself paying pretty close to local prices. And if it's something that doesn't fit quite right, doesn't work, or needs to be exchanged for some reason, you'll wind up paying shipping costs more than once.

Always beware of off-brand merchandise. These things can have some very attractive prices, but be advised that parts and service can be difficult, if not impossible, to obtain. With all mechanical objects, complexity equals vulnerability to failure, so the more complex the equipment, the more concerned you should be about follow-up service availability.

Whether you deal with your local marine retail store, discount house, or mail-order house, be aware of the different levels of expertise and service. As in so many other instances, you *generally* get what you pay for.

4
ACCESS

REPAIR AND maintenance work on boats is frequently complicated by poor access to equipment. Whether it's a routine maintenance job like changing oil or filters, or a repair job like fixing a wiring problem or a leaking water tank, in order to do the job you first must be able to get to it.

There are several reasons why access is such a problem. For one thing, most designers aren't mechanics. They design a boat to sail and handle well, to look good, and to provide comfortable living accommodations. There's a limited amount of space in the hull where they have to make room for a lot of large, heavy, awkwardly shaped equipment.

Builders are also part of the problem. They'll frequently change a designer's specs in order to save money and time in the building process. Also, if a boat has a production run of several years, equipment and accessories will change and be installed in spaces not necessarily designed for them.

For instance, if a boat is designed with a Perkins engine in mind, the engine room and access are laid out accordingly. A couple of years down the line, if customers want the same boat with a Volvo engine, and it will fit into the hull, in it goes. The fact that the engine now must be pulled out to change the oil filter might not be considered.

The other guilty party in the equation is the buyer. Hang around a boat show or busy dealership sometime and listen to the questions that prospective buyers ask, and you'll see why service access isn't a top priority with designers or builders. People looking at boats want to know how many berths it has, how many heads, how many it will seat for dinner, how fast it will go, and what the cruising range is.

These demands from the boating public force boat builders and designers to make numerous compromises. When you have to design a twenty-four-foot sailboat to accommodate five or six berths, a full head, shower, hot water, and other conveniences, something's got to give, and that something is usually service access.

So much for reasons and excuses. Your problem is a repair job in a seemingly inaccessible location. What should you do first? It's important that you learn to completely survey the problem before you start taking things apart. Look at the situation from all angles, and then sit back and *think* about what you're going to do before you do it.

Train yourself to ask a lot of "What if?" questions, such as "What if I cut a great big access hole here? Will I be able to repair it, will it be visible, will it affect the integrity of the surrounding structure, will it cause the boat to sink?"

This approach is easy to talk about but difficult to apply in specific circumstances. When you look at a repair job, especially one that presents an access problem, you're struck by two conflicting urges.

The first impulse, of course, is to just flat give up. "This can't be done, I can't do it, I'd better call someone else, if I ignore it it'll go away." In especially difficult circumstances, this urge can be nearly irresistible.

The other urge is to jump in headfirst and just *do it!* This impulse, except in the most simple or familiar of tasks, is to be mightily resisted. It's all too easy to leap into a job with tools (and curses) flying and find out later that there was an easier and less painful way to do it, if only you had taken a little more time to look at it carefully from all the possible angles. Sometimes the improbable or unconventional approach can be the most successful.

Before doing any major surgery on an access problem, look to see if the builder made the access difficult for structural reasons or just because it was easier and cheaper to build the boat that way. You want to make things better with your modifications, not worse.

Access problems should also be taken into account when evaluating boatyard bills. It's all too common for yard managers to hear customers screaming when presented with a bill detailing six or eight or twelve hours of labor to replace something like a broken two-dollar fitting on a water tank. Let's look at a hypothetical, but entirely realistic example.

Typically, water tanks, especially on sailboats, are placed underneath settees that double as berths. When the boat is being built, the tank has the fittings and hoses installed. The tank is placed in position, and usually secured with base cleats and tie-down straps. Then, the surrounding woodwork is put in place, and either screwed down, glued or fiberglassed in place. Then, if the berth is a slide-out type, that mechanism is installed. Finally, the finish trim, paint, and upholstery are applied.

Now, in order to get at and replace that broken two-dollar plastic elbow, all of the above has to be taken apart, the elbow replaced, and then everything redone. If the job is done well, there will be no visible evidence that a large section of your boat's interior was completely dismantled. All you're left with is a bill for three or four dollars for parts, and $400 in labor.

Providing reasonable access is where some of the "invisible" costs in boat building become apparent. It often takes extra time, and therefore money, to design and install equipment in such a way that access is easy and repair costs are minimized.

OVERHEADS

To gain access to deck hardware and some wiring and leaks, you will probably have to remove the cabin overhead. This is one area where cheap construction methods make a big difference in the cost of repairs or installing additional equipment.

The Esprit 37 is one sailboat whose designers showed uncommon foresight in the construction of its overhead. When this boat first appeared in our yard, all the riggers went down to give it the usual once-over. As you can imagine, people who spend all of their working time aboard a wide variety of boats can be pretty jaded when it comes to looking at new ones.

But when the salesman pointed out the overhead to us, the collective attitude changed. It was made up of a series of padded panels secured with Velcro®. Access was as easy as pulling off a panel, doing your work, and putting the panel back in place. Needless to say, we were impressed. It was as if a group of surgeons were shown a new, improved human body with zippers installed near all the major organs.

However, this kind of construction is obviously expensive, and it's the kind of expense that's bound to be unappreciated by the vast majority of boat owners. So, when it comes to dealing with overheads in most boats, it's back to the real world.

One-piece fabric overheads are inexpensive, they look nice, and are easy enough to install on a production line. They're also relatively easy to take down when you need access. They are not, however, easy to replace. There's quite a lot of stretching and fine-tuning required, and it's definitely not a one-person job. If you *must* take down a fabric overhead, your best bet is to seek the help of a good upholstery shop. This is a job where amateurs can get in over their heads (no pun intended) trying to take care of a simple-looking job, and wind up making a mess of things, and calling in a professional to fix their mistake. Better to recognize your limitations, bite the bullet, and pay the going rate right off the bat. You'll wind up saving some money, and *lots* of aggravation.

An unfortunate trend in cabin overheads, especially on boats built in Asia, is the use of wood panels, screwed, or even, heaven help us, *nailed* in place, then covered with a decorative veneer glued down to cover everything. With teak trim battens and plugged screw heads included, you've got an overhead that's a nightmare to work on.

If you have to remove any kind of overhead covering, proceed very slowly. Look at every detail of the construction *before* you take it apart. Take measurements, notes, and if possible, Polaroid pictures. Look to see what is connected to what, and how it will all go back together once it's all disassembled.

TEAK PLUG DETAILS

If you have to disassemble interior trim work or exterior teak pieces like rails or coaming caps, you'll need to know how to remove and replace teak finishing plugs. These plugs are installed over countersunk screw heads to achieve a smooth, uniform, visually pleasing finish.

To remove the plugs, first sand the varnish from the plug and the adjacent wood. Varnish is adhesive and will hold the plug in place. Use a fine-grit paper, such as 220-240 grit, and sand *with* the wood grain, not across it.

Next, drill a ⅛-inch hole in the center of the plug, stopping when the drill bit hits the underlying screw head. Screw a number 8 sheet-metal screw into the hole, and the plug will back out as the screw bottoms out on the fastener head beneath the plug.

If the plug has been glued in, things get just a little more complicated. You can either drill out the entire plug with a countersink bit, or you can use a small screwdriver. Make a " + " in the center of the plug with a ⅛-inch screwdriver blade by tapping the screwdriver handle with your hammer. *Gently* pry the plug out with a small screwdriver, trying not to damage the hole's margins. Now you can clean out the exposed screw head and back the fastener out. So much for the easy part.

The tricky part is getting plugs replaced and refinished and looking like new. Before you do this, though, ask yourself if you'll have to remove the trim again. If so, how important is it for these screw holes to be plugged and refinished? In many cases, if the job will be repeated, you might be better off with a different arrangement. You can use brass or silicon-bronze fasteners with heads that fill the old plug hole, or you can use stainless fasteners and finish washers. These fasteners can look as good as the originals and take considerably less time to remove.

If you decide to replace the plugs, here's the routine:

With your countersink bit, drill out the old plug hole. This removes bits of glue and varnish that can make replacing the plug difficult. (See Figure 4.1.) Replace the fasteners, making sure that they're snug. Don't run them in too tightly, or you'll crack the wood. Before tapping the plug into the hole, line up the grain pattern of the plug with the grain pattern of the trim piece. Then, tap the plug into the hole.

Place a *sharp* wood chisel flat along the trim piece, parallel to the grain of the wood. *Gently* tap the chisel handle, knocking off the protruding portion of the plug. There will probably be a small raised portion of the plug remaining. Shave that down with the chisel, or sand it flush. Once the plug is sanded smooth, varnish or oil it to match the adjacent woodwork, and allow it to dry.

An alternative to removing and replacing the same interior woodwork over and over again is the use of access ports and panels. While access panels are something that you have to make and install yourself,

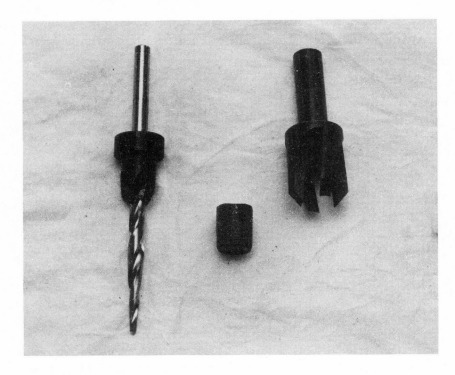

Fig. 4.1.   Left to right—*a countersink bit, a teak finishing plug, and a plug cutter.*

access ports, such as those made by Beckson, and the Pyhi brand made by Bomar, are readily available from marine dealers. (See Figure 4.2.)

Occasionally you'll come across an access problem that really does defy solution. Not that it necessarily can't physically be done; but rather the only possible way to do the job is prohibitively expensive.

For example, if you have a boat that was literally built around a leaking water tank, it might be *possible* to remove the deck from the hull and tear out $5,000 worth of interior joinerwork in order to get at the tank, but it's not a terribly practical idea. In cases like this, you have to be creative and, rather than attacking the problem head-on, look for ways around the problem. Here you could look for places to install a new tank instead of trying to get at and repair the old one. Lockers and storage spaces can be used, and flexible tanks can be very adaptable in these situations.

Fig. 4.2. *Access ports are available in a variety of types and sizes.* PHOTO COURTESY OF BOMAR, INC.

If you've traced a short in a wire that's inaccessible, rather than tearing up the joint, see if you can't just run a new wire. (If you decide to go this route, be sure to shut off power from the troublesome section.)

Once again, this kind of an approach relies on thinking the problem through before you start. As above, when solving a wiring problem, the solution may be more easily found if you ask yourself, "How can I provide the needed electricity to this appliance?" rather than, "How do I repair this particular wire?" You should be open-minded about troubleshooting and look for less than obvious solutions.

RUNNING WIRE

When you're trying to run wires through a long, blind channel, you'll need a "fish wire." It should be rigid and narrow enough to get through with the wire or a length of string taped to it. The plastic tubing supplied with trim tabs is especially good for this purpose. Do not use anything rigid or sharp enough to sever or damage wires already in place.

Once you've run your fish wire, and pulled the new wire through the difficult section, pull an extra length of string through and tie it off at both ends. That way, the next time you need to run a wire through, you'll already have a tag line in place.

Another possibility, if you can't negotiate the wiring run with a fish wire, is to use one of the existing wires as your tag line. After first making sure that you've got enough slack in the wire to leave you some margin for error, and to allow you to crimp a butt connector in place after you're through, cut the wire at one end. Tape your tag line to it and pull through. Then, tape the new wire and a second tag line to the one you cut and pull everything back through. Reconnect the cut wire, and you've got the new wire run and a tag line in place for the next time.

After you begin taking care of some of the routine maintenance chores on your boat, you'll find that your standards concerning boat construction and layout begin to change. When looking at other boats, you'll be seeing things like engine installation, tank placement, and wiring runs with a much more critical eye. Construction details that were formerly unknown or hidden will leap out at you, whether they're indications of care and quality or of slipshod, bubbleheaded planning.

If the engine is installed in such a way that simple chores like changing oil will require excessive time and effort, you can bet that the jobs won't get done as often as they should. A used boat that has an engine installed in such a way that changing the oil filter is a six-hour job is a boat that hasn't had its filter changed very often. And won't have in the future.

This is not to say that ease of access will become your only or even your most important criterion in evaluating boats. But it will color your opinion when looking at boats other than your own, especially any boat you might be considering for purchase. You'll have acquired a skill that will help you to look past the flash and glitter that's so often used to disguise quick and dirty construction methods or serious flaws in a boat's layout.

5
DIESEL ENGINES

T HIS CHAPTER is intended as a supplement to your owner's and shop manuals. Owner's manuals usually cover only engine operation, and shop manuals are written for the professional mechanic. This chapter aims to bridge the gap between the two, without serving as a substitute for either. It's very important that you consult the manuals for your engine before performing any of the tasks we recommend. Read all of the available instructions, carefully survey the parts to be worked on, and ask lots of "What if?" questions.

We'll cover only basic maintenance in this chapter. We won't get into valve adjustment, injector pump timing, turbocharger service, or engine overhauls. Most owners won't feel comfortable digging that far into an engine's innards, and there are some areas, such as injector pumps and turbochargers, where the untrained should *never* venture.

There are a few terminology variations that you should be aware of before you start reading up on your diesel engine. Some of the differences are between American and British texts, and some are regional.

The pump that draws fuel from the tank and delivers it to the injector pump is referred to as the lift pump, feed pump, fuel pump, transfer pump, or low-pressure pump; the individual injectors are called injectors, atomizers, or fuel nozzles; return lines are sometimes called leak-off pipes or lines; the injector pump is also sometimes referred to as the high-pressure pump.

We'll use *lift pump* for the low-pressure pump, *injector pump* for the high-pressure pump, *return lines* for the fuel return lines, and *injectors* for the individual fuel atomizers.

Briefly, both gas and diesel engines take in fuel and air, and mix them together. Pistons compress the mixture in cylinders, the mixture is ignited, expands, and moves the piston down. The piston rotates a crankshaft that turns a drive shaft.

The main difference between diesel and gas engines is that gas engines use an electrical system (coil, distributor, and spark plugs) to ignite the mixture, while diesel engines use the heat generated by high compression. The diesel motor is simpler, since it doesn't depend on a finicky electrical system.

Diesels use a lift pump to draw fuel from the tank, through (ideally) two filters, and on to the injector pump. The injector pump meters minute quantities of fuel, supplying it to the cylinders at very high pressures, precisely timed through individual injectors. Excess fuel is then routed back into the system through the fuel return lines. The fuel injector pump is an extremely precise and complex mechanism, and should *never* be tinkered with by untrained people.

While we're on the subject of things to leave alone, include turbochargers. If your manual indicates that you've got a filter to change on the turbo, then change it. Otherwise, there's nothing owner-serviceable on a turbocharger.

The modern diesel motor is engineered to give thousands of hours of trouble-free service with a minimum of maintenance. While it's a low-maintenance power plant, this doesn't mean that it's a *no*-maintenance power plant, a distinction that many boaters, and especially sailors, too often fail to make. The most common cause of diesel engine problems is the failure to take care of even these few requirements.

It's pretty safe to generalize that there's a difference between the way engines are viewed by sailors and by powerboat owners. Powerboaters think of their motors as their lifeline to shore. If the motors don't work, they don't go anywhere. Sailors, on the other hand, think of their auxiliary motors as noisy, dirty, smelly chunks of iron that live *somewhere* down below. Their sails are their primary means of transportation, and the engine is too often an afterthought. They turn the key to go, and when it doesn't go, they call the mechanic in to fix it. Given the abuse and neglect that most diesel auxiliaries suffer, it's a wonder any of them work at all.

Most diesel auxiliaries suffer from underuse and misuse rather than overuse. Their lives consist of short warm-up times, running under load long enough to get past the breakwater, abrupt shutdown, repeat to get back to the slip. They undergo an oil change every season (or so), and a visit from the mechanic when something goes wrong.

Proper use consists of knowing how to start, run, and shut down the motor, along with taking care of routine maintenance at the prescribed intervals.

STARTING

Starting a diesel engine is usually pretty straightforward, although you should check your owner's manual for variations. Normally, you advance the throttle slightly, turn the ignition on, and then engage the starter, either with the key switch or with a separate starter button. Engines equipped with glow plugs use an intermediate step of preheating for twenty to thirty seconds. Some engines not equipped with preheaters have a modified routine or a mechanical device on the injector pump for use in cold-weather starting. Check your manual.

If the engine doesn't start after a couple of tries, close the raw-water sea cock as mentioned in the section on exhaust systems (see page 69).

It's also important to reduce wear on the starter motor if you're having starting difficulties. Don't crank for more than twenty to thirty seconds without allowing a couple of minutes' rest for the starter. This will allow excess heat to dissipate, prolonging starter life and reducing wear on the entire starting system. It also gives the starter battery a breather.

The engine should be warmed up before getting under way. This normally takes fifteen to twenty minutes, depending on the engine's mass. Because of the high compression ratios used by diesel engines, their internal metal structures are thicker than similar parts in gasoline engines, and it takes considerably longer for the engines to heat through and achieve a stable, constant temperature. Once your gauge indicates that your coolant has warmed up, get under way slowly, allowing time for the motor to warm thoroughly. Don't assume that a gauge reading of 160 degrees means that the engine is ready for high-speed, high-load operation.

A good starting routine is to make a quick check of engine oil, transmission fluid, and coolant levels as soon as you arrive on board. Then start the engine, checking exhaust water flow and gauge readings. Make sure that you're secured to the dock, and run the engine at fast idle speed (under 1,000 rpm). Then load provisions and passengers. By the time you've got everything aboard and secured, your engine will be warm and ready to go.

STOPPING

It's as important to know how to stop your motor properly as it is to know how to start it. Some engines use manual kill switches, and others use electric solenoids. Each has advantages and disadvantages.

Manual systems consist of a cable that's pulled with a T-handle at the helm station, shutting off the fuel supply. Electric systems use a stop button to activate a solenoid on the engine, shutting it down.

You should know how to circumvent your system, since cables break and pull loose, terminal fittings fail, electrical components corrode, and connections break.

If you've got an electric kill switch, turn the ignition switch to the "On" position, but don't start the motor. Get down next to your injector pump and have someone hit the kill switch, making careful note of exactly what your kill switch does. (For a manual system, of course, there's no need to turn the ignition on.) Now, if your kill switch or cable fails, you'll know how to stop your engine without waiting for it to run out of fuel.

It's good practice to let the engine idle for five minutes or so before shutting down. This allows temperatures to stabilize before shutting down the system.

RUNNING

The proper cruising speed for a boat depends on a number of factors, such as engine horsepower, reduction gear ratio, propeller diameter and pitch, hull shape, bottom fouling, and boat weight. Ideally, your boat and engine combination, operating with a normal load and a relatively clean bottom, should allow your engine to just reach the listed maximum revolutions per minute (rpm). You'll find this figure in your owner's manual under "Technical Data." If your boat and motor combination can't achieve the rpm figure listed in the manual for maximum horsepower, you're not using all the power you've paid for. Either your boat's overloaded, the bottom is fouled, or your propeller is damaged or not properly matched to your boat.

Matching the correct propeller diameter and pitch to any one boat and motor combination is at least as much art as science. Most boats come from the factory with an installed prop that's proved to be adequate for most other similar setups. No one prop, however, is going to suit every owner's loading and use patterns, so some time spent with a knowledgeable propeller technician can pay off in increased efficiency, higher speeds, or lower fuel consumption. This is even more highly recommended with a boat you've purchased used, since there's no telling whether the installed prop is a good one.

Somewhere between running full-out and idling along at a snail's pace is the ideal operating speed for your motor. When you're under way, in calm water and carrying a normal load, and the engine's up to operating temperature, run full throttle for a short stretch to determine your boat's maximum rpm figure. The rule of thumb is that diesels are most efficient at about 80 percent of full throttle. So, figure 80 percent of your maximum rpm attainable, and that should be your best cruising speed.

MAINTENANCE

The diesel fuel system and filters are covered in detail in other chapters. While these are probably the most important maintenance items, there are others that also demand attention.

Routine maintenance consists of changing lube and transmission oils; filters for fuel, air, and oil; checking and replacing cooling system zincs; checking and replacing coolant in freshwater-cooled engines; checking belts and hoses for wear; checking hose clamps for tightness; checking electrical connections for corrosion and integrity; and looking over the entire engine for leaks, drips, and other trouble signs.

Your owner's manual should contain a maintenance schedule, listing the proper intervals between services. While some powerboats can put in fifty hours of service over a long weekend, some sailboat auxiliaries might not see fifty hours of use in three years. If your motor is used infrequently, perform all of your service functions such as oil and filter changes, fuel filter replacement, and coolant renewal at least once a year.

If you've purchased a new boat, pay special attention to the services required to keep your warranty valid. Requirements to have work performed by your dealer or by factory-authorized people should be taken seriously. Trying to save a few dollars by doing those jobs yourself and thereby voiding your warranty is a false economy. Even if you perform the maintenance jobs correctly, the factory has no way of knowing that, and may balk at paying any subsequent claims.

If your main engine doesn't have an hour meter, install one. It serves the same function as the odometer on your car, telling you how much use the engine is getting and when to perform maintenance jobs. For boats, maintenance intervals are measured in hours run rather than miles traveled, and installing an hour meter saves a lot of guesswork and tedious log keeping.

Also keep in mind that your gen set use is independent of your main engine use. While it might be more convenient to service all your engines at the same time, if your boating style dictates that your gen set gets twice as much or half as much running time as your main engines, you have to adjust service intervals accordingly. If your generator doesn't have an hour meter, install one.

COOLING AND EXHAUST SYSTEMS

Cooling systems are divided into two groups—freshwater and raw-water. A raw-water system pumps seawater from outside the hull, circulates it through the engine's water jacket and manifold, and expels it through the exhaust.

A freshwater cooling system circulates a water-antifreeze mixture through the water jacket. A heat exchanger cools the mixture with seawater. The seawater is then injected into the exhaust system and overboard.

The benefit of the raw-water system is that it's cheap. That's about it for benefits. Freshwater systems, while initially more expensive, offer significant advantages. The most obvious is that you're not circulating highly corrosive salt water through your expensive, cast-iron

Fig. 5.1. *Exterior raw-water screen.*

engine. The other advantages to freshwater cooling are the ability of the system to more reliably control engine temperature, and the exposure of fewer engine parts to contaminants in seawater that may get past the strainer.

Every system, whether raw-or freshwater-cooled, should have a seawater strainer installed near the intake sea cock. This will remove most debris from the water before it has a chance to get into your water jacket. Check the strainer and clean it frequently.

There should also be a screen or strainer over the outside of the raw-water intake. (See Figure 5.1.) When the boat is out of the water for painting, check this screen for obstructions. If it's removable, pull it off to make sure that there's nothing growing behind it. Also, make sure that the openings aren't clogged by repeated applications of bottom paint.

If your engine overheats, approach the problem logically and methodically. Check the obvious, easy things first, and work your way through the system until you find the cause.

Check your exhaust first. No water flowing out, or a much smaller stream than normal, tells you that there's an obstruction in the raw-water side of the system. Normal water flow tells you that your problem is probably on the freshwater side.

If there's no water coming out, start at the beginning of the system, the raw-water intake. Inspect your strainer for debris. If that's clear, close the sea cock and remove and inspect the hoses on both sides of the strainer. Also, open and close the sea cock *quickly* to see if it's clear. Replace the hose on the through-hull fitting, and proceed.

Next, check the raw-water pump. Close the sea cock, and mark the pump cover and housing with adjacent scratches. Remove the cover and check the impeller for missing or damaged vanes. If it's intact, replace the gasket and cover, lining up the scratch marks.

If the impeller needs replacement, check your spare impeller to see how it's secured inside the pump. Most impellers have a flat side on the inside diameter corresponding to a flat side on the drive shaft. If this is the case, or if the shaft is keyed in some way, you have only to slide the old impeller off. If there's a set screw, loosen it and then slide off the old impeller.

If there were vanes broken off, and you can't find all of them inside the pump, they've traveled downstream. For example, a freshwater-cooled engine will require that the heat exchanger and oil cooler be disassembled in order to find the missing parts, a job probably best left to your mechanic. If the missing pieces are small enough, there's a possibility that they'll pass through the system and out the exhaust, doing no damage. If your engine swallows impeller parts, and you can't recover them, monitor your water temperature closely to detect any overheating problems.

A raw-water-cooled engine can ingest the pieces into the water jacket deep inside the engine, and then you can have *real* problems. There's not a lot that can be done, except hope that the system clears itself without causing any overheating problems.

If the only problem is damaged vanes, or if you can locate all of the impeller pieces inside the pump housing, pull out the old impeller, grease the shaft, and put in the new one. When replacing the cover, it's a good idea to replace the cover gasket, too. You should buy a gasket with each spare impeller, and have some spares on board as well, for times when the cover is removed but the impeller isn't replaced.

To refasten the cover plate, first start all the screws without tightening them. Snug them up in a crisscross pattern, like tightening lug bolts on a car wheel.

If you've got an older boat, check the inside of the raw-water pump cover. This cover is also a wear plate, and in time will allow considerable water blowby, reducing the effectiveness of the pump. If the plate shows noticeable wear, replace it.

Nine times out of ten, the above approach will cure water-flow problems.

If exhaust water flow is normal, the problem is in the freshwater side, where the most frequent cause is a faulty thermostat. The thermostat controls engine temperature by opening and closing to regulate the amount of coolant that flows through the water jacket. To test your old one, pull it out (*after* the engine has cooled off) by unbolting the housing, a bulbous fitting usually near the front of the cylinder head. Remove the thermostat, noting the opening temperature stamped on it, usually in degrees Celsius.

Put it in a coffee can or old metal pot about half full of water. (Don't use a regular cooking pot for this—antifreeze is poisonous!) Insert a cooking thermometer that reads to over 200 degrees Fahrenheit, and begin heating the water. When the water temperature reaches the thermostat's opening temperature, it should open fully. If it doesn't, replace it. If it does open normally, then your problem is elsewhere. Replace the thermostat and the housing gasket, and bolt it down snugly.

Another possible trouble spot on the freshwater side is a loose belt running from the crankshaft pulley to the water pump. Check the pump drive belt, and tighten as necessary. (See below for procedure.)

If you've got adequate raw-water flow, your thermostat and pump drive belts check out, you've tested your gauge and sender (see page 76), and you've still got an overheating problem, call your mechanic. Overheating problems that don't yield to the procedures already outlined can be very troublesome, and some engines have cooling system idiosyncrasies that only a trained mechanic can sort out. Don't continue to operate a motor that's running hot.

Another maintenance item to check on periodically is the condition of the zinc pencils in the heat exchanger. These are sacrificial anodes that perform the same function in the cooling system that exterior zincs perform for your running gear. Seawater circulating through the heat exchanger will corrode the internal metal parts if zinc maintenance is neglected.

Check your owner's manual for the locations. There's usually one in the heat exchanger, and one or more installed in the water jacket. Also, some engines have zincs in the oil cooler and also in metal mufflers. Check all of them at least annually, and replace when they're 50 percent gone. Carry spares!

Some engines, such as certain Ford Lehman models, require the removal of some cooling hoses in order to replace alternator belts. This means draining the coolant, removing hose clamps, separating hoses, removing and replacing the belt, reconnecting the hose, and refilling the coolant. Obviously, if the belt breaks while you're under way, this drill will be at least moderately inconvenient.

The thing to do, then, is to keep a close eye on belt wear, and replace old ones before they break. Then, when you replace a belt, slip a spare one through with the new one and secure it out of the way with tape or wire ties. Now when a belt breaks, you've already got your spare in a place that doesn't require disassembling the cooling hoses.

Coolant wears out, and should be replaced annually. The ideal coolant mix is a ratio of 50 percent antifreeze and 50 percent water. The coolant protects against freezing, boiling over, and corrosion, and also lubricates moving parts.

The typical marine exhaust system injects exhausted cooling water into the gases from the exhaust manifold, through a muffler and overboard. There are a number of things to look for in the system.

When the system is cool, squeeze the exhaust hose along its length, looking for soft spots. Replace any hoses that become either soft or brittle with age. Tighten all hose clamps, and look for evidence of leaks.

Check the alternator belt for wear and tightness if it's driving a pump or pumps. If there are cracks or worn spots, replace it. The rule of thumb for belt tightness is to push down on the belt at the midpoint of its longest span. If moderate pressure deflects the belt more than ¾ inch, tighten it. If it moves less than ½ inch, loosen it. A belt that's too loose will slip, while one that's too tight will wear out the bearings in the alternator.

To adjust belt tension, there are two bolts that hold the alternator in place. One is usually threaded into the block somewhere, and the other rides along a curved strip of metal that protrudes from the engine. Both fasteners are loosened, and the alternator pried so that the adjusting fastener slides along the curved path until the belt is tight enough. When the proper belt tension is reached, tighten the adjusting bolt first to hold everything in place, and then tighten the bolt that's threaded into the block.

When you're working around the alternator, keep metal objects well clear of the terminals on the back. They're usually exposed, and usually hot.

Be careful when prying the alternator. A block of wood or a short length of broom handle is ideal, both to avoid electrical complications and to avoid damaging the alternator case.

One thing to keep in mind, should you have trouble starting your engine: When the starter is turning the engine over, the raw-water pump is turning, even if the engine isn't running. Since the exhaust gases aren't forcing the water out through the exhaust pipe, the system downstream of the water injection point is filling with water, and can eventually back up into the engine, filling your cylinders with water. Needless to say, this situation is to be avoided. If your engine doesn't start after several tries, close the seawater intake. Open it again after the engine is running.

TRANSMISSIONS

The standard marine transmission is also referred to as the gearbox, reverse gear, and reduction gear. The majority of transmissions in use today are hydraulic units, using oil under pressure to keep the clutch disks in place.

There isn't a lot of maintenance to do, but it's important to do the minimum. That consists largely of checking the oil level occasionally, and maintaining the oil cooler, if present.

An important item that's frequently overlooked when new boats are commissioned is the adjustment of transmission detents. Borg-Warner gearboxes use a system that snaps an indicator ball into a series of holes (detents) in the shift lever mounted on the transmission to indicate full gear engagement. (See Figure 5.2.) This adjustment must be maintained, since failure to completely engage the transmission when running will result in excessive wear and an early demise of the gearbox. Recheck this adjustment annually, since cables can be bent or stretched, changing the effective length and adjustment.

Detent adjustment consists of moving the cable terminal back and forth until the indicator ball snaps into place for forward, neutral, and reverse positions. Throw the shift lever into each gear, checking for engagement. If your boat has dual helm stations, the adjustment has to be checked and corrected for both stations.

This is a job that's best done by two people, and with the engine cooled off and not running. Putting the transmission in gear, crawling down into position next to the gearbox, looking at the indicator ball, climbing out, changing gears, climbing back down again, and so on, can take hours. On a boat with a flying bridge and multiple helm stations, this process can get old in a hurry.

If the indicator ball isn't centered in the hole, the shift cable will have to be adjusted by removing the terminal fitting from one end, and threading it up or down on the shaft. The detent adjustment must be checked with the shift levers in each gear at each helm station.

Some transmissions use automotive automatic transmission fluid (ATF), some use motor oil in a separate reservoir from the engine, and some use the engine's crankcase oil. Check your manuals to see what your setup is, and service accordingly. Pay special attention to *exactly* what kind of lubricant is called for, whether it's ATF Type F, Type FA, or a Dexron® II or Mercon® equivalent. Also check the API

Fig. 5.2a. *Photo and drawing showing detent positions on Borg-Warner transmission.*

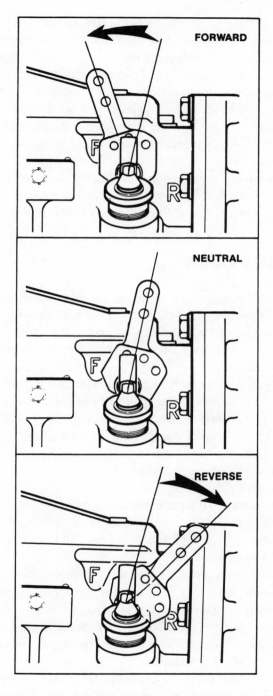

Fig. 5.2b.   DRAWING COURTESY OF BORG-
WARNER CORP.

(American Petroleum Institute) rating for the oil or fluid, to see if it coincides with the gearbox manufacturer's recommendation.

Also note your transmission's oil-check procedure. Most gearboxes use a dipstick attached to the fill cap and marked with the appropriate oil level. However, some systems require you to check the level with the cap fully inserted, and some have you set the cap loosely on the transmission. Also be advised that some manufacturers require that the transmission be engaged in order to check fluid level. Know which way is proper for *your* transmission.

Some transmissions are equipped with a separate oil cooler and heat exchanger. Zincs will need to be replaced regularly, and your shop manual will outline any additional maintenance requirements.

CONTROL CABLES

Control cables transmit the throw of throttle and shift levers to the engine and transmission. When you move the throttle or shift lever forward, the end of the lever moves a rigid wire inside a hard plastic sheath, and transmits the motion to the appropriate lever on the motor. (See Figure 5.3.)

Control cables can't be repaired; cracked or separated jackets, bent terminal rods, burned or melted cable, or blisters in the jacket indicating underlying corrosion necessitate replacement. Don't delay needed cable replacement—loss of one or more of your engine controls can be disastrous. Lubrication is not recommended, either. Excessive friction indicates that something is broken or worn and that the cable should be replaced soon.

The most common type of cable used on pleasure boats is the Morse Type 33C Red-Jaket®. In most instances, controls and cables built by other companies, such as Teleflex, Vetus, and OMC, are interchangeable with Morse equipment.

If a control cable breaks or wears out, replacement can be pretty straightforward, or it can be a nightmare, depending on how much care was taken when the boat was designed and built. With small boats having one engine and one helm station, problems are usually minor. As boat size and complexity increases, so do the number and seriousness of attendant problems.

Unless you have good reason to believe that the cable installed on your boat is the wrong size, always replace control cables with units

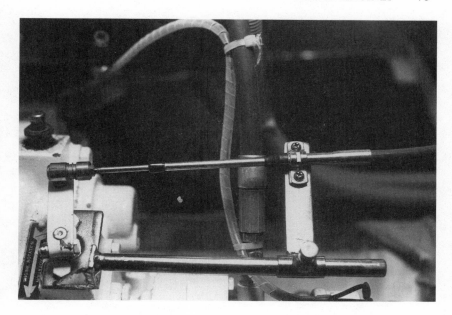

Fig. 5.3. *Typical control cable shift lever installation.*

of the same length. Control cable isn't like rope or wire, where you can just cut off or coil up any excess. If your shift cable is seventeen feet long, an eighteen-foot cable might fit, and then again, it might not. Too much cable can be just as much of a problem as too little, if there's no room to loop or otherwise contain excess cable.

Most cable is marked at both ends of the jacket with the manufacturer's name, the cable type, and the length. If your cable isn't marked, if you can't locate the markings, or if they're worn off, you'll need to take the old cable into the parts store in order to buy a replacement.

When you remove control cables, tie or tape a length of line to the end being pulled out. That way, you can use the line to snake the cable back through its original pathway.

If the shift lever on the transmission or the throttle fitting on the motor isn't traveling far enough in one direction or the other, the cable terminal fittings will have to be adjusted. By loosening the lock nuts and moving the terminal up or down the threaded end of the cable, the cable throw can be altered.

Trial and error is the name of the game, but be sure that, after you're finished, the terminal isn't so close to the end that it's likely to pull off under stress. Morse Controls recommends that the thread engagement length be equal to one and one-half times the thread diameter. (For example, ³⁄₁₆-inch threads should be engaged for a length of at least ⁹⁄₃₂ inch.) Remember to tighten the locking nuts when finished.

A common trouble spot on terminal fittings is the circle clip, or E-ring, that secures the cable terminal to the engine or transmission. These handy little items can be the weakest point in the system, and have been known to pop off at inappropriate times. Even when they don't fall off on their own, they're a pain in the neck to work with, exhibiting an annoying tendency to fly off to really inaccessible places when you're trying to remove them, and to mightily resist replacement once they're off.

But despair not—there is a better way. By drilling a small (³⁄₃₂-inch or so) hole in the post and inserting a cotter pin, you can transform a potential trouble spot into a foolproof, easily manipulated fitting. (See Figure 5.4.)

CONTROL PANEL

The typical engine control panel has a tachometer, ignition switch, engine preheat switch, start and stop buttons, water temperature and oil pressure gauges, volt and/or amp meters, and an alarm buzzer. Large powerboat engines might have a few other options, but these are the basics.

The tach uses electrical impulses from the alternator or a mechanical cable to count engine rpm. Some tachs include an integral hour meter. The ignition switch, preheat switch, and start and stop controls are self-explanatory. The water temperature and oil pressure gauges are attached to sending units installed in the engine block. A few engines use mechanical oil pressure systems, but the majority are electrical. The thing to keep in mind when monitoring gauges isn't always the actual numbers indicated. Since gauges and sending units vary noticeably in their accuracy and sensitivity, what's important is what's normal for your boat.

One way to determine normal readings for your boat and your boating habits is to keep notes under various conditions. When your engine is warmed up and running at cruise, what are your temp and oil pressure readings? How about when running at half throttle, idling in gear, and idling prior to shutdown?

Fig. 5.4. *Cotter pin installed to secure control cable terminals.*

Once you've got a feel for your normal ranges, use thin strips of tape to mark the normal highs and lows on the gauges. Now you'll be able to see at a glance if a gauge reading begins to stray from normal, and take corrective action before something expensive develops. This is an especially good procedure if several skippers run the boat.

This supposes, of course, that your instrument panel uses gauges rather than warning lights. If you only have lights, you need to be more vigilant of fluid levels, belt tensions, exhaust water flow, etc. Unfortunately, warning lights discourage rather than encourage this attitude. It's much too easy to fall into the lazy mental habit of assuming that as long as the lights and buzzers aren't going off, everything's fine in the engine room.

Check your warning lights for proper operation. Turn the ignition switch to the "On" position, but don't start the engine. All of your indicator lights should come on. If not, you've got a malfunction somewhere, such as a burned-out bulb or a loose wire. Investigate and repair.

When a gauge, light, or alarm indicates that there's a problem, there are two possibilities—either there really is a problem, or there's something wrong with the indicator system.

If the indicator system is working properly and you really do have the problem, it will obviously need to be taken care of immediately. If there's something wrong with the indicator, the need for repair is less pressing, but should still be taken care of as soon as it's convenient. A broken oil pressure gauge is not as serious a problem as the loss of engine oil pressure. Until you investigate, however, you won't know which problem you've got.

If your system indicates a problem, analyze the circumstances. If you've been running for a while, and your water temperature slowly rises to the point where your gauge indicates a reading outside the normal range, you've probably got a problem with your cooling system.

However, if you come down to the boat, turn on the ignition switch for the first time that day, and the temp gauge immediately jumps up to indicate 240 degrees, you've obviously got a malfunction in the indicator system. There are basically three things that can be at fault in a gauge, warning light, or alarm that's not working. Either the instrument has failed, the sending unit has failed, or the wiring is faulty.

Finding the sending unit can be a problem. Most manuals don't identify them, and there's almost no information available on their maintenance, or even their existence. The most common sending units installed on engines are for water temperature and oil pressure. They are typically threaded into the engine block, and have terminals at the top to attach a wire connecting it to the instrument. (See Figure 5.5.)

The water temperature unit usually is located near the thermostat housing, and the oil pressure unit is somewhere farther down on the block, but of course there are exceptions. To see which is which, you can compare the color of the wires from the sender with the color of the wires attached to the instruments. If your builder has saved money by using the same color of wire throughout the boat, you'll have to remove the units and see whether the bottom of the unit is covered with antifreeze or oil (oil is black, antifreeze isn't).

Checking instrument and sender functions is easy on twin-engine boats. You've got identical setups at hand for exchanging parts and investigating anything that looks or acts unusual. For example, say you go down to your Seaslug 30 on a Saturday and crank up the motors for a day trip. Right away, being a vigilant, conscientious boat owner, you notice that the oil pressure gauge on your port engine is reading 60 pounds or so, and the gauge on the starboard engine reads 0. Now, the last time you were out, both gauges read normal throughout your

Fig. 5.5. *Water temperature and oil pressure sending units.*

trip. Have you all of a sudden lost your oil pump, resulting in a reading of 0, or is there something wrong with the indicator system?

Chances are that it's in the gauge, sender, or wiring, since oil pumps don't *usually* just decide to quit one day. It's more normal for them to wear out gradually, on the infrequent occasions when they wear out at all.

If there's easy access to the back of your instrument panel, have a look back there and see if any wires have worked loose or been broken off. If not, take a look at the engine.

First, check the oil level on the suspect engine. No oil will equal no oil pressure every time! If you have adequate oil, remove the oil pressure sending units and switch them between engines. Start the motors, and check the gauges. About eight times out of ten, you'll find that the suspect gauge reading will have switched as well. You've just discovered a bad sending unit.

If the 0 reading doesn't change when you reverse senders, you've either got a bad wire, a bad gauge, or your oil pressure really is 0! Now, the troubleshooting procedure is the same as for a single-engine boat.

First, check the wiring. You'll need to test the wire for continuity. Detach the wire from the sending unit and from the gauge. Run a length of jumper wire from one end, leading it to the other end, close enough for you to attach both probes from the omhmeter. Set your multitester to "Ohms," and check for resistance. It should be near 0. If it reads ∞, there's a break somewhere in the wire, and it needs to be repaired or replaced.

Finally, you're left with two possibilities. Either the gauge is broken, and your oil pressure is fine, or your gauge is right and you've got no oil pressure.

The only way to know for sure is to check the pressure by an alternate method. Most auto parts stores sell manual oil pressure gauges. These consist of a threaded fitting, a gauge, and a connecting tube. Thread the sender into your engine block, using a bushing or adapter if necessary. (Take your suspect sender with you to the auto parts store to compare sender diameters and threads. If the parts shop doesn't have the appropriate bushing or adapter, check with a plumbing supply house.)

If the gauge shows a normal reading when the engine is running, replace the faulty gauge. If it still shows no oil pressure, call your mechanic before running your engine again.

The same basic procedure can be used for a suspect water temperature reading. With a raw-water-cooled engine, remove the water temp sender, thread a manual gauge into the hole, and check the reading.

With a freshwater-cooled motor, remove the cap from the expansion tank and check the temperature there with a thermometer that reads in the 200- to 300-degrees-Fahrenheit range.

While we're on the subject of sending units, there are a few things that you should know before you go out looking for a replacement.

Sending units are matched to the instruments, not to the boat or the engine. They also differ for gauges and warning lights, for systems with and without alarm buzzers, for single and dual helm stations, etc. For instance, a Seaslug 30 with GM engines will use one sender for

VDO single-station gauges, another for Stewart-Warner gauges with dual stations, and still another for a builder-installed warning light.

Diesel engine maintenance is important, but the procedures and practices we've outlined here aren't hopelessly complex. If you haven't done any of your own work before, start out with the jobs that seem uncomplicated and work your way up to the more challenging jobs.

Keep records of what jobs you've performed and when, and make notes on part numbers, dealer's names, and other important information. Also note any changes made in the engine's original equipment. These notes will prove to be invaluable the second time you have to perform a maintenance chore or make a repair.

Drawings and diagrams can also be very useful if you get started on a job, get in over your head, and have to call in a mechanic. If he doesn't have to start from absolute scratch, it will save you time and money.

Before taking apart or removing things like carburetors and alternators, mark the wires, hoses, etc. White electrical tape is good for this, since you can write on it with ball-point pen, and stick it almost anywhere. It's also useful for leaving notes on ignition switches and on equipment under repair.

For especially complex jobs, a Polaroid picture can save hours of grief when reassembling things, especially if there's a long lag time between taking things apart and putting them back together. Frequently, things seem to make perfect sense as we're taking them apart, but after having everything disassembled and lying in a heap, details are forgotten.

You'll eventually acquire a familiarity with your engine and associated systems that will enable you to maintain your engine and to troubleshoot and repair a wide variety of mechanical problems.

6

DIESEL FUEL SYSTEMS

L AWS AND guidelines covering the installation of gas and diesel fuel systems differ greatly. Gasoline, being more volatile and flammable, is subject to more and stricter laws than is diesel fuel.

For boats with inboard gasoline engines, the Coast Guard has adopted specifications for the installation of fuel and electrical systems. These specifications are federal law and their standards must be met in order for a gas-powered boat to be sold in the United States.

Boats with diesel engines are another matter. As long as a diesel-powered boat does not carry passengers for hire, its fuel and electrical systems do not have to meet federal specifications. However, the National Fire Protection Association (NFPA) and the American Boat and Yacht Council (ABYC) publish *guidelines* for fuel and electrical systems, engines, hulls, etc., that outline generally accepted industry practices. These are the standards by which most marine surveyors determine the safety, value, and insurability of small craft.

Most boat builders follow these recommendations closely, but since they are not required by law to do so, they have considerable latitude in determining which practices they'll follow and which ones they won't. It's a good idea to be familiar with the standards, especially if you've purchased a used boat. Most boat owners and, unfortunately, many boatyards are unfamiliar with them, so copies of the NFPA and/ or the ABYC standards make worthwhile additions to your on-board reference library. Addresses for these organizations are listed in the Sources of Information.

FUEL TANKS

Fuel tanks in powerboats are fairly standard in size, shape, and location, while sailboat tanks are frequently designed to fit into odd-shaped compartments. Their locations are varied, with the most common places being under quarterberths, settees, V-berths, and cabin soles. Access is usually limited, and in some cases nearly nonexistent, but surrounding panels and bulkheads are sometimes removable. You may need power tools, pry bars, and a sizable collection of swear words, but then we never said this was going to be easy.

Inspect the tank and fittings regularly, especially just after the tank has been filled, to check for leaks while the fittings are under stress. Even if the tank is made of a supposedly corrosionproof material, regular, careful inspection of the system is prudent. Inspection should include hoses and clamps, tank hold-downs, fuel gauge sending unit seal, fuel shutoff valve, feed and return line fittings, grounding of the tank and deck fitting, and general tank condition.

If your tank was designed to fit snugly into its own compartment, additional hold-down devices are usually unnecessary. However, if the tank is sharing a compartment with other equipment, there will be some means used to secure it against movement. Typically, this system will consist of cleats around the tank base that keep it from sliding and some sort of strapping material to hold it down.

If metal strapping material is used, it should be padded to prevent chafe and metal-to-metal contact. The padding should be inspected regularly and replaced when worn.

The fuel fill tube is usually a 1½-inch flexible hose, secured to the tank and to the deck fill fitting with hose clamps. There should be two clamps at each end of the hose, and the worm gears (tightening screws) for each pair should be positioned opposite each other. (See Figure 2.5.)

The clamps should be snugged down firmly, but please, resist the temptation to put a huge wrench on your screwdriver and tighten the screws until hose material oozes out through the holes in the clamp. Hose clamp care is covered in the "Fasteners and Clamps" chapter, on page 41.

Make sure that the metal fuel tank *and* the deck fill fitting are grounded. (If your tank is made of fiberglass, no grounding is possible or necessary. Just check your fill fitting.) This will prevent sparks caused by static electricity buildup when filling the tank.

To check grounding, get out your VOM and set it on ohms, as described in the "AC and DC Electrics" chapter (see page 130).

Touch one probe to the tank, and the other to a good ground. You should get a reading of less than 100 ohms. (The Coast Guard fuel standard requires that "each metallic component of the fuel fill system and fuel tank which is in contact with fuel must be statically grounded so that the resistance between the ground and each metallic component of the fuel fill system and fuel tank is less than 100 ohms.")

Next, check the metal body of the deck fill fitting. The reading should be the same. If not, there's a fault in your grounding system. The most common problem is that the grounding wire attachment is either loose or corroded. Tighten the connection, replace the terminals, or replace the ground wire, as necessary.

The tank vent is usually a ¾-inch hose that runs from the tank to a fitting that spills fumes and excess fuel overboard. It's very important that this line have no valleys or low spots in its run, and it should form an upward loop just before it reaches the through-hull fitting. If water or fuel gets into the hose, it will collect in low spots and block the vent. If the vent is clogged, fumes won't escape overboard, and filling the tank will be difficult, if not impossible, because of built-up air pressure.

If you have a fuel gauge included with your engine instruments, it will be connected to a sending unit in the tank. The sending unit consists of a float attached to an electrical device that measures resistance, and the whole works is inserted into the tank through a hole in the top. It is typically secured to the tank with five self-tapping screws fastening the flange to the tank, and sealed with a gasket. (See Figure 6.1.)

If you discover a leak at the sending unit during one of your regular full-tank inspections, try the easiest remedy first. Tighten the screws firmly, but carefully. Overtightening can distort the gasket material or strip the screw threads, so take it easy. Start with one fastener, then tighten every other one in a clockwise rotation until all five are done. Take up a little more slack each time around until all the screws are

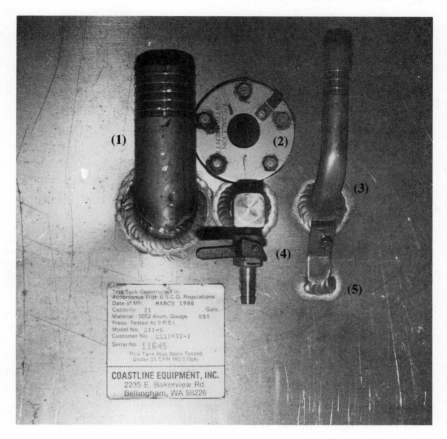

Fig. 6.1. *Fuel tank fittings: (1) fill pipe, (2) sending unit, (3) vent fitting, (4) fuel pickup and shutoff valve, (5) grounding tab.*

evenly and firmly secured. If the leak persists, you probably need a new gasket.

Run some fuel out of the tank before removing the sending unit. Next, with a pencil or a scratch awl, mark a spot on the sending unit flange opposite another mark on the tank. The five-hole pattern looks symmetrical, but isn't. If the unit isn't replaced in exactly the same position in which it was removed, it *will* leak.

Fuel tanks are made of stainless steel, aluminum, black iron, or fiberglass. (If you bought a used boat that was converted from gas to diesel power and you have an internally galvanized tank, read no further. You've got a bigger problem than this chapter will be able to solve. Galvanized steel is *not* compatible with diesel fuel. Seek professional help soon!)

Black iron is the only tank material that will require much external maintenance. (If you're unsure whether your tank is made of iron, check it with a magnet.) Inspect it regularly and take care of any signs of rust or corrosion promptly. Iron tanks are usually painted with a rust-resistant paint, but the protection is far from perfect. If the paint is chipped or worn away, rust will soon gain a foothold.

Blisters in the paint indicate rust. Scrape, prime, and repaint the affected area. Inspect closely any areas that are subject to exposure to seawater. Tanks that are located in engine compartments can be very susceptible to corrosion, owing to temperature changes, condensation, and spray thrown off because of leaky packing glands.

Tank tops can be a trouble spot when water collects and forms puddles. Also, tanks that are in lazarettes can take a beating from having gear thrown on them, and from the dampness that's usually present.

FUEL LINES

The fuel line runs from the pickup tube on the tank, through an emergency shutoff valve, and in turn to the fuel filters, to the lift pump, the injector pump, and the injectors. The return lines take excess fuel from the individual injectors back into the system at the filter or into the tank.

In older boats, these lines are usually made of copper tubing, but many builders now use reinforced rubber hose. If your boat does have copper lines, the final foot or so of fuel line at the engine should be flexible hose, suitable for use with diesel fuel. This isolates engine movement and vibration from the fixed copper line, preventing metal fatigue. Check this feature on both feed and return lines.

Inspect copper fuel lines regularly for corrosion. The first sign of corrosion on copper is a green film, which usually indicates exposure to seawater or battery acid. Clean the copper with a solution of baking soda and water and keep an eye on it. If the problem reoccurs, you'll probably have to reroute the line to keep it out of trouble. Don't even *think* about wrapping the line with tape; that just hides the problem, and will make matters worse by trapping moisture.

When rubber fuel lines pass through a bulkhead or panel, it's important that there be some sort of antichafe material present, either

Fig. 6.2.   *Chafing gear protecting fuel lines that pass through a bulkhead.*

wrapped around the line or permanently secured to the panel, to prevent the hose from wearing through. A layer or two of rubber or vinyl hose works well. (See Figure 6.2.)

Whether the lines are made of copper or rubber, they should be supported by corrosion-resistant hangers or clips to prevent movement. Long runs of fuel line should have hangers installed at fourteen- to eighteen-inch intervals.

The feed line that runs from the tank to the engine should have a shutoff valve at the tank end, and if the tank is more than twelve feet from the engine, there should be another one at the engine end. During inspections, check to make sure that the valves operate freely.

MULTITANK SYSTEMS

Many twin-engine boats use a two-fuel-tank arrangement that facilitates tank location and load balancing. On many of these systems, the arrangement is pretty straightforward: The port tank feeds the port engine, and the starboard tank feeds the starboard engine. This is simple enough.

Where complications can set in is with the addition of a generator that draws from one tank. Running the gen set for prolonged periods can create an unbalanced load, or cause one of the engines to run out of fuel long before the other one does.

Another potential complication is a contaminated tank. Frequent causes include taking on contaminated fuel, having a "helpful" passenger fill one of the fuel tanks with water while you're not looking, or leaving a fuel cap off after fueling and loading the tank up with spray or rainwater.

To isolate the fouled tank and draw fuel for your main and generator engines from the other tank, you need a crossover line and valve system. This is the simplest and most common setup, but variations are possible, including the addition of more tanks, gen sets, etc. If you have such a system, don't leave the crossover valve open all the time, as many boaters do. Leaving it open only sabotages its function of isolating the different fuel supplies.

Many systems also include valves that enable you to direct the flow from the fuel return lines to different tanks. Follow your system from end to end, and make a diagram of it to help you understand every different combination of open and closed valves. If an emergency arises, you'll be able to isolate and contain any contamination.

FUEL PUMPS

While a few engine manufacturers supply electric lift pumps with their motors, most use mechanical pumps. Electric pumps can be more convenient when bleeding the fuel system, but they're also more complex and more susceptible to breakdown.

If your engine is installed in such a way that bleeding is particularly difficult or time-consuming, you might want to consider adding an electric priming pump to supplement the mechanical one. Although details are beyond the scope of this book, the installation is not especially complex. Such a system would allow you to use the electric pump for bleeding, and as a backup should the mechanical one fail. Consult your local mechanic for details.

As the heart of a diesel engine, the fuel injector pump is the most critical part of the system. It is engineered and built to astonishingly precise tolerances, and is very intolerant of contaminants like dirt and water. Its internal parts should *never* be tinkered with by untrained people. The pump measures tiny amounts of fuel and supplies it to the injectors at exact intervals, and any damage is likely to be very costly in terms of engine performance and repair.

FUEL SYSTEM BLEEDING

Whenever any part of the fuel system between the tank and the injector pump has been disconnected, when there's a leak in the fuel line, or when the fuel tank has been run dry, air gets into the fuel line. Air can also get into the system if the tank is low on fuel, the engine is running, and the boat is rolling severely or is heeled hard over. Once air gets into the system, you'll have to bleed it out.

It would be hard to overemphasize the importance of knowing how to bleed air out of your fuel system. All it takes is a small bubble of air to completely disable a diesel engine, and no amount of cranking, swearing, or beating will get it restarted, so no responsible boat owner should ever leave the dock without the knowledge and the tools necessary to perform this basic maintenance task. The only way to get a diesel engine going after it has swallowed an air bubble is to follow the proper bleeding procedure, carefully and in sequence.

There are so many different kinds of injector pumps and bleeding methods that it's impossible to cover them all here. That's why it is very important that you read and understand your owner's manual and the bleeding procedure for your engine. Better yet, get the shop manual for your motor. It'll have much more useful information than an owner's manual, and should be a part of every boat owner's *on-board* equipment.

Although bleeding procedures vary, some general points can be made. Follow directions for the procedure exactly *and in sequence*. Taking shortcuts will only result in frustration.

The usual sequence starts at the engine fuel filter, then goes to the injector pump and, in some cases, to the injectors themselves. Generally, you'll loosen a bleed screw on the fuel filter and operate the lift pump until a stream of fuel free of air bubbles flows out. (Electric lift pumps are usually activated by turning on the ignition key, and mechanical pumps are operated by priming levers.) Then you'll close that screw and do the same thing with one or more bleed screws on the injector pump. Again, there are almost as many variations to this operation as there are engines, so it's crucial that you read and follow *in sequence* the proper procedure outlined in your engine manual.

When loosening bleed screws, back them out just enough to send a thin stream of fuel out when you operate the lift pump, usually no more than a turn or two. Something to watch out for when bleeding, especially if you have an electric pump, is the tendency for fuel to squirt out in a stream that has a real affinity for soaking shirt sleeves.

If your engine has a mechanical lift pump, it's possible that you'll get no pumping action when you operate the priming lever. This happens when the pump's cam is centered on its high point. Bump the ignition and turn the engine over a partial turn—the pump should then operate properly.

MISCELLANEOUS FUEL SYSTEM HINTS

Keep your tank full, especially if the boat's going to be laid up for any length of time, and especially in cold weather. This reduces condensation and water buildup in the fuel.

If you need to carry fuel in cans or auxiliary tanks, make sure that they're as clean and dry as possible before you put any fuel in them. Don't make life any tougher for your filters than you have to.

The most common type of diesel fuel sold for use in boats is number 2 diesel. Unless you're a frequent cold-weather boater, this is probably the only fuel grade you'll ever use. However, below temperatures of about 32 degrees Fahrenheit, number 2 fuel becomes thick and waxy and can clog your fuel system. If you'll be doing much cold-weather boating, give your local fuel distributors a call and ask about their recommendations for cold-weather fuels and/or additives. For boats that spend a lot of time running in cold climates, a fuel-line heater is a good investment, especially if you have diesel-powered accessories such as stoves and cabin heaters.

One problem of diesel fuels is that, given the right conditions, bacteria can grow inside fuel tanks, producing a slime that clogs filters, reduces fuel flow and filter effectiveness, and generally creates a gooey, sloppy mess. Growth is slow under normal conditions, but if the boat is idle for any length of time, and if you've got just the right amount of water suspended in your fuel, you've got great conditions for producing your own little science project.

Obviously, winter is a good time for this, but a few precautions can head off the problem. Before laying your boat up, fill the tank to reduce condensation, and add a biocide to the fuel. Biocides are fuel additives that prevent bacterial growth in the fuel, and are usually available from fuel distributors and engine parts houses.

Because of the way that sailboat engines are typically used, another problem presents itself. Diesel fuels vary in the amounts of sulfur residues present, and a high sulfur content combined with relatively cold cylinder walls causes the sulfur to condense, creating sulfuric acid, which accumulates in the crankcase, and eats away at the crankshaft and bearings. When a diesel engine is run at idling speed without load, or when it is run in short spurts without being thoroughly warmed up, sulfuric acid formation is accelerated. (Diesel motors are heftier than gasoline engines, and the thicker metal components take more time to warm through.)

There are several ways to avoid this problem. You could burn only low-sulfur fuel, you could run your engine for longer periods of time and only under load, or you could change your lube oil more often.

The first solution is impractical. Most boaters have a limited choice of fuel brands, and getting objective answers to questions about sulfur content from your local fuel dealer won't be easy.

Good intentions notwithstanding, the second solution probably isn't any more practical than the first. Although you might try warming up your engine more thoroughly whenever you use it, it's the nature of sailboat engines to be used lightly and for shorter periods of time than engines in powerboats.

The thing to do is to change your engine oil regularly. Sulfuric acid buildup isn't the only reason to do this, but it's one of the better ones. To maximize time between oil changes without jeopardizing your motor's health, have your lube oil analyzed, as mentioned in the ''Filters'' chapter (see page 168).

Diesel fuel additives on the market include cetane boosters, biocides, water removers, cold-weather additives, and others. As you might expect, there is quite a range of quality involved, from those that can be essential under certain circumstances, to others that are useless and, in some cases, downright harmful. Some filters contain gasket and sealant material that can be damaged by some additives. Before using any fuel additive, check with your engine dealer and with your filter manufacturer or dealer.

Diesel engines are much less maintenance-intensive than gasoline engines, but they aren't maintenance-free. Most of the common engine malfunctions are directly related to problems with contaminated fuel. If you observe a few simple preventive maintenance procedures, including periodic inspections, filter care, and some precautions when laying the boat up, you'll find that engine problems will be greatly reduced and your peace of mind and confidence in your motor greatly enhanced.

7
GASOLINE ENGINES

SAFETY CONSIDERATIONS

IF YOU'RE accustomed to working on diesel engines or on automotive gas engines, working on marine gasoline engines requires some adjustments in work habits and attitudes.

The most obvious characteristic of gasoline, and the one that everyone is more or less aware of, is that gasoline vaporizes and forms explosive fumes.

The not so obvious characteristic of gasoline is the fact that gas fumes are heavier than air. This concept can be hard to visualize, since many of us have this cartoon image of fumes as a bunch of wavy lines, rising up and disappearing into the atmosphere. This doesn't hold true with gasoline. Gasoline is a volatile liquid, meaning that when it is exposed to air, it evaporates rapidly. The fumes created are heavier than air; therefore, they sink.

When working on cars, this seldom presents a problem. The bottom of the engine compartment is open, and the fumes fall out and dissipate.

In a boat, however, the fumes fall and collect like puddles. If such a "puddle" forms in the engine compartment, which, given the location of fuel lines and filters, is very likely, you've got a potential problem. A stray spark near a pocket of gas fumes can cause an explosion. Therefore, the fuel system must be designed to prevent leaks, and the electrical system must be designed to prevent sparks in case there are leaks. Also, the engine compartment must be ventilated so that fumes and heat can escape from the hull. This system consists of a bilge blower, ducting, and openings to the atmosphere that allow for both powered and natural ventilation.

The NFPA and ABYC standards for hull ventilation are detailed and precise, and should be consulted before making any modifications to your engine compartment or to any of the ventilation components. A few general points can be made, however.

The free end of the blower intake hose should be secured in place as low as possible in the bilge, but where it won't be blocked by bilge water. Too many hoses are just left to dangle around loose in the engine room, or are secured in such a way that the end is submerged in bilge water under normal operating conditions. The same rules apply for the nonpowered ventilation system hoses.

From time to time, check your exhaust fitting when the blower is running, to be sure that the blower is working, and that it's moving the air in the proper direction. Reversed wiring or an improperly installed blower unit can cause the system to operate backward. Too many boaters assume that if the unit is making noise when it's turned on, everything's fine.

Even with all the proper equipment functioning and correctly located, don't assume that it's okay to just hop on board, run the blower for five minutes, and then crank up the motor. We recently read a newspaper report of a boat explosion at a fuel dock. The owner fueled up, turned on his blowers, and started one engine. No problem. Started the other engine, and the boat exploded. Surprisingly, no one was killed or seriously injured, and in a postexplosion interview, the guy said something like, "I don't understand what went wrong, my blowers were working fine."

What did go wrong? For starters, even if we assume that the blowers were turned on for the recommended five minutes before starting the engines, and were actually operating, and were moving the fumes in the proper direction, that doesn't mean that the blower hoses were properly located or even still attached, or that the standard five-minute interval was sufficient. If you've got a gallon of fuel spilled in the bilge, five minutes of blower time isn't going to make much of a dent in the accumulated fumes.

Before starting your engine, open the engine compartment or go down into the engine room. Get your nose as far down into the bilge as practical and sniff. A fuel leak serious enough to cause an explosion will have a noticeable odor. When you're satisfied that all is well, run the blower for five minutes, and then start the engine. It may sound inconvenient, but it's not nearly as inconvenient as an explosion.

LAWS AND STANDARDS

The Coast Guard has written a set of regulations governing the fuel and electrical systems for gas-powered boats. When performing maintenance and repair on gas boats, these standards must be followed to ensure a safe, legal installation. Information on how to obtain copies of the standards is in the Sources of Information.

All electrical components must be ignition-protected or isolated from fuel sources by bulkheads, decks, or open atmosphere. Wiring, batteries, fuses, circuit breakers, and every part of the fuel system, from tanks and filters to carburetors and hoses, must conform to the Coast Guard regulations.

Many of the provisions of the law are a bit arcane and intended for manufacturers, such as: "Polyurethane cellular plastic used to encase metallic fuel tanks must have a density of at least 2.0 pounds per cubic foot, measured under ASTM D-1622, 'Apparent Density of Rigid Cellular Plastics.' " However, the sections that do apply to the kind of work we're dealing with cover things like fuel hoses, fuel filter installation, and tank grounding, and must be taken into account when you're installing or replacing parts of the fuel or electrical systems.

There are also standards published by the ABYC and by the NFPA. Both sets of standards closely parallel the Coast Guard standards, without going into many of the concerns that are of interest only to builders. The NFPA standards, published as "NFPA 302—Pleasure and Commercial Motor Craft," cover hulls, engines, fuel and electrical systems, and fire protection systems.

The ABYC standards are much more inclusive, covering everything from the items covered by the NFPA and USCG standards, as well as standards for helm visibility, bilge pumps, flotation, boat trailers, etc.

The addresses for these organizations are listed in the Sources of Information.

GAS FUEL SYSTEMS

Gasoline tank materials, grounding, tie-downs, gauges, sending units, and fill and vent systems are nearly identical to those outlined in the chapter on "Diesel Fuel Systems," but gasoline's volatility and flammability demand some extra precautions. For example, all openings in the tank, such as fill, vent, and supply lines, must be on the top of the tank, while many diesel tanks have openings cut into the tanks' sides. Clean-out plates, common on diesel tanks, are also prohibited.

The multitank arrangement pictured in the "Diesel Fuel Systems" chapter is applicable to gas systems, as long as the crossover valve is approved for use with gasoline. If you have an older boat with copper fuel lines, make sure that there's a section of flexible, USCG-approved fuel hose separating the engine from the copper line. Without the flex section, engine movement and vibration can fatigue and break the copper line.

Every component of the fuel system must be Coast Guard approved for use in gasoline systems, including tanks, hoses, valves, etc. Before replacing or repairing any part of the fuel delivery system, read the regulations and standards carefully. The stakes involved are too high to allow for ignorance or sloppiness.

GAS-ENGINE MAINTENANCE

Because of the large number of basic engines, marinizers, accessories, etc., this chapter will not address some of the details peculiar to each engine. To really become familiar with your motor, you should have a copy of the engine's shop manual, available from the engine dealer or distributor. The manual might seem a bit pricey, but compared with forty- to fifty-dollar-an-hour shop rates, it will probably pay for itself the first time you use it.

While shop manuals are excellent sources of information on maintenance requirements, specifications, and procedures, they tend to be written for mechanics. What this chapter will try to do is to make some of the basic jobs more understandable.

The gas engines installed in boats come from a variety of sources. Most of them began life as car, truck, or tractor engines, and were marinized, or converted to marine use. Very few were actually designed and built for marine work.

Marinized automotive engines, such as those sold by OMC, Mercury, Crusader, and Volvo, look nearly identical to their original versions, but a number of important changes have been made. Dissimilar metals in the engine block have been changed to reduce the potential for galvanic corrosion, and the transmission and cooling systems are different. However, the most significant changes are in the fuel and electrical systems.

Carburetors are modified to vent internally, and fuel pumps are changed to lessen the potential for leaks and drips. Additional fuel filters are added to the system to remove water from the fuel.

Electrical accessories also must be modified to operate safely in a potentially explosive atmosphere. Starters, alternators, voltage regulators, etc., must be shielded so that they don't produce open sparks.

This is an area where economizing unwisely can have disastrous consequences. Inexperienced mechanics will recognize an automotive engine and compare prices for what appear to be identical parts from marine and automotive suppliers. They'll note that the marine part is more expensive, and decide to save a few dollars by buying from the local Chevy dealer rather than from the OMC dealer. If the part is a valve cover gasket, no big deal. If the part is an alternator, very big deal.

We had one potential customer who did just that. Reasoning that a Chrysler marine engine was no different from the one in the family Dodge, he went to the local Dodge dealer when his alternator went bad. When we arrived to do some work on his electrical system, and noticed blue sparks visible inside the alternator when the engine was running, we immediately shut everything down and had a talk with him. No amount of reasoning, however, could convince him that we weren't trying to sell him an overpriced piece of equipment that he didn't need. He figured that his alternator worked fine and hadn't blown anything up so far, so what was the problem? Needless to say, he had to find himself another mechanic—one willing to take dangerous chances.

There are some areas where it's possible to save money safely, especially on tune-up parts.

Spark plugs are spark plugs, whether they're installed in marine engines or automotive engines. The owner's manual will list the correct plug for your motor, and you can usually find the same plug (or its equivalent from another manufacturer) in an automotive supply store or discount store. Advertising copy aside, all brand-name plugs are quite good, and your parts house will have a pamphlet listing equivalent model numbers for Champion, AC, Autolite, and NGK plugs.

If your boat uses electronic gear such as depth-sounders, Loran, VHF, or CB radios, etc., use resistor plugs. They reduce the amount of electronic interference, and typically only cost ten to twenty cents more per plug. They're usually identified by the letter "R" added to the plug's model number.

Points, condensers, rotors, and distributor caps can also be found in automotive stores, although you may have to look a bit harder. If you know who made the distributor and have the model number, a knowledgeable parts person can usually find the appropriate items for you. One thing to beware of is distributor caps with aluminum contacts, since they don't hold up in the marine environment. Check the inside of the cap to be sure that the metal contacts are brass.

You can also save money on fuel and oil filters. These can usually be found in discount houses, and if you buy them by the case, your savings increase dramatically. Don't store large numbers of them aboard the boat, however, since the moisture in the air can cause them to break down prematurely. Keep one or two spares aboard and store the rest in a cool, dry place. Again, as with spark plugs, there are several name brands that are comparable in quality, and dealers will have listings showing equivalent model numbers.

While fuel filter change intervals aren't quite as critical in gas engines as in diesels, they are still important, and manufacturers' recommendations should be followed. Likewise, oil and air filter changes should be done according to recommendations. Compared to the costs of performing major repairs, filter costs are inconsequential and amount to cheap insurance for your engine. Details and tips on changing engine oil and transmission fluid can be found in the "Filters" chapter (see page 166).

Another adjustment that has to be made when going from car to boat work results from the lack of standardization. When trying to buy parts, you'll soon realize that you need detailed information when dealing with boats. For instance, if you want to buy a new distributor cap for your 1986 Ford, usually all you need is the engine year, number of cylinders, and possibly engine size.

Take that same information to your marine parts store, and you'll find the counter person asking you a lot of questions. If you don't have the correct answers, you wind up making aggravating trips back and forth between boat and store. To keep those trips to a minimum, know exactly what you need before you go in.

When dealing with parts such as carburetors, distributors, and alternators, you need to go in with as much information as you can gather. If you can't take the unit in with you, get every part, model, and serial number you can find; know your engine's maker, marinizer, serial number, model number, year, horsepower, cubic inches, and rotation. Some marinizers play little tricks like painting over the ID plates on distributors, but once you're wise to them, things get easier.

When trying to find sending units for the engine instruments, refer to page 78 in the "Diesel Engines" chapter for help. For more information on some of the pitfalls of parts purchasing, see the "Spare Parts" chapter (page 47).

TUNE-UP

Tuning a gas engine consists of cleaning or replacing spark plugs, cleaning or replacing and adjusting breaker points on engines without electronic ignition, checking and adjusting ignition timing, checking and adjusting the carburetor, and taking care of belts, hoses, and any other parts that are subject to wear.

Before getting into the mechanics of a tune-up, there are a few common terms that need to be defined.

Spark plugs supply the spark that ignites the gas-air mixture in the cylinder. The spark arcs across the gap between the center electrode and the side electrode. In order for a spark plug to operate efficiently, or at all, the gap must be properly matched to the engine. Your owner's manual will provide that figure for your motor, expressed in thousandths of an inch.

Breaker points, or ignition points, are located inside the distributor. A cam on the distributor's central shaft opens and closes the points to fire each cylinder. When the points are closed, the necessary low-voltage electrical flow is built up. When the points open, the high current is discharged, then distributed to the proper spark plug. Electronic ignition systems eliminate the need for points.

"Dwell," or dwell angle, is a measure of how long the points remain closed during each cylinder's cycle. To adjust the dwell angle, the point gap is changed.

Ignition timing determines where in the piston's compression stroke the spark plug fires. Measured in degrees BTDC (before top dead center) of the piston's travel, timing is adjusted by rotating the distributor and checked by illuminating the timing mark with a *timing light*.

An engine's rotation refers to the turning direction of the crankshaft. Engines, like boats, have only one left and one right side. That might sound laughably obvious, but some circumstances can confuse matters.

For example, on V-8 motors, the number-one cylinder is the first one on the left bank, and the number-two cylinder is the first cylinder on the right bank. Now, is the left side of the motor the left side facing forward, or the mechanic's left as he faces the engine's front end? What if the engine is equipped with a V-drive, and is installed facing aft?

If you were to sit on the carburetor (which we do not recommend, by the way—we're just trying to illustrate a point here), facing the front of the engine, your left is the engine's left. That applies if the engine is installed facing frontward, backward, sideways, or upside down.

TUNE-UP TOOLS

Some specialized tools are needed in order to tune your engine.

A dwell tachometer measures engine rpm and dwell. The more sophisticated (and expensive) "engine analyzers," which can also test alternators, diodes, electronic ignition modules, etc., are usually unnecessary for basic tune-up work.

Timing lights are used to check ignition advance. Most of the units on the market have inductive pickups that clamp around the spark plug wire. They're much more convenient to use than the old type that require you to remove a plug wire and insert the pickup into the plug boot.

Loosening the retaining bolt on the distributors of some automotive-based engines is made easier with a special offset distributor wrench, available from most brand-name toolmakers. Know which engine block your motor uses, since different makes require different wrenches.

A remote starter switch can be a time saver if you're working on the motor unassisted. Trying to stop the motor right at top dead center by running back and forth between engine and helm station gets old in a hurry. Buy a good-quality, heavy-duty switch from an auto parts store. We've used lightweight units that, unlike M&M's, *do* melt in your hand. Also, be very careful when connecting the switch. An improperly installed switch can cause a dead short.

A compression gauge is also useful for evaluating wear in valves and piston rings. The easiest to use are the ones that screw into the spark plug holes, and these usually are adaptable to different spark plug thread sizes.

There are two ways to look at the "How often do I tune my engine?" question. There's the "frequent, preventive maintenance" school, and there's the "if it works, don't fix it" school. Most of us tend toward the "FPM" idea in theory, and the "IIWDFI" school in practice.

So we're going to recommend that you service your motor regularly, and conscientiously observe all the recommended service intervals, keeping an eye out for signs of potential trouble.

A good tune-up is in order *at least* once a year. This entails: replacing spark plugs and points, checking ignition timing, adjusting the carburetor, changing oil and filter, changing fuel filters, checking and adjusting belts and hoses, checking transmission fluid level, checking coolant level and effectiveness, replacing cooling system zincs, checking distributor cap and rotor, checking plug wires, removing rust, and applying touch-up paint.

It sounds like an awful lot of work, especially if you've got a pair of V-8s, but once you're familiar with the drill, you should be able to tune an eight-cylinder motor in a couple of hours, with another hour or two spent on other maintenance.

There's the preferred sequence to follow when tuning a gas engine's electrical system.

1. Replace and/or gap the spark plugs.
2. If your engine has breaker points rather than electronic ignition, set your point gap and adjust the dwell.
3. Finally, check and adjust the ignition timing. The first two steps are pretty much interchangeable, but timing adjustment must come *after* dwell adjustment.

To pull spark plugs, first remove the plug wire. This is done by pulling and twisting on the boot over the plug, *not* by pulling on the wire. Pulling directly on the wire can damage it, resulting in rough running that's very hard to troubleshoot.

Loosen the plug with a socket wrench, and clean away any loose gunk around the plug base before removing it completely. A small paint brush or a blast of canned air will get rid of the chunks of dirt and rust that tend to accumulate there.

If you don't plan on doing a compression test, gap and install the new plug, reinstall the plug wire, and go on to the next cylinder. If a compression test is on the agenda, mark and number the plug wires, remove all the old plugs, and proceed with the test (see page 105). Then, gap and install the new plugs.

Normally, a used plug will have a dry, light-brown deposit over the tip. Variations, such as black, oily deposits, cracks in insulator tips, etc., indicate a variety of engine ailments. Check all your plugs, and note especially if one cylinder or bank of cylinders shows any variation from the norm.

Don't automatically assume that the correct plugs are installed, especially if you've purchased a used boat. Check the manual for the proper plugs and the correct gap setting, and check the gap before installing new plugs.

When replacing spark plugs, treat them gingerly. Dropping or otherwise knocking them around can crack the insulators or cause internal damage that can drive you nuts trying to track down. Some particularly fastidious mechanics throw away any dropped spark plugs, figuring the expense to be well worth the headaches avoided.

In theory, you should always use a torque wrench when installing spark plugs, and torque each plug to factory specs (check your manual —torques can vary from 15 to 30 foot-pounds). In practice, however, most mechanics either just set the torque by feel or by degrees of rotation.

If you aren't familiar with the procedure, use a torque wrench until you acquire the feel. Plugs that are too loose will get looser owing to vibration, and will leak pressure. Tighten a plug too tight, and you run the risk of stripping the threads in the cylinder head, or breaking the plug, or at the very least, making removal very difficult.

Some of the newer engines use tapered spark plugs that have no sealing gaskets. If you are replacing standard plugs with tapered plugs, make sure that the old sealing gasket isn't left attached to the cylinder head when the old plug is removed.

(If you manage to get some plug wires crossed, which is fairly easy to do, refer to page 107 below for the proper procedure for sorting them out.)

After installing new spark plugs, the next step is determined by the type of ignition system your motor uses. If you've got electronic (or capacitor discharge) ignition, there aren't any points to adjust or dwell angles to set, so you move on to ignition timing. (Some electronic ignitions call for an air gap adjustment. This is usually performed with a special brass feeler gauge. Check your owner's manual for details.)

If you have breaker points, they must be adjusted and the dwell set *before* you check the ignition timing. Unscrew the fasteners on either side of the distributor cap and remove the cap. Without removing the plug wires from the cap, set it out of the way. The distributor's innards are now exposed, revealing the rotor, points, shaft, and cam. Some distributors have a cover plate over the points—remove the rotor by pulling up on it, and then remove the plate.

Inspect the metal tip on the rotor, and the metal contact points on the inside of the distributor cap. If they are severely worn, fouled, or pitted, replace rotor and cap. If they're only slightly discolored or corroded, touch them up with a piece of fine sandpaper and some electric contact cleaner.

Ignition points must be properly gapped, be correctly aligned, and be clean and not corroded. Replace them annually—they're inexpensive but vital. Carry a spare set on board as well.

To check the point gap, the engine must be rotated until the rubbing block is resting on one of the cam's high points. There are three ways to accomplish this.

If you've got a small, four-cylinder motor, or if all of the spark plugs are removed, you can turn the engine over by hand, either by putting a wrench on the nut at the center of the crankshaft pulley or by turning the pulley itself. When using this method, make sure before you start that you know the proper rotation direction for your motor, and *don't* turn it backward.

An easier method is to attach a remote starter switch to the starter motor and solenoid, and "bump" the engine with the switch until it stops at the proper place.

The final, and least efficient, method is to turn the engine over with the ignition switch. If you're alone, this entails going to the helm station, hitting the ignition for an instant to move the distributor shaft a tiny bit, going below, looking at the rubbing block, saying a dirty word, going back to the helm, hitting the ignition again, etc.

If you've got a helper or can recruit some unsuspecting soul to stand at the helm while you watch the rubbing block, the third method is modified slightly.

Once you've got the rubbing block resting on a high point, measure the gap with a feeler gauge. Your owner's manual will give you the exact figure—usually around 0.018 inch. Make sure that there's no grease or oil on the feeler gauge—you don't want to gum up the points. If in doubt, wipe the gauge clean with a solvent such as acetone, alcohol, or electric-contact cleaner. Measure the gap by inserting the proper size gauge between the points. Make sure that the gauge is parallel to the flat surfaces of the points. You should feel a slight drag on the gauge if the gap is correct. This is another instance where a certain feel has to be learned, somewhere between too much drag and not enough.

Most systems use two mounting screws, one of them serving as a pivot point, the other sitting in an oval or oblong hole, allowing adjustment movement. Some use a two-screw system where one of the fasteners secures the points to the base plate, and the other screw is actually a cam device that adjusts the point gap. Your manual will describe which system your engine uses.

Loosen the pivot screw just barely enough to allow movement when making the adjustment. If it's too loose, it's hard to hold in place when adjusting the gap. Then loosen the other screw. Adjustment is accomplished by inserting a screwdriver blade in the appropriate slot and turning very slightly, or by turning the cam screw. Once you've got the proper gap, tighten the screws firmly, and recheck the gap.

To remove a set of points, loosen the fastener on the side of the distributor body that secures the wire running to the points. Then, remove both screws securing the points to the distributor and remove them. Install the new set, and then adjust the gap.

Once you've got the gap set, it's time to check it with the dwell meter. Replace the cover plate, if there is one, the rotor, and the distributor cap.

Don't set the cap on the distributor loosely—tighten the fasteners. Connect the dwell meter according to instructions, and start the motor. Check the dwell reading on the appropriate scale (four, six, or eight cylinder). If the reading isn't within a degree or two of the figure in your owner's manual, the point gap needs adjustment.

Shut off the engine, remove the distributor cap, and turn the engine over until the points open. Loosen the screws securing the points, and adjust. (There's an inverse relation between gap and dwell reading. To increase the dwell, decrease the gap.)

After adjusting, replace everything, start the engine, and check again. After a bit of practice, you should be able to hit the correct setting with one or two tries.

If the gap-adjusting procedure is too time-consuming for your taste, there are aftermarket electronic ignition systems available that are reliable and inexpensive. Depending on local prices and which engine you own, you can sometimes buy an entire new distributor for only a little more than the cost of the electronic ignition package, although installation of a distributor is best left to a pro.

Replace the condenser at every tune-up. It's inexpensive, and there's no practical way to gauge wear. Condensers either work, or they die completely, without warning. Save yourself some aggravation, and replace them.

To check ignition timing, connect the timing light terminals to the battery terminals (red to positive, black to negative or to ground), and attach the inductive pickup around the number one spark plug wire. There should be an arrow on the pickup, pointing toward the spark plug—don't install it backward. Attach your dwell tachometer also, and set it to read engine rpm.

Once everything is attached, and you're sure that the wires are clear of all moving parts, start the motor and allow it to warm up. While it's warming, check your owner's manual under "Tune-up Specifications." Ignition timing is usually given in degrees before top dead center at a given rpm: for example, 8 degrees BTDC at 700 rpm.

Now find your timing marks. Most engines use a mark on the crankshaft pulley that lines up with figures on a plate mounted on the engine block, while some use a mark on the flywheel. (Check your owner's manual for specifics.) If the marks on the pulley or the plate are dirty, clean them off before starting the motor. Sometimes it's helpful to touch up the timing mark with a dab of white paint for better visibility.

Once the engine has reached operating temperature, bring the engine to an idle and check your tachometer. Adjust the idle speed to correspond with the speed given in your timing specification. If the engine won't idle at the speed given in the manual, adjust the idle with the appropriate screw on the carburetor (see page 104).

Then point the timing light at the timing mark. As if by magic, moving parts seem to stand still. The strobe light is being fired once on every engine revolution, momentarily freezing the mark on the pulley or flywheel. If the mark on the pulley lines up with the proper number on the plate, your timing is set. If it's off by more than a degree, adjustment is necessary.

Using a socket or combination wrench, or one of the special wrenches mentioned on page 97 above, loosen the fastener holding the retaining plate at the base of the distributor. Not too loose, just enough so that you can rotate the distributor by hand. With the timing light shining on the timing marks, move the distributor slowly back and forth until the pulley mark lines up with the figure given in your manual.

On some motors, especially in dual-engine installations where one of the engines uses left-hand rotation, the manufacturer will install symmetrical timing mark plates that don't indicate which direction is *before* top dead center and which is after. To check the proper direction, point the timing light at the mark, and speed up the engine slightly. The mark will advance, or move in the direction of BTDC.

Tighten the bolt at the distributor base and recheck. (Occasionally, tightening the bolt moves the distributor just enough to disturb the setting.) Once you've checked and adjusted or replaced plugs, points and condenser, and reset the timing, the basic tune-up work is done. What's left is routine maintenance.

A frequently neglected maintenance chore is checking the spark plug wires. As they age, they may crack and leak voltage, resulting in missing and rough running. You can replace them every year or so as a precautionary measure, or purchase an inductive plug wire tester and check them periodically. If the wires leak, replace them, along with the high-tension lead between the coil and distributor. They're not only inefficient, they could arc to the engine and cause a fire or explosion.

CARBURETORS

Carburetors differ from the fuel injector pumps on diesel engines in several ways, one of which is that, unlike fuel injection pumps, it's practical for the mechanically inclined boat owner to perform regular service. Carburetor service and overhaul isn't the kind of thing to take lightly, but it's not rocket science, either. A rebuild kit, shop manual, a few specialized tools, such as a set of calipers and some small screwdrivers, and a clean, well-lighted place to work are all that are required to do the job.

Some carburetor adjustments such as idle speed and mixture adjustments are simple and should be checked regularly. You'll need a tachometer to check idle speeds, and, for some carburetors, a vacuum gauge to check mixture adjustments. Check your shop manual for details, and follow procedures carefully.

One of the more common problems, especially when setting mixture adjustments on four-barrel carburetors, is the tendency to jump in and start turning the mixture and idle screws at random. Before you know it, things are worse than when you started, and you're totally lost.

A better approach is to read through the procedure completely before you start, familiarizing yourself with the locations of all the appropiate parts. Then proceed slowly, step by step, *writing down* every turn of every screw. There can be half a dozen screws to adjust, and if you document every move you can return everything to its original setting in the event that things get worse before they get better.

Most manuals instruct you to adjust mixture screws by first turning them in until they seat, and then backing them out a prescribed number of turns. When doing this, be careful to avoid damaging the screws by overtightening them. The screws are actually tapered needle valves that can be ruined by overtightening.

Before purchasing a rebuild kit, write down the ID number on the metal tag attached to the carburetor. Use this number rather than the manufacturer's name and model, as marine and automotive kits differ significantly.

Look over the instructions, familiarize yourself with parts and procedures, and see if the directions are clearly written and understandable. If you feel comfortable that your skill level is up to the task, go to it. If not, have a mechanic do it for you.

When removing a carburetor for rebuilding or major servicing, disconnect and mark the cables, fuel lines, and any other connections. Disconnect the fasteners securing it to the intake manifold, then gently lift it free. If it refuses to budge, gently pry with a piece of wood, don't just smack it with your hammer. (You'd be surprised at how many people need to be told these things!)

Before disassembling the carburetor, reread all the instructions. Then take it apart carefully. There are usually springs and check balls inside that are just waiting to leap out and scurry underneath shop furniture, so proceed slowly and carefully.

When working on carburetors and fuel pumps, be sure to use only gasket sealers and materials approved specifically for gasoline systems. Many sealants are gasoline soluble, turning them into unsealants in short order.

Flame arrestors sit on top of the carburetors, where the air cleaner is located on automotive engines. They are usually cleaned by washing with cleaning solvent or kerosene—check owner's manual. When replacing them, make sure that they're properly seated on the carburetor.

COMPRESSION TEST

As an engine ages, it gradually loses cylinder compression through valve and piston ring wear, resulting in oil blowby in the cylinders and reduced power. If you check your compression annually and track the results, you can frequently see trouble coming before it becomes critical. This helps in planning downtime and your maintenance budget, and avoids emergencies and inconvenience.

To check compression, you'll need a compression gauge, a spark plug wrench, a pencil and paper for notes, some way to mark the plug wires (white electrical tape or masking tape), and a small squirt can filled with motor oil. A remote starter or an assistant are convenient but not essential.

Start with a warm engine. First, number and mark all your plug wires. Then carefully pull out the plugs. Remove the high-tension lead between the coil and the distributor, grounding the distributor end on the engine. This prevents unwanted sparks.

Starting with cylinder number one, screw the gauge into the plug hole (hand tighten only), and turn the engine over three or four turns. Record the reading. Push the release button to zero the gauge, and repeat for each cylinder. Then repeat the procedure for each cylinder after squirting a small amount of motor oil (a couple of teaspoonfuls should do it) into the cylinder, recording the reading again. Repeat for all cylinders.

To analyze the readings, first look at the numbers for the dry test. If there's no more than a 10 percent difference between the high and low numbers, you're in good shape. A wide variation in the dry numbers indicates wear, either in the valve train or inside the cylinder, usually the piston rings. To determine which is the case, check the readings for the wet test. If the numbers didn't improve appreciably, the low compression is probably a result of wear or sticking in the valves.

If the numbers did improve with the addition of oil, it indicates that your low compression is probably due to worn piston rings. The oil in the cylinder forms a temporary seal around the piston, duplicating the effect of an unworn ring.

The difference between the two problems is that to repair valves, you only have to remove the cylinder heads and take them in for reconditioning. The degree of difficulty of this job depends on the size of your engine, and access. Worn rings, on the other hand, generally mean that an engine overhaul is in your future. To replace the rings, the engine must be pulled out and completely torn down. When you've got a motor in that stage of disassembly, it's silly to replace only the piston rings.

The smart thing to do, once the engine is torn down, is to replace and recondition those now-accessible items that are subject to wear and failure. This includes replacing the engine's main bearings and cam bearings, regrinding the crankshaft and camshaft, reconditioning the cylinder heads, and grinding the valves.

Removing the cylinder heads for valve work can be a bit time-consuming, but it's not really complicated. As always, when disassembling things, mark everything with tags or tape, take notes, and, if possible, take Polaroid photographs. It's always tempting to look at assembled components and think, "I'll remember how this all goes together. It's so obvious!" After things are disassembled, however, parts taken to the shop, left for a few days or weeks, and then brought back, the stuff that looked so incredibly obvious before has turned itself into an incomprehensible mess. After taking the necessary precautions, go ahead and remove the cylinder heads, according to the instructions and sequences given in your shop manual.

Be advised before you start that you'll need to purchase new gaskets for the heads and manifolds (many builders sell a "valve grind" kit that includes everything necessary for this particular job) and a torque wrench for reassembly.

Also, pay close attention to the head bolt tightening sequence given in your manual. Follow this pattern closely and torque the bolts down in thirds, applying one third of the final setting on each of three passes.

It's also generally recommended to retighten the head bolts after fifty to one hundred hours of running time, and to check and tighten them annually. Remember, whenever the heads are tightened appreciably, valve adjustment needs to be checked as well.

SORTING OUT CROSSED PLUG WIRES

If, in the course of performing a compression test or replacing spark plugs, you manage to remove the plug wires without marking them, or if the wires become attached to the wrong plugs, there's a fairly simple procedure for sorting them out.

You need to know two things—your engine's firing order, and the location of your number-one cylinder. The firing order is given in your owner's manual, the shop manual, and in most cases, is also stamped on the intake manifold. A typical four-cylinder firing order is given as 1-2-4-3, while an eight-cylinder order might be 1-8-4-5-6-2-7-3.

Twin-engine boats equipped with engines that rotate in opposite directions will have different firing orders. Owner's manuals, shop manuals, engine tags (sometimes marked RH and LH), and flywheels (sometimes marked with arrows) will help determine which engine is right-hand rotation and which is left-hand.

The cylinders on the left side are numbered 1-3-5-7, and on the right side, 2-4-6-8 (for V-6 engines, omit 7 and 8). In-line motors are numbered in a straight line, front to back. If your engine deviates from this standard, your manuals should so indicate.

To help you find the number-one cylinder location on the distributor, some manufacturers mark the terminal on the distributor cap. For most engines, however, some detective work is in order. Remove the spark plug from the number-one cylinder. Put a wrench on the nut at the center of the large pulley on the front of the motor. Turn the engine over slowly, making sure that you're turning in the proper direction.

With large six- and eight-cylinder engines, you'll probably have to remove all the spark plugs in order to turn the engine over. Four-cylinder engines can usually be turned without removing the plugs, and they frequently come equipped with hand cranks for use in starting the engine manually.

Make sure that the ignition is off before trying this—otherwise you could start the engine inadvertently, although anyone who has tried to do this on purpose would quote some pretty long odds against its happening by accident. Use your finger to seal the plug hole of cylinder number one while turning the engine. As the piston moves up in the cylinder, you'll feel air pressure on your finger when the piston approaches the top of its reach on the compression stroke. (During this operation, make a note of the rotation direction of the rotor, clockwise or counter clockwise. It might help to put a piece of tape on the cap, and draw an arrow for future reference.)

Bear in mind that on your basic four-stroke gasoline engine, the piston makes four strokes (two ascending and two descending) in each cycle, every other ascending piston stroke being a compression stroke. On the compression stroke, you'll feel the air pressure through the spark plug hole.

The timing mark that you used to set your ignition timing will tell you when the piston is at top dead center. When the timing mark on the crankshaft pulley is aligned with the 0 or TDC mark, and the piston is on the compression stroke, the rotor will be pointing at the distributor terminal for the number-one cylinder.

You can then replace the distributor cap and the spark plugs. Connect the plug wire from the number-one distributor terminal to the number-one spark plug. Then, following the direction of the rotor and the firing order, replace the rest of the wires. For example, with a four-cylinder firing order of 1-3-4-2 and a clockwise rotor direction, you'd attach the wire from the number-three cylinder to the next distributor terminal in line, then the number-four wire, and so on.

Continue until all are attached, and start the engine to test. Any flaws in your performance will be immediately obvious, since the engine either won't start at all, or will pop and spit when it does turn over.

REFUELING

Refueling a gas-powered boat is like walking through a mine field. Doing *almost* everything right can get you into just as much trouble as doing nothing right, the end result being an explosion.

Before refueling, extinguish *all* flames, pilot lights, cigarettes, anything that could produce a spark or flame. Turn off the battery switch, and any 12-volt equipment that's not wired through the switch. For example, some boats have 12-volt/110-volt refrigerators that automatically revert to 12-volt when the shore power is disconnected. They are sometimes wired directly to the battery, so that they can be run with everything else shut off through the switch. If your boat has an arrangement like this, you have to turn the refrigerator off whenever you refuel, and remember to turn it back on afterward.

Also, if you have a propane-powered refrigerator or water heater, remember to extinguish the pilot lights.

Likewise with bilge pump float switches. Typically they are three-position switches, labeled "Off," "On," and "Automatic," and wired directly to the battery. Turn them off before refueling. If there is no "Off" switch, you'll need to disable the float switch, either by disconnecting it, or placing a heavy object on it. These precautions will keep the refrigerator motor or the bilge pump from cycling on while you're refueling.

When you're secured to the fuel dock, get everyone off the boat, turn off the batteries, extinguish all lights, and kill the refrigerator and bilge pump. Close all windows, hatches, portholes, and doors open to the outside. Then, and only then, refuel.

When fueling, be sure that the fuel nozzle is touching the metal part of the fill tube. Gasoline running through the hose can build up a static charge, and if the nozzle isn't grounded against the fill tube, a spark can arc across the gap. To check the fill tube for grounding, see the "Diesel Fuel Systems" chapter (page 82).

When refueling is complete, open all doors and hatches and go below. Don't blindly rely on your bilge blowers to remove all the fumes before you start your motor. Get your nose down as low as you can get it in the bilge, and sniff. If you smell fuel, find the source and take care of it *before* starting the engine. There are a number of gas-sniffing devices on the market, but none of them is as good as your own nose. Gas fumes (or propane fumes) in sufficient concentration to explode will be very noticeable.

It's a good idea to leave the boat, get outside and breathe fresh air for five or ten minutes before sniffing for fumes. If you're filling the tanks, it's easy to become accustomed to the smell of fumes to the point where they're no longer noticeable.

This is also a good time to visually inspect your fuel tank, fill hose, and fittings. Leaks will be most apparent when the tank is topped off.

When you're sure that everything is safe, turn on the battery switch and start the blower, running it for at least five minutes. Start the engines and get your passengers back on board.

With planing powerboats, keep the blower running until after the boat is up on plane. These hulls normally sit bow-down when at rest. It's possible for gas fumes to collect in the bow, only to roll aft once the boat's up on plane. Obviously, this could be dangerous, if there's an ignition source back there and the blower isn't running.

MISCELLANEOUS

In addition to the maintenance requirements included in this chapter, there are a number of mechanical details that are common to both gas and diesel engines.

Cooling systems and exhaust systems are the same on both types of motors. Both raw-water and freshwater cooling systems are used, and hoses, sea cocks, seawater strainers, heat exchangers, zincs, and similar parts are the same. Gauges, sending units, instruments, motor mounts, and engine alignment are also similar or identical, as are the on-board AC and DC electrical systems.

The sections of this chapter dealing with the hazards of gasoline aren't intended to serve as scare tactics. The point we're trying to make is that while gasoline is a potentially dangerous substance, a boat owner who is aware of the dangers involved can take the proper precautions when doing maintenance and repair work. The boater who isn't aware of the consequences of mistakes, or who becomes careless and slipshod in his work habits, is a danger to himself and to his passengers.

8
BATTERIES

THE 12-VOLT batteries installed on most boats have two functions —starting the engine and supplying power to accessories. Once the engine is running, the alternator, driven by the engine, provides current that travels through a voltage regulator and back to the battery, recharging it.

Batteries don't generate electricity—they temporarily store it using a system of lead plates and an electrolyte of sulfuric acid and water. The chemical interactions are well documented in *Your Boat's Electrical System,* by Conrad Miller and E. S. Maloney (see Sources of Information), in case you're interested in battery theory.

Batteries are rated in terms of their "reserve capacity" and their "cold cranking amps" (see page 126 for definitions). The requirements for these ratings are such that a high rating in one category dictates a lower rating in the other. When purchasing a battery, consult your dealer and outline your intended use to determine which combination of qualities is best suited to your needs.

As a battery ages, its components break down and its capacity gradually diminishes. Eventually, it will no longer hold a charge, and

111

must be replaced. Besides the gradual deterioration of the battery as a whole, it's possible for a single cell of the battery to short itself out owing to internal damage. The dead cell can be discovered by hydrometer testing (see page 115 and page 122) of the battery, with the dead cell recording a significantly lower specific gravity (see page 126) than the others.

A dead cell in a battery is incurable—the charger will sense 10 volts or so from the battery, and try to bring it up to 12 volts. It will then continue to overcharge all of the good cells, eventually destroying them.

In the simplest system, a single battery provides the power to start a single engine, and also provides the necessary DC voltage to run the boat's accessories. Complications enter the picture in the form of additional engines and batteries, gen sets, 110-volt chargers, etc. Diagrams illustrating several different setups are shown in Figures 8.1 and 8.2 on pages 119 and 120.

SAFETY PRECAUTIONS

Since batteries are filled with lead and sulfuric acid, they're heavy, awkward, and extremely dangerous if you drop them. While many large batteries come equipped with handles, most of the smaller ones do not, and smaller doesn't necessarily mean easy to handle. There are battery handling devices on the market, but beware of any that pick the battery up by its terminal posts. That's like picking a dog up by its ears—not recommended for the long-term health of the pickee.

Baking soda dissolved in water is an effective neutralizing agent for battery acid. Make some up and keep it handy if you'll be working on batteries or moving them around.

Wear eye protection and rubber or plastic gloves—there's no sense having your fingerprints eaten off unless you plan to crack safes to pay for your boat.

Gases given off during battery charging are explosive, so avoid any open flames or ignition sources when batteries are charging.

Nonmetallic covers should be secured in place on the battery except when working on it. A metal object can touch a positive terminal and arc. When installing or removing terminals, be aware that while the wrench is on the positive terminal nut, it's an extension of the terminal, so don't allow the free end of the wrench to contact metal while you're working.

The NFPA code calls for batteries to be installed in liquid-tight trays or battery boxes made of electrolyte-resistant materials. Some builders use wooden boxes, especially for large batteries. Wood is a less than ideal material, since it can retain moisture almost indefinitely, to the detriment of the battery. Wooden boxes should be coated with fiberglass or epoxy, making them acid-resistant.

Smaller, standard-sized batteries are usually housed in plastic, commercially available boxes, complete with ventilated covers and tie-down straps. These should be checked regularly to see if there's any liquid accumulating inside, and the acid removed if any is found.

Check the fasteners on the strap anchors. A couple of number 10 screws in a piece of plywood aren't going to be much of a deterrent to a ninety-pound battery being buffeted around in a seaway.

When soaking up spilled electrolyte, wear rubber or plastic gloves and eye protection. Make up a baking soda and water solution, heavy on the baking soda. Dip a rag or sponge into the solution, and wring it dry. Soak up as much electrolyte as the rag or sponge will hold, and rinse it out in the baking soda solution. Wring dry and repeat until all the acid is soaked up.

AUTOMOTIVE VERSUS MARINE BATTERIES

Automotive 12-volt batteries are identical in some respects to the batteries used in boats, but there are significant differences in operation and construction. The main difference between automotive service and marine service is that a car battery's primary function is to start the engine. After the motor is running, the 12-volt accessories are powered by the engine's alternator, with the battery serving as a kind of buffer or well for the electrical energy, parceling it out at a steady rate.

On boats, batteries start the engines, but are also called upon to operate the 12-volt accessories for long periods of time when the engines aren't running. This function demands some physical changes in the batteries.

The lead plates need to be thicker, in order to better sustain extended periods of voltage drain. Marine "deep cycle" batteries can stand long cycles of discharge and recharging that would damage standard automotive batteries.

Some 12-volt batteries are advertised as "sealed," "low-maintenance," or "low-water-loss" batteries. As far as routine maintenance on sealed batteries is concerned, there's not a lot you can do. Check the terminal connections, clean as necessary, and charge according to manufacturers' directions. Some differences in charging procedures might be necessary.

Hydrocap® battery caps fit over the individual cells, and capture escaping gas, chemically recombining it into water, allowing it to return to the cell. They greatly reduce electrolyte loss, but don't relieve you of the responsibility of occasionally checking fluid levels.

The newest type of battery on the market is the "gel cell" battery. These units are also advertised as being maintenance-free, probably with quite a bit more justification than the low-water-loss batteries. The electrolyte is a sulfuric acid solution that's suspended in a gel rather than in liquid, and sealed. In case of severe overcharging, vents are installed to prevent explosion, but other than that, there are no provisions for replacing the electrolyte. These batteries are quite a bit more expensive than standard units, but they advertise deep-cycle capabilities, long service life, and complete freedom from maintenance. The advantages seem impressive, but your own cost-benefit ratio will determine whether or not they're right for you.

Finally, a marine battery's internal structures and case must be sturdier than those of automotive batteries because of the severe pounding experienced aboard boats. Your garden-variety car battery would have a pretty short life expectancy aboard an oceangoing boat.

On the other hand, if your type of marine use closely approximates automotive use, you might be able to get by with an automotive battery. Just be aware of the differences, and don't expect a $50 car battery to give the same length or quality of service as a $150 deep-cycle, marine item. Avoid long discharge cycles, treat it gingerly, and maintain it carefully.

BATTERY MAINTENANCE

There are a couple of additions to your tool kit required for day-to-day battery maintenance. A terminal cleaner can be purchased at an auto parts store, and makes short work of keeping battery and cable terminals in good shape. If you don't have one aboard, use sandpaper.

Inspect the battery terminals from time to time for corrosion and tightness. If the open ends of the cable terminal clamp jaws are touching, install a smaller-diameter terminal, or file down the inside edges of the cable terminal. A gap in the open end is necessary to be sure that the terminal clamps tightly.

Corrosion at the terminals is common, which is why you bought the terminal cleaner recommended above. Once a year or so, and more often if corrosion is visible, remove the cable terminals and clean their inside surfaces as well as the battery terminal posts. Tighten the clamps securely—good contact between cables and batteries is important.

Before you remove cables from a battery, mark them plainly, and make certain that you *never* connect them backward. Even a momentary application of reverse voltage to your electrical system can cause damage to any electronic devices on board.

To check battery fluid levels, remove the cap for each cell. (The individual cells aren't connected, so each one must be checked separately.) Look into each cell with a flashlight if necessary, and don't even *think* about using a match or lighter! Each cell has a tube or well-extending part way down into the cell. The electrolyte should reach the bottom of the tube. If the fluid level drops so low that the lead plates are uncovered, the dry sections will become sulfated and incapable of holding a charge. On the other hand, don't overfill, either. As the battery is charged and warms up, the fluid expands and will leak from the vents, spilling battery acid.

Wipe the battery down occasionally with a rag dipped in a baking soda and water solution, being very careful not to let any of the solution get into the battery cells. Batteries can sweat with use, and wiping them down neutralizes the mild acidic residue on the battery case.

Hydrometers for testing battery electrolyte can be purchased in auto parts stores, in varying degrees of technical sophistication. The simplest and least expensive battery testers consist of a large eyedropper-type tube containing four colored balls. The percentage of a battery's charge is measured by the number of balls floating when electrolyte is drawn into the tube. All four balls floating equals a 100-percent charge, three balls floating equals a 75-percent charge, etc. These deals are a bit better than nothing, but leave something to be desired in terms of accuracy.

Real hydrometers give readings in specific gravity of the electrolyte. They're more expensive, but also give you detailed information on your battery's condition. Choose your equipment according to how serious you are about monitoring the health of your batteries.

Some thought should be given to hydrometer storage after use. They tend to be fragile, and should be thoroughly rinsed out after use. Throwing a glass hydrometer dripping with battery acid into a toolbox is a great way to break the hydrometer, and also to eat up everything around it. One idea is to mount a section of PVC or plastic pipe on a bulkhead near your batteries. Cap the bottom, and rinse the hydrometer out after each use. Slip it into the pipe after rinsing, and it'll be near at hand and ready for use.

Most drinking water is acceptable for use in batteries. Distilled water is best, and well water or any hard water having a high mineral or chlorine content is worst. In a pinch, any water is better than none if the electrolyte levels threaten to drop below the tops of the plates, but for routine topping up, why not splurge and use distilled water? If it gets to the point where your distilled water bill is cutting into your beer money, then there's definitely something wrong with your batteries, your charger, or both.

(Note—don't check electrolyte condition immediately after adding water to the cells, during charging, or immediately after a heavy discharge. Some stabilizing time is necessary to ensure accurate readings.)

Don't add acid or electrolyte to the battery—good water, followed by regular charging will suffice. Mixing electrolyte is dangerous, and unnecessary for our purposes.

Most builders are well aware of the physical and legal implications of loose batteries, and so are generally careful to be sure that they are well secured. Nobody's perfect, however, so you should inspect your battery tie-down system to be sure that things were done right at the factory, and that no subsequent work has been done to "improve" the arrangement.

The perfect location for batteries is low in the bilge, but above normal bilge water levels. (On sailboats, this means taking extreme angles of heel into consideration.) The batteries should be as near the longitudinal centerline as possible, secured in acid-resistant boxes, with covers that allow easy access, while preventing stray objects from reaching the terminals. There should be enough room above the batteries to allow escaping gases to dissipate, and also to afford easy access to all the cells and terminals for routine maintenance. Finally, the batteries should be close enough to the engines, battery switches, and battery charger that cable runs are minimized.

Space and access considerations being what they are aboard boats, very few installations will meet all of these criteria perfectly, but the closer your installation comes to the ideal, the better off you'll be.

BATTERY SWITCHES

Most boats are equipped with switches to turn the batteries on and off, and to select which battery to use in multiple-battery systems. These switches are available in different amperages and configurations.

The switches installed by builders tend to be the minimum acceptable size. If you're adding a switch, or replacing a defective one, buy the one with the highest amperage ratings available. Most of the standard switches are rated at about 250 amps continuous, and 360 amps intermittent load, and some are rated as low as 175 and 325 amps, respectively. Current surges higher than these ratings will simply blow the switch. We've seen cheap switches on sale that don't have any ratings listed. Avoid these pieces of junk—in this instance, no news is bad news.

By contrast, the Guest Corporation, as well as several others, makes heavy-duty and extra-heavy-duty switches rated as high as 600 amps continuous and 1,000 amps momentary. The extra protection afforded by these switches can be very useful in an emergency, and you only have to need the protection once in order for the thing to pay for itself.

The higher ratings are important if you've been adding accessories to your system, especially if you've added a large-capacity alternator.

The simplest arrangement is an "On-Off" switch for a single-battery, single-engine setup.

Next in complexity is a single-engine, dual-battery switch. This one will have settings labeled "Off," "1," "All," and "2," indicating that either battery can be selected individually, or they can both be used in parallel.

Connecting batteries in parallel is familiar to anyone who has ever jump-started a car. Connect the positive terminal of one battery to the positive terminal of another battery, and connect the negative terminals to each other, and you've in effect created a bigger 12-volt battery. This allows you to jump-start the motor so that the alternator can continue the charging process.

By comparison, two batteries connected in series creates a battery that adds the voltages together. This is occasionally seen when two

6-volt batteries are connected to make a 12-volt battery. It's also illustrated when you put batteries into a flashlight. A pair of 1.5-volt dry cell batteries connected positive to negative produces 3 volts for the bulb.

Some boats use a simpler system employing a single "On-Off" switch for each battery, and a separate battery parallel switch. An example of this system would be two batteries and two engines, with one of the batteries supplying one engine, and the other battery supplying the other engine, as well as the 12-volt ship's service. If the ship's service battery is drained, the other engine is started first, and then the parallel switch used like jumper cables to start the engine with the discharged battery. (See Figures 8.1 and 8.2.)

With battery switches, there are some common mistakes and misconceptions. Too many boaters just turn the switch to "All" for starting and running, and leave it at that. In most situations, this practice doesn't present any problem.

Where you can get into trouble is starting and running with the switch set on "All," then turning off the engine and running 12-volt accessories without resetting the switch. This uses both batteries to power the accessories, and will eventually drain them both. A better system is to start and run on "All," but switch to one battery or the other after the engine is shut off. Then you'll have a fresh battery to start the engines should your accessories drain one battery.

Unless you're absolutely certain that your switch is of the type known as an "alternator field disconnect" model, and is correctly installed, don't ever switch the batteries off when the engine is running. To do so pretty much guarantees that you'll damage your alternator, necessitating an expensive trip to the shop.

We've also seen wiring harnesses melt on diesel engine installations when a boater turned off the battery switch in an attempt to turn off the motor.

Many of the switches on the market today are known as "make-before-break" switches. This means that the switch makes the next connection before breaking the previous one, so that you can switch between any of the running positions ("1," "All," or "2") while the engine is operating. However, even if you're sure that your switch is of this type, it's not a good habit to get into. There have been cases in the past where make-before-break switches and some field-disconnect models were defective, causing a series of blown alternators. As

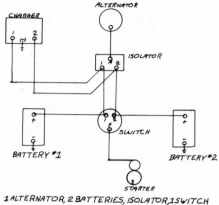

1 ALTERNATOR, 2 BATTERIES, ISOLATOR, 1 SWITCH

Fig. 8.1. *Drawing showing typical setup for one-engine, two-battery system, with charger.*

a general practice, turn off the engine before changing battery switch positions.

BATTERY CHARGING

The primary means of charging batteries is the engine alternator. If the batteries are used only when the engines are running, or are used for short periods of time when the engines are off, followed by fairly long running times, additional means of charging the batteries might be unnecessary. After all, how often does your car battery need to be charged? Powerboats that spend little time running accessories with the engines shut down closely approximate automotive use patterns.

Cruising sailboats that spend considerable time at anchor or under sail, operating lights, pumps, etc., and running the engine only minimally, represent the other extreme. Here, an additional means of keeping batteries charged is essential.

Most boaters' 12-volt use falls somewhere in between the extremes, and many boats require some type of battery charger eventually. Unfortunately, charging batteries is an area filled with erroneous information and bogus "common sense."

Because of mechanical and cost considerations, the perfect, completely automatic, foolproof, zero-maintenance battery charger doesn't

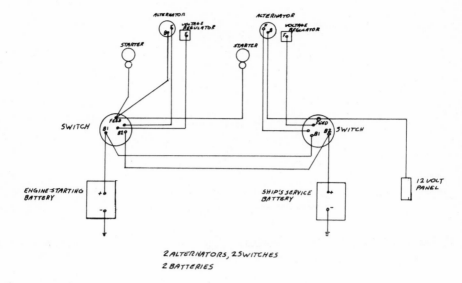

Fig. 8.2.   *Typical two-engine, two-battery system.*

exist, and one of the most common pitfalls is the false sense of security generated by the purchase of an "automatic" battery charger. Too many owners take the adjective literally, and assume that all they have to do is to hook up the charger, turn it on whenever they're connected to shore power, and their batteries will live happily ever after, courtesy of the automatic battery charger.

But alas, life—like your boat—is never so simple. Automatic chargers come in varying degrees of "automaticness," and you pretty much get what you pay for. It would be nice if you could find a $200 charger that does everything that a $600 unit does, but you won't. Technical sophistication and advanced features cost money. However, this is not to say that everybody needs the $600 unit. Knowledge of charger functions and uses, coupled with an appraisal of your needs, will enable you to buy one that is tailored to your boat and budget.

When a battery is being charged, whether from an alternator, a 120-volt charger, solar cells, or some other source, electrical current is directed into the battery, and the battery becomes charged. As the battery is used, it discharges. This charge-discharge cycle constitutes a battery's life.

If we use more electricity with our accessories than the alternator can replace while the engine is running, a battery charger is needed.

Both voltage and amperage must be regulated for effective charging of a battery, and the necessary value of each will vary at different times in the cycle.

Chargers are usually listed in terms of amperage, giving the maximum rate at which voltage is supplied. When a battery is severely discharged, high current flow is necessary to bring the battery up to snuff. As full charge approaches, the rate should taper off. If the battery is charged at too high a rate, usually at over 14 volts, the electrolyte will begin to bubble and gas. The gas escapes through the cap vents, reducing the fluid level.

A good automatic charger senses low voltage, directs current at the appropriate voltage and amperage into the battery, then shuts itself off when the cycle is complete. It will then maintain the charge at a level known as "float" voltage, around 13.2 volts. This level is considered ideal for the battery's long-term health.

Inexpensive chargers compromise on all that sensing and turning on and off by supplying voltage at a level higher than the ideal float voltage, but just short of the gassing point. This system is inexpensive and doesn't cause immediate harm to the batteries, but the high voltage is detrimental to long battery life.

Some automatic chargers taper the current as the battery is charged, but reduce the rate to a trickle rather than shut the charger off completely. When charging is complete, they trickle a constant voltage at a low rate, eventually causing a breakdown of the battery's internal components.

Ideally, your charger should have a gauge showing the output amperage, and an adjustable "float" setting, allowing you to tailor the voltage to your system.

A typical use pattern for a boat equipped with an automatic battery charger goes something like this: The owner plugs in his shore-power cord on Sunday, turns on the automatic charger, and goes home. The following Friday, he comes back, fires up the motors, unplugs the shore-power cord, and takes off.

Now, as long as he never lets the boat sit without the engine running and without the charger plugged in, his batteries could be nearly dead, and he'll never know. Not until he anchors up somewhere for a while and then tries to restart the engines after running the 12-volt accessories will he come to realize the error of his ways. The automatic charger has successfully masked the imminent death of the batteries. What's needed is to occasionally let the batteries sit for a day or so without running the engine or charger, and then measure the specific gravity of each cell with a hydrometer. A specific gravity reading of 1.265 indicates a full charge, 1.225 equals a 75 percent charge, 1.190 equals a 50 percent charge, 1.155 equals a 25 percent charge, and a reading of 1.120 indicates discharge. These readings must be corrected to account for electrolyte temperature, so check the instructions on your hydrometer for the proper method.

Generally, with a hydrometer calibrated for 80 degrees Fahrenheit, .004 points are added for each 10 degrees above 80 degrees, and .004 points subtracted for each 10 degrees below.

If any one cell reads .050 points lower than the others, it's probably going bad. Charge the battery, and recheck. If the reading stays lower than the other cells, you're going to have to replace the battery.

ADDING A CHARGER

Before buying a charger, carefully consider your situation. First of all, do you really need a charger? As mentioned earlier, if you own a powerboat that seldom sits at anchor using lots of 12-volt power, your alternator may be able to keep your batteries topped off.

If your alternator isn't quite doing the job, maybe you just need a different alternator, rather than a 120-volt charger. There are aftermarket alternators and voltage regulators out there that do a much more efficient job of charging batteries than the standard units, which are really not much more than marinized automotive parts. These high-output alternators can recharge batteries with much less engine time, and in some cases allow you to manually vary the rate according to conditions.

If you add an accessory alternator, be sure to match it according to manufacturer's specs with the proper voltage regulator, isolators, wiring, etc.

Battery isolators are solid-state devices that function as check valves in a battery system. They allow you to charge two or more batteries more efficiently by parceling out charging current to each battery individually, rather than averaging the needs of batteries at different states of discharge. An isolator will also prevent a low battery from discharging a good battery wired in parallel. Be advised, though, that isolators are available in a variety of current ratings, and must be carefully matched to your system. They also cause a .5- to .7-volt drop in voltage, so adjust your calculations accordingly.

If you decide that you do need a 120-volt charger, do you need the kind of ideal, fully automatic, and expensive charger described above? Do you put your boat in the water at the beginning of the season, then use it nearly every weekend until fall? If so, is an expensive charging system necessary?

Automotive trickle chargers are sometimes used by boaters as an inexpensive method of keeping batteries topped off. There are several problems with this approach. The most obvious one is that they have no means of sensing the battery's state of charge and shutting themselves off at the proper time. The other drawbacks are that they are not ignition protected, nor are their materials designed to stand up to the marine environment.

With a normal self-discharge rate of between 3 and 10 percent, a healthy, fully charged battery at an average temperature of 75 degrees Fahrenheit should still have a 50 percent charge after six months. If your batteries are run down after a week or two at rest, either a current draw is draining the batteries, or they are old and near the end of their useful lives.

If your automatic bilge pump is running too often and running down the battery, you need to find and repair the leak, not rely on a battery charger to keep the boat afloat. We know of at least one situation where a boater was doing just that. He'd tied up to a dock where electrical outlets were scarce, plugged in his boat, and left. The pump and charger did their respective jobs, until someone needed to use the outlet, unplugged his shore-power cord, and forgot to replace it when he was done. The boat sank.

Does your boat sit in the water for months on end, seldom visited? If so, you'll need a top-of-the-line system of low- or zero-maintenance batteries and an excellent charger, or someone to check on the boat periodically. Leaving a second-rate charger on constantly under those conditions is pretty much going to guarantee a short life span for your batteries, if not for your boat.

CHARGER CHOICE AND INSTALLATION

Battery chargers must be carefully sized to the system, taking into account the number of batteries on board and their sizes (capacities). Know the sizes of your batteries when you go shopping for a charger, and read the charger's specs before you buy. When installing a charger, there are a number of considerations to keep in mind.

Since chargers tend to be on the hefty side, make sure that they are well supported and through-bolted, with large washers or a backing plate in place.

Sometimes the charger can be mounted near a 120-volt outlet, and simply plugged in. This is convenient, but don't let convenience override other important considerations. The best method is to have the charger wired into its own circuit from the AC panel.

Another consideration is distance from the batteries. As the distance increases, so does either voltage drop or physical size of the wire required (see "AC and DC Electrics," Tables 9.4 and 9.5 on pages 141 and 142). The large-diameter cable required for remote charger installations is not only very expensive, it's also a *real* pain in the butt to work with! Terminals are difficult to find and to secure on to the cable, and the cable itself is thick, inflexible, and difficult to route and to handle.

Other important factors are heat and air flow around the unit, and possible presence of explosive or flammable gases. Most chargers are *not* ignition protected, and so cannot be mounted in engine rooms of gas motors, directly over the batteries, or in places where gas or propane fumes are likely to collect. Consult the owner's manual for specific recommendations.

Once you've made the decision, purchased and installed your charger, familiarize yourself with it. Don't just plug it in, turn it on whenever you're connected to shore power, and forget it. Check to see how it operates on your boat, with your batteries. Check electrolyte level frequently, especially at first, and check battery condition with a good hydrometer. Acquire a feel for how often your batteries need water, and note any change in frequency of water need.

Additional aids to battery maintenance include battery and electrical system monitors that can supply important information. They can indicate voltages on each battery, alternator-charging rates, AC voltage and current, and can even show how many amp hours have been used from a battery. The degree of sophistication you can buy is limited only by your checkbook!

INVERTERS

A fairly recent development in the boating industry is the popularity of inverters as a source of AC power. Basically, these devices take DC electricity and "invert" it, changing it into 120-volt AC power. Installation and maintenance of inverters is beyond our scope in this book, but a brief word is in order.

The nice thing about inverters is that they provide an alternative to gen sets, either as substitutes for generator purchase, or to reduce generator running time. A generator is a noisy, smelly, expensive, high-maintenance way to obtain AC power. Inverters are quiet, clean, and, in many cases, less expensive than gen sets. There are some other considerations to keep in mind, however.

Nothing is free, and the cost of an inverter can be measured not only by purchase and installation price, but also as a function of wear and tear on your battery system. Using batteries as a source of additional power will add to the number of charge-discharge cycles your batteries endure. A battery only has so many of these cycles in it before it dies, and marginally adequate batteries will have their life spans reduced dramatically by repeated inverter use.

If your charging system of alternators and 120-volt charger aren't up to the added strain, something will give eventually, and it will probably be something expensive.

With this in mind, however, inverters, properly installed and used in a well-designed system, can provide added flexibility and functions to your battery system.

Battery use and maintenance is simple and straightforward, provided you understand the principles involved, and keep an occasional eye on the system. No combination of batteries, alternators, and chargers is going to be completely maintenance-free, and while you can reduce the amount of care you must give to the system, a certain level of upkeep and monitoring is essential. Batteries are expensive, and good care will extend their lives considerably.

DEFINITIONS

Ampere-hour (Amp-Hr, AH): This is a unit of a battery's electrical storage capacity. A battery that delivers 5 amps of current for 20 hours has supplied 100 Amp-Hrs of capacity.

Capacity: A battery's capacity indicates its ability to deliver a certain amount of current at a specified rate over a definite period of time. Its reserve capacity rating is the time in minutes that a battery at 80 degrees Fahrenheit will deliver 25 amps. A battery's capacity is determined by size, weight, temperature, age, etc.

Cold-cranking rating: Number of amps a battery at 0 degrees Fahrenheit can deliver for 30 seconds while maintaining a voltage of 1.2 volts per cell.

Specific gravity: The ratio of the density of a liquid such as battery electrolyte to the density of water. A hydrometer reading of 1.2 means that the volume of electrolyte being measured is 1.2 times as dense as the same volume of water.

9
AC AND DC ELECTRICS

T HIS CHAPTER will describe and outline the basic 12-volt direct current (DC) and 120-volt alternating current (AC) systems found aboard most pleasure boats. For boats using 24- and 32-volt DC, or 240-volt AC, most of the information also applies, with relevant exceptions noted.

The standards and practices outlined follow the recommendations of the American Boat and Yacht Council, the National Fire Protection Association, and the federal regulations enforced by the U.S. Coast Guard. Some of the material standards also refer to standards published by Underwriter's Laboratories (UL) and the Society of Automotive Engineers (SAE). Information on how to obtain copies of these recommendations and standards is found in the Sources of Information.

Many of these standards and practices are requirements under federal law for boats using gas-powered inboard engines, but the ABYC and NFPA recommend applying the standards to diesel-powered craft as well. If you own or operate a diesel-powered boat, these practices are optional, but highly recommended. Cutting corners to save a dollar here and there is possible, but do so at your own peril.

We don't want to sound like alarmists, but after seeing what some people consider to be "acceptable" practices, we cannot recommend that people ignore the standards and just use common sense.

You should also be advised that any work that doesn't meet these standards is likely to be rejected by marine surveyors. If your boat requires a survey for insurance purposes, for refinancing, or for resale, nonstandard work will have to be corrected before the boat will pass. Save yourself time, money, inconvenience, and possibly disaster, and do it right the first time.

While the AC and DC systems aboard boats have many principles in common with household AC systems and with automotive DC systems, there are significant differences in practice. Wire, wiring connections, switches, and all other components must be compatible with marine use. The greatly increased corrosion factors involved, as well as the possibility of contact with flammable liquids and explosive fumes, demand that items of appropriate qualities and materials be used.

While there are some areas where nonmarine parts and accessories can be used, it's not a good idea to assume so in all cases. Where it's possible, we'll mention it—if it's not specifically noted that household or automotive units are acceptable, don't use them.

The subject of electricity doesn't lend itself well to oversimplification. An understanding of some of the theory involved is essential in order to comprehend what's going on in a system of invisible forces. On the other hand, it's easy to get bogged down in explanations of theory and definitions of terms. So we're going to try to keep theoretical discussions to a minimum, explaining only what we think is essential in order to understand the mechanics of what we're doing.

In some cases, this will mean that you're just going to have to play along. Should your intellectual curiosity demand more detail, we'll recommend the sources we use for clearing up mysteries.

TEST METERS

As mentioned in the "Tools" chapter, a good crimping tool and a multitester (also called multimeter, VOM, or volt-ohm-milliam-meter) are essential for electrical work. Using a multitester is simple, as long as you take a few precautions and learn to decipher the different symbols and abbreviations used.

The most frequently used functions of a multitester are the volt- and ohmmeters. The voltmeter functions, both AC and DC, are used to check for "hot" wires and outlets, and the ohmmeter function is used to check wires for continuity, and to test the integrity of ground wires and straps.

There are many different types and manufacturers of multitesters, so we're going to fall back on our old, worn-out advice that you check your owner's manual for details of use and care. Beyond that, however, we can offer a few suggestions.

A fifteen-dollar analog multimeter with six or eight scales will probably be all the sophistication you'll ever need. The ability to test 12-volt DC, 120-volt AC, and a simple ohmmeter will probably be the extent of your multitesting. When buying an analog meter, try to find one that has a 0- to 15-volt DC scale. Some meters have 0- to 10- and 0- to 50-volt scales, but a 0- to 15-volt scale is much more useful when working with 12 volts.

If you plan on doing some of the precise voltage testing necessary to evaluate a battery charging system (as mentioned in the "Batteries" chapter), a digital meter will probably be necessary. Inexpensive digital meters can be found for under fifty dollars.

Always check your scale settings before touching the probes to any wires. Don't just assume that the setting is okay, or that it's still in the same position where you last remembered using it. Frying a perfectly good meter by trying to test a 120-volt circuit with the meter set on ohms has been known to happen.

Common abbreviations on meters include AC and DC, V for volts, A for amps, mA for milliamps (thousandths of an amp), $\overline{=}$ or − for ground, + for positive, Ω for ohms, ∞ for infinity, and K for thousand.

On small meters, scales are usually selected by inserting the probes into the appropriate sockets, while more complex meters with more scales use a combination of sockets and a dial.

In most cases, there is one socket for the negative probe, and it's usually marked " − " or "Com" or both. There may also be separate negative sockets for AC and for DC and ohm readings.

Before testing a circuit with the voltmeter, calibrate the meter by setting the needle to zero with the adjusting screw on the meter's face. (The thin mirror strip on the meter face is used to visually line up the needle with its mirror image to check the pointer position accurately.) Set the meter to the scale for the highest voltage likely to be encountered. For example, if there's a possibility of hitting a 240-volt reading when testing an AC circuit, set your meter on a high enough register before testing. Then, if you see that the scale is too high when you take the reading, you can reduce it to a more readable scale without damage to the meter.

The ohmmeter tests a conductor or connection for resistance to circuit continuity by sending an electric current, provided by an internal battery, through one probe, and reads how much of that current returns to the other one, indicating the value on the ohms scale. Similarly, the amount of electrical resistance can be measured in a circuit, as can the amount of resistance offered by a path to ground.

To test resistance, the ohmmeter is calibrated by inserting the probes into the proper sockets (check the meter's owner's manual if you're unsure or if the meter markings are confusing), adjusting the dial to the correct range, and then touching the free ends of the probes together. The needle should swing over to the right-hand side of the ohms scale, and is then adjusted to the zero position with the "Ohms [or Ω] Adjust" dial.

The ohmmeter function requires the use of an internal battery. If you find that you're unable to calibrate the ohmmeter, a weak battery is usually the cause.

The ohmmeter function is the only one where the polarity, whether positive or negative, of the test probes is irrelevant. In all other functions, use the black wire for negative, the red one for positive.

A particularly handy idea is to make up a wire with an alligator clip in place of the negative probe. You'll find that there are more than a few instances where three hands are required for manipulating the two probes and the meter, and the alligator clip makes for easier handling. The clip can then be attached to any good ground, and voltage readings taken by touching the positive probe to the hot wire. Either cut off the probe supplied and crimp or solder a clip in its place, or make up another probe wire with parts from an electronics supply house. Take your meter in with you if you're going to buy parts, since there are several sizes of plug-in jacks available.

Testing voltages is pretty straightforward, both for AC and DC circuits. Set your meter to the appropriate scale, and clip your negative probe to the ground wire or insert it into the ground socket in the outlet. Then use the other probe to test the hot wire for voltage. Since the AC and DC grounds are separate, or at least should be, you need to use an AC ground source for checking AC voltage, and a DC ground for DC voltage.

When testing resistance, most of the time you'll be trying to determine if a wire is intact from end to end. Calibrate your meter and touch the probes to the opposite ends of the suspect wire. If the needle jumps, the wire's okay—if it just lies there, the wire's broken.

Where you might want a bit more precision is in determining fuel system grounding, as mentioned in the "Diesel Fuel Systems" chapter (see page 82). This assures that any static charge generated by the fuel-filling operation has a low-resistance (less than 100 ohms) path to ground. To check, set your meter to "Ohms." If your meter has more than one ohms scale (usually designated as RX1, RX10, RX100, and RX1K) set it to the most sensitive scale (in this case, RX1). Calibrate the meter as mentioned above. Touch one probe to the item being tested, and the other to a good ground. A reading of 100 ohms or less means you're okay. A higher reading indicates that the path to ground is of too high a resistance, and must be looked into.

MATERIALS

All wire used on boats must be insulated, stranded copper. The solid wire common in house construction is unacceptable since it's liable to break after being flexed a few times. Boats, being a bit more active than your average three-bedroom home, demand the use of stranded wire. It should also be double insulated, meaning that insulated wires are enclosed in an additional layer of insulation.

The term *wire* is somewhat imprecise, since it can apply to any number of different configurations of wire, insulation, etc. Textbooks and industry standards prefer to use the term *conductor*. For example, with a length of wire consisting of two insulated "wires" encased in an additional sheath of insulation, the entire piece can be considered a wire, as can each of the individual wires inside. The conventional means of referring to these items is that the whole piece is a length of "duplex" wire, or double-insulated wire, but the separate wires are referred to as conductors.

The wire and insulation must also meet certain standards for use aboard boats. Again, these standards are mandatory only for boats with gasoline engines, but recommended for all boats. Marine-grade wire

Table 9.1   SAE CONDUCTORS

TYPE	DESCRIPTION	AVAILABLE INSULATION TEMPERATURE RATING PER SAE J378b
GPT	Thermoplastic Insulation, Braidless	60°C (140°F) 90°C (194°F) 105°C (221°F)
HDT	Thermosplastic Insulation, Braidless	60°C (140°F) 90°C (194°F) 105°C (221°F)
SGT	Thermosplastic Insulation, Braidless	60°C (140°F) 90°C (194°F) 105°C (221°F)
STS	Thermosetting Synthetic Rubber Insulation, Braidless	85°C (185°F) 90°C (194°F)
HTS	Thermosetting Synthetic Rubber Insulation, Braidless	85°C (185°F) 90°C (194°F)
SXL	Thermosetting Cross-Linked Polyethylene Insulation, Braidless	125°C (257°F)

Figs. 9.1. and 9.2. *Tables listing conductor insulation types and temperature ratings.* TABLES COURTESY OF AMERICAN BOAT AND YACHT COUNCIL (ABYC).

sold in chandleries will generally meet these requirements, but if in doubt, check the markings on the wire against Tables 9.1 and 9.2 (Figures 9.1 and 9.2).

The standard of measurement for wire is the American Wire Gauge (AWG) system. Larger gauges are indicated by smaller numbers. The size of wire needed is determined by how much current the accessory uses, how far it is from the electrical power source, and how much voltage drop is acceptable. See Tables 9.4 and 9.5 for details.

Connecting one section of wire to another and attaching terminal fittings is most commonly accomplished with solderless crimp fittings. These fittings come in a wide variety of types and sizes, and should only be attached with a crimping tool made for the job. The most common crimp fittings include butt connectors for joining two lengths of wire together, ring connectors for attaching wire to screws in terminal blocks, and male and female spade connectors for wire connections that will be disconnected frequently. (See Figure 9.3.) The twist-on connectors and wire nuts used in home construction are *not* acceptable for any wiring done on a boat.

The fittings are color-coded for the appropriate sizes of wire to be used. Pink fittings are usually used only in electronics work, since

Table 9.2   CONDUCTORS

TYPES (SEE NOTE)	DESCRIPTION	AVAILABLE INSULATION TEMPERATURE RATING
THW	Moisture and Heat-Resistant, Thermoplastic	75°C (167°F)
TW	Moisture-Resistant, Thermoplastic	60°C (140°F)
THWN	Moisture and Heat-Resistant, Thermoplastic	75°C (167°F)
XHHW	Moisture and Heat-Resistant, Cross Linked Synthetic Polymer	90°C (194°F)
MTW	Moisture, Heat and Oil Resistant, Thermoplastic	90°C (194°F)
AWM STYLE NOS: 1230 1231 1275 1345	Moisture, Heat and Oil Resistant, Thermoplastic, Thermosetting	105°C (221°F)
UL 1426	Boat Cable	(See UL 1426)

NOTE: Some of the listed types are not commonly available in stranded construction for sizes smaller than 8 AWG. However, these types are acceptable if obtainable.

they're designed for use with 22- to 18-gauge wire. Blue fittings (14- to 16-gauge) and yellow fittings (12- to 10-gauge) are the ones most commonly used, with some larger sizes found occasionally. The connections must be strong enough to resist being pulled off the wire, as listed in the accompanying Table 9.3 (Figure 9.4).

After a crimp connector is applied, wrap the joint with a few firm turns of electrical tape. This covers any exposed wire and helps to keep corrosion out. Electrical tape is used to provide electrical insulation where a wire's plastic insulation has been stripped away to make a connection. Use a good grade of tape and don't substitute friction tape, duct tape, etc. It also comes in a variety of colors, useful for color-coding wire functions. It is *not* meant to be used to hold lengths of wire together in place of a crimp connector.

Solder is sometimes used to join wires together, although with the advent of crimp connectors, it's rare to find soldered joints aboard pleasure boats. Some folks prefer it, though, and in some cases the type of connection desired makes solder the material of choice. When

Fig. 9.3. *Solderless crimp-on connectors, including ring terminals, butt connector, and spade terminals.*

using solder in electrical work, be sure to use only rosin core solder. Acid core solder is only used to repair nonelectrical items, and will corrode quickly if used aboard your boat.

Solder alone is not acceptable as a means of providing mechanical connections. In case of high current flow, enough heat can build up to melt solder, so wires must also be joined with crimp connectors.

Heat-shrink tubing and tape are used to make wire connections waterproof and to insulate them. With tubing, a length equal to the length of the exposed wire, plus a half inch or so on either end, is slipped over one of the wires before the connection is made. After joining the wires, slide the tubing over the connection and heat the tubing with a heat gun or a soldering iron held next to it. For connections that are already made or are more complex than a simple wire-to-wire joint, heat-shrink tape is available. Wrap it around the connection securely, and heat carefully. The tubing will shrink tightly to cover the connection.

Wire ties or cable ties come in a variety of lengths, both with and without screw holes for mounting, and are useful for bundling wires,

Table 9.3 **TENSILE TEST VALUES FOR CONNECTIONS**

CONDUCTOR SIZE GAGE	TENSILE FORCE Pounds/Newtons		CONDUCTOR SIZE GAGE	TENSILE FORCE Pounds/Newtons	
18	10	44	4	70	311
16	15	66	3	80	355
14	30	133	2	90	400
12	35	155	1	100	444
10	40	177	0	125	556
8	45	200	00	150	667
6	50	222	000	175	778
5	60	266	0000	225	1000

Fig. 9.4. *Table showing recommended attachment strength of crimp-on terminals.* COURTESY ABYC.

securing them up and out of the way, and for dozens of other fastening chores aboard the boat. They're very strong, nonconducting and non-corrosive, their only drawback being that they don't stand up well to sunlight and tend to get brittle with exposure. (See Figure 9.5.)

Circuit breakers are fast replacing fuses as the most common means of overcurrent protection. Fuses are cheaper, to be sure, but once a

Fig. 9.5. *Back of a typical electrical panel, showing banks of circuit break-ers, and wiring neatly bundled and secured with wire ties.*

circuit breaker is installed, it's much less trouble to maintain than a fuse. Differences and uses are explained below.

Switches need to be suitable for the marine environment, whether for AC or DC use. You can buy cheap and simple push-pull or toggle switches in hardware and auto parts stores, but their life expectancy aboard a boat is bound to be short. Marine switches are usually made of brass, ensuring longer life.

Switches are also subject to amperage ratings, which must be followed if the installation is to be a safe one. Hooking a 6-amp switch into a 20-amp circuit will result in "southern fried switch," considered a delicacy by parts supply houses.

AC switch types are classified into single- or double-pole and single- or double-throw categories. Consult a parts supplier or electrician if in doubt about the proper type of switch.

For high current loads, continuous-duty, heavy-duty switches are required. In applications where use of such switches is inconvenient or impossible, relays and solenoids can be used as alternatives. Consult an experienced marine electrician for details.

Finally, switches installed in engine rooms or other areas where gasoline fumes are likely to be encountered must be ignition protected.

The terms used in electrical work are defined more or less in relation to each other. For example, a volt is defined as the unit of electromotive force, or electrical potential, that will cause a current of 1 amp to flow through a conductor with 1 ohm of resistance. An ampere, or amp, is a unit of electric current, equal to the current that passes in a resistance of 1 ohm when 1 volt is applied. An ohm (we know you can see this coming) is the resistance in a conductor in which 1 volt of force produces a current of 1 amp.

In DC electrics, appliances are usually described in terms of how many amps they draw. In AC electrics, appliances are more likely to be rated in terms of watts, a unit of measure arrived at by multiplying amps by volts.

12-VOLT DIRECT CURRENT

The most basic concept in understanding and working with direct current (DC) electricity is the circuit. Electricity starts at the power source, flows through a conductor to the appliance, and back to ground. Interrupting the circuit with a break in the conductor causes the flow of electricity to stop. Of course, technology being what it is, there are numerous additions, refinements, and other complications that will enter into the picture, but we've found that most problems in troubleshooting and installing 12-volt equipment stem from a tendency to overcomplicate things. DC electricity is a very simple, straightforward system, and the best way to solve problems is to keep the system's simplicity in mind.

The 12-volt systems used on the vast majority of powerboats and sailboats built in the United States, Europe, and the Orient are very similar to automotive 12-volt systems. The principles are the same, but some practices are significantly different.

All the elements of the circuit must be compatible in order for things to work. The appliance must be matched to the voltage supplied, the conductors and circuit protection must be adequately sized for the current involved, the ground must be a good one, and all the connections have to be tight.

Fuses and circuit breakers guard against failures by acting as the weak links in a circuit. In case of a surge of current, the fuse will blow or the breaker will trip, stopping the flow of electricity before the other parts of the system can be damaged.

A fuse is a metal strip with a low melting point inside a glass tube, attached at both ends to metal caps. The fuse is installed in the line, and the current flows through it as it flows through the wire. In case of a current surge, the metal melts through, stopping the flow. The fuses are rated in terms of amperage, and a 10-amp fuse will blow if the current exceeds 10 amps. Some accessories such as pump motors specify slow-blow fuses that allow for a certain amount of current surge as the motor starts up. Substituting standard fuses for slow-blow fuses is not recommended.

There are also fuses with ceramic or fiber bodies that can substitute for the glass types. They work on the same principles, and are interchangeable, as long as the current ratings match. By matching the fuse to the circuit and the equipment, motor failures, melted wiring, and possible fires are avoided.

There are several different devices commonly used to hold fuses, including fuse blocks, in-line holders, and holders installed in panels. (See Figure 9.6.)

One warning about using in-line fuse holders: The size of the wire supplied with the holder must be taken into account. For example, a circuit with a 10-gauge conductor and a 20-amp in-line fuse contained

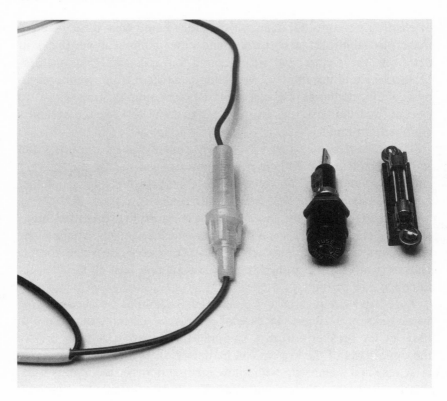

Fig. 9.6.   Left to right—*In-line fuse holder, panel-type fuse holder, and single-fuse block.*

in a holder supplied with 14-gauge wire is destined to cause a problem. That section of 14-gauge wire, no matter how short, is now the weak point in the circuit, and will cause the fuse to blow prematurely by restricting current flow.

On all fuse holders, you should mark the proper fuse size somewhere on the holder, whether with a label, a piece of tape, or scratched onto the holder itself.

Circuit breakers perform the same safety function as fuses, but in a slightly different way. They use magnetic or thermal sensing devices to detect current, and when the current flowing through the breaker exceeds its rating, it trips the breaker, interrupting the flow. When the problem is remedied, the switch on the front of the breaker is reset, and life goes on.

Circuit breakers should be of the type known as trip-free. These breakers can't be circumvented by holding the switch in the "On" position—the fault must be remedied for the breaker to remain in the "On" position.

The advantage to using fuses is that they're very cheap and yet effective. The disadvantage is that they can be a problem to place in a convenient location. For electrical accessories buried behind panels or in a boat's bilges, do you install the fuse holder near the equipment, where troubleshooting access is likely to be a problem? Or, do you install all the fuse holders in a convenient working area, far from the equipment, and try to remember which is which?

The other problem with fuses is carrying a large enough supply of every fuse on board. It's common when troubleshooting an electrical problem to go through a trial-and-error process, blowing a fuse with each trial. By the time you track down the cause of the trouble, you can run through a hefty supply of fuses.

What most people do when they run out of the right size fuse is to just substitute the next greater size—a *very* dangerous practice! The problem with this approach is that you're bypassing the circuit's safety feature. If the fuse is no longer the weakest link in the electrical chain, then failure will occur elsewhere if excessive current flows through the circuit and may cause a fire. And, no matter how sincere your intentions of replacing the fuse with the proper one "as soon as we get back to the marina," it's all too easy to forget about it, and just let it ride. A circuit designed for a maximum of 10 amps carrying a 20- or 30-amp fuse is an accident just waiting to happen.

Circuit breakers are much more convenient to use and to work with. They're conveniently located on the main breaker panel, they double in function as circuit protection and as on-off switches, and there's no limit to how many times they can be tripped and reset when you're tracking down a troublesome electrical problem. The disadvantage is cost. A fuse holder and fuse can be had for a dollar or two, and boxes of fuses for another dollar or so, while a trip-free marine circuit breaker can set you back fifteen dollars or more.

Most boats now come from the factory with panels of circuit breakers installed, usually with room for adding more breakers to allow for expansion. If you're adding circuits to such a system, it makes sense to go with the existing arrangement. Fifteen dollars won't break you, and from a convenience and resale point of view, will probably pay off in the long run.

However, if you've got a boat that already uses a fuse system, and doesn't have a breaker panel, or doesn't allow for easy expansion, it might make sense to go with fuses. Just be aware of the possible pitfalls, and always carry *plenty* of spares for each fuse used on board.

ADDING EQUIPMENT AND CIRCUITS

Tables 9.4. and 9.5 (Figures 9.7 and 9.8) show the minimum wire size to use in a DC circuit, considering the length of the circuit, the current that the appliance will draw, and the allowable voltage drop. Some accessories, such as interior lights, will work well with a 10 percent drop, while others, such as pump motors, work better with only a 3 percent drop. If there's any doubt about whether the wire size is big enough, go to the next size up (smaller gauge number).

Wire that's too small results in excessive voltage drop, which can cause electric motors to run poorly, and to wear out prematurely. It also results in excessive heat generation in the wire itself.

Table 9.6 (Figure 9.9) gives the maximum allowable current for different size wires and types of insulation in DC systems.

When figuring circuit lengths, always measure the distance from the power source to the appliance, and back again. In other words, a bilge pump that's ten feet away from the power source (usually a circuit breaker on the DC panel) demands that you use the wire gauge under the twenty-foot conductor length in the table. Some tables don't make this distinction clear, and it's easy to mistake wire length from appliance to voltage source for circuit length.

And that's twenty feet as the wire travels, not measured in a straight line. The pump can be two feet away from the breaker, but if the wire has to run behind panels, through bulkheads, and around stringers, you must use the actual wire length in your figuring, not just the physical distance between accessory and breaker.

When running wire to a new accessory, it's important that you run both hot and ground wires to their proper terminals. For example, if you're installing a bilge pump, it's possible to make it work by running a single hot wire from the breaker to the pump, and then running a ground wire from the pump to another ground in the system, such as the engine, a gas tank, etc. This will save you a few pennies on wire, but it can cause other problems. For one thing, troubleshooting becomes a nightmare, with wires running to ground all over the place. The more serious reason, though, is that running wires to ground in

Table 9.4   CONDUCTOR SIZES FOR 10% DROP IN VOLTAGE

Length of Conductor from Source of Current to Device and Back to Source—Feet

12 Volts—10% Drop Wire Sizes (gage)—Based on Minimum CM Area

TOTAL CURRENT ON CIRCUIT IN AMPS	10	15	20	25	30	40	50	60	70	80	90	100	110	120	130	140	150	160	170
5	18	18	18	18	18	16	16	14	14	14	12	12	12	12	12	10	10	10	10
10	18	18	16	16	14	14	12	12	10	10	10	10	8	8	8	8	8	8	6
15	18	16	14	14	12	12	10	10	8	8	8	8	8	6	6	6	6	6	6
20	16	14	14	12	12	10	10	8	8	8	6	6	6	6	6	6	4	4	4
25	16	14	12	12	10	10	8	8	6	6	6	6	6	4	4	4	4	4	2
30	14	12	12	10	10	8	8	6	6	6	6	6	4	4	4	2	2	2	2
40	14	12	10	10	8	8	6	6	4	4	4	4	2	2	2	2	2	2	2
50	12	10	10	8	8	6	6	4	4	2	2	2	2	2	2	1	1	1	1
60	12	10	8	8	6	6	4	4	2	2	2	2	1	1	1	1	0	0	0
70	10	8	8	6	6	6	4	2	2	2	2	1	1	1	0	0	0	0	0
80	10	8	6	6	6	4	2	2	2	2	1	1	0	0	0	2/0	2/0	2/0	2/0
90	10	8	6	6	6	4	2	2	2	1	1	0	0	0	2/0	2/0	2/0	2/0	3/0
100	10	8	6	6	4	4	2	2	1	1	0	0	0	2/0	2/0	2/0	3/0	3/0	3/0

Figs. 9.7. and 9.8.   *Minimum conductor sizes for 12-volt circuits, based on circuit length, current draw, and voltage drop.* COURTESY ABYC.

Table 9.5 CONDUCTORS SIZES FOR 3% DROP IN VOLTAGE

Length of Conductor from Source of Current to Device and Back to Source—Feet

12 Volts—3% Drop Wire Sizes (gage)—Based on Minimum CM Area

TOTAL CURRENT ON CIRCUIT IN AMPS	10	15	20	25	30	40	50	60	70	80	90	100	110	120	130	140	150	160	170
5	18	16	14	12	12	10	10	10	8	8	8	6	6	6	6	6	6	6	6
10	14	12	10	10	10	8	6	6	6	6	4	4	4	4	2	2	2	2	2
15	12	10	10	8	8	6	6	6	4	4	2	2	2	2	2	1	1	1	1
20	10	10	8	6	6	6	4	4	2	2	2	2	1	1	1	0	0	0	2/0
25	10	8	6	6	6	4	4	2	2	2	1	1	0	0	0	2/0	2/0	2/0	3/0
30	10	8	6	6	4	4	2	2	1	1	0	0	0	2/0	2/0	3/0	3/0	3/0	3/0
40	8	6	4	4	4	2	1	1	0	0	2/0	2/0	3/0	3/0	3/0	4/0	4/0	4/0	4/0
50	6	6	4	4	2	2	0	0	2/0	2/0	3/0	3/0	4/0	4/0	4/0				
60	6	4	2	2	2	1	2/0	2/0	3/0	3/0	4/0	4/0	4/0						
70	6	4	2	2	1	0	3/0	3/0	3/0	4/0	4/0								
80	6	4	2	2	1	0	3/0	3/0	4/0	4/0									
90	4	2	2	1	0	2/0	3/0	4/0	4/0										
100	4	2	2	1	0	2/0	3/0	4/0											

Table 9.6 ALLOWABLE AMPERAGE OF CONDUCTORS FOR UNDER 50 VOLTS

TEMPERATURE RATING OF CONDUCTOR INSULATION

CONDUCTOR SIZE ENGLISH (METRIC) SEE TABLE IV	60°C (140°F)		75°C (167°F)		80°C (176°F)		90°C (194°F)		105°C (221°F)		125°C (257°F)		200°C (392°F)
	OUTSIDE ENGINE SPACES	INSIDE ENGINE SPACES	OUTSIDE ENGINE SPACES	INSIDE ENGINE SPACES	OUTSIDE ENGINE SPACES	INSIDE ENGINE SPACES	OUTSIDE ENGINE SPACES	INSIDE ENGINE SPACES	OUTSIDE ENGINE SPACES	INSIDE ENGINE SPACES	OUTSIDE ENGINE SPACES	INSIDE ENGINE SPACES	OUTSIDE OR INSIDE ENGINE SPACES
18 (0.8)	10	5.8	10	7.5	15	11.7	20	16.4	20	17.0	25	22.3	25
16 (1)	15	8.7	15	11.3	20	15.6	25	20.5	25	21.3	30	26.7	35
14 (2)	20	11.6	20	15.0	25	19.5	30	24.6	35	29.8	40	35.6	45
12 (3)	25	14.5	25	18.8	35	27.3	40	32.8	45	38.3	50	44.5	55
10 (5)	40	23.2	40	30.0	50	39.0	55	45.1	60	51.0	70	62.3	70
8 (8)	55	31.9	65	48.8	70	54.6	70	57.4	80	68.0	90	80.1	100
6 (13)	80	46.4	95	71.3	100	78.0	100	82.0	120	102.0	125	111.3	135
4 (19)	105	60.9	125	93.8	130	101.4	135	110.7	160	136.0	170	151.3	180
2 (32)	140	81.2	170	127.5	175	136.5	180	147.6	210	178.5	225	200.3	240
1 (40)	165	95.7	195	146.3	210	163.8	210	172.2	245	208.3	265	235.9	280
0 (50)	195	113.1	230	172.5	245	191.1	245	200.9	285	242.3	305	271.5	325
00 (62)	225	130.5	265	198.8	285	222.3	285	233.7	330	280.5	355	316.0	370
000 (81)	260	150.8	310	232.5	330	257.4	330	270.6	385	327.3	410	364.9	430
0000 (103)	300	174.0	360	270.0	385	300.3	385	315.7	445	378.3	475	422.8	510

Fig. 9.9. *Table listing maximum current for DC systems, based on conductor size and insulation temperature ratings.* COURTESY ABYC.

a haphazard manner creates a lot of stray current. The negative conductor in a two-wire system doesn't carry voltage, but it does carry current, and the current carried by the negative conductor will greatly accelerate galvanic corrosion of your underwater metal parts. (This concept is hard to grasp, and in fact some of us never do really understand the physics involved. Fortunately, it's one of those things that you don't have to understand, you just need to take it on faith and incorporate it into your work habits.)

The other point that has to be made about the current-carrying capability of the ground wire is that in a two-wire system, both wires need to be the same size. Don't try to save pennies by running the proper size hot wire and a smaller gauge ground wire, reasoning that since the ground wire doesn't carry voltage, size doesn't matter.

Let's go through a hypothetical installation of a 12-volt pump, just to illustrate all the necessary steps and calculations involved. After finding an appropriate location for our pump, making sure that the pump and its attendant plumbing fittings will fit into the space we've got in mind, it's time to figure out how to wire it. The first thing to check is the rating of the pump motor. On a typical 12-volt pump, the specs might give both motor draw and fuse size, such as "$5/7.5$." In this case, the manufacturer is telling us that the pump draws 5 amps, and is recommending a 7.5-amp fuse, the 2.5-amp difference allowing for start-up surge and for the heavy loading on the motor as the pressure builds to the cutoff point.

Next, we need to find out what size wire to use. Measuring the distance from our prospective location to the breaker panel, we find a distance of fifteen feet, *as the wire travels,* not in a straight line! If the pump is going to be the only thing on the circuit, our recommended fuse (or circuit breaker) size tells us that 7.5 amps will be our maximum draw.

Next, we consult Table 9.5 (Figure 9.8). A fifteen-foot wire run gives us a total conductor length of thirty feet. Since there is no listing for 7.5 amps, we take the next size up, which is 10 amps. Consulting the 3-percent voltage drop column, since we want our motor to run as efficiently as possible, we find that we need 10-gauge wire.

Finally, we must also consider how certain we are that this is the only item that we'll ever want on this circuit. Is there a good chance that we might eventually want a larger pump installed? With those questions in mind, would it be more cost- and effort-effective to wire for the larger current now, rather than going through the drill all over again in the future?

Is cost of materials an object? The difference between thirty feet of 10/2 (10-gauge duplex or double-insulated) wire and thirty feet of 14/2 wire isn't likely to be more than a couple of dollars. But, when you start getting into wire that's bigger than 10-gauge, costs start to escalate rather quickly.

Choose a switch of the proper type and size. In this case, a two-position (off-on), push-pull switch rated at 12 volts, 7.5 amps or greater, will work. If using a circuit breaker rather than a fuse, an additional switch isn't necessary.

Locate the fuse in an accessible, easy-to-remember position. If your fuse panel has a vacant slot, no problem. Remember that the accessory has to be connected to both ground and hot, so locate your fuse block or holder near a convenient ground connection.

If you're using an existing fuse panel, there will be a ground connection on the panel, either in the form of a large stud or bolt, or a brass strip.

If installing a fuse elsewhere, you may have to add a ground connection for convenience, especially if installing a fuse block with several holders. There are numerous combinations of fuse and terminal blocks available (Figure 9.10), so match them to your installation, keeping in mind the possibility of future expansion.

Don't wire accessories directly to the batteries. The reason that you have a battery switch on board is so that you can throw that switch and know that everything on the 12-volt system is shut off, whether for emergency or convenience.

If the main battery switch is to be bypassed for automatic bilge pumps, automatic fire extinguishers, or burglar alarms, wire them to the hot terminals on the switch. This keeps the battery terminals uncluttered, and work can be done in the cabin, rather than down in the bilge. When wiring equipment around the switch and main panel, remember to fuse all such circuits.

All that's left, then, is to actually do the work. Secure your pump in place, and run the plumbing. Attach the wires to the pump, either with butt connectors or quick-disconnect spade terminals. Run the wire to the power source, securing it in position with wire ties, and adding chafe protection where it runs through bulkheads. Then wire in the fuse or circuit breaker, and hit the switch.

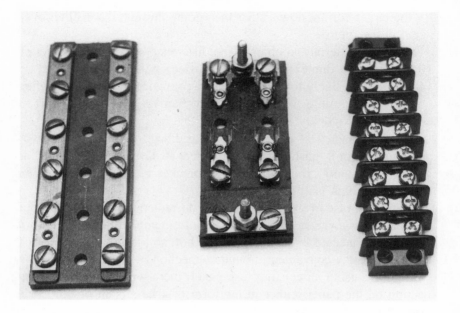

Fig. 9.10.   Left to right—*Terminal block, combination fuse and terminal block, independent hot-feed terminal block.*

12-VOLT TROUBLESHOOTING

Table 9.7 (Figure 9.11) lists the recommended wiring color code used by most domestic manufacturers. It can help in identifying wire functions, but shouldn't be taken as gospel. Production line shortages, repair work done since the boat was commissioned, and just plain mistakes can cause your boat's color code to differ from the standard. Use the table as a general guideline for troubleshooting, and to choose the proper color code when you're installing equipment.

Finding the source of 12-volt problems is not terribly complicated, but there are times when it's easier than others. The basic task of locating and repairing simple faults can be complicated by access difficulties and by nonstandard practices of previous repair people, but for the most part, it's a very simple process.

(When working on DC accessories where fumes may be present, turn off the battery switch and disconnect the negative battery terminals. This will ensure that even accessories that are wired backward will be neutralized.)

Table 9.7   RECOMMENDED MARINE WIRING COLOR CODE
DIRECT CURRENT SYSTEMS—UNDER 50 VOLTS
(No diagram required if wiring is in compliance with Tables I and II)

COLOR	ITEM	USE
Yellow w/Red Stripe (YR)	Starting Circuit	Starting Switch to Solenoid
Yellow (Y)	Generator or Alternator Field	Generator or Alternator Field to Regulator Field Terminal
	Bilge Blowers	Fuse or Switch to Blowers
Dark Gray (Gy)	Navigation Lights	Fuse or Switch to Lights
	Tachometer	Tachometer Sender to Gauge
Brown (Br)	Generator Armature	Generator Armature to Regulator
	Alternator Charge Light	Generator Terminal/Alternator Auxiliary Terminal to Light to Regulator
	Pumps	Fuse or Switch to Pumps
Orange (O)	Accessory Feed	Ammeter to Alternator or Generator Output and Accessory Fuses or Switches
	Accessory Common Feed	Distribution Panel to Accessory Switch
Purple (Pu)	Ignition	Ignition Switch to Coil and Electrical Instruments
	Instrument Feed	Distribution Panel to Electric Instruments
Dark Blue	Cabin and Instrument Lights	Fuse or Switch to Lights
Light Blue (Lt Bl)	Oil Pressure	Oil Pressure Sender to Gauge
Tan	Water Temperature	Water Temperature Sender to Gauge
Pink (Pk)	Fuel Gauge	Fuel Gauge Sender to Gauge

Fig. 9.11. *Marine wiring color code.* COURTESY ABYC.

For example, let's suppose that a 12-volt cabin light is out. Question number one should be, "Is the light turned on?" Always check the easiest, most obvious possibilities first—failure to observe this most basic of rules can result in unnecessary and embarrassing repairs.

If the battery switch is on, the light switch is on, and the breaker is on or the fuse is good, and still no light, then it's time to proceed. Is the bulb burned out? A light bulb is a miniature circuit, with current flowing from the contact point on the base, through the filament, and back to ground, either through the brass base or through a second contact point on the base. When a bulb fails, it's because the filament has broken, breaking the circuit. To check the bulb, set your VOM to "Ohms" and touch one probe to each contact point on the base—you will get a reading of near 0 ohms from a good bulb, and ∞ (infinite) ohms from a burned-out one. (If the bulb has only one contact point on the base, touch one probe to it and the other to the brass casing.)

A frequent cause of lamp failures is corrosion of the bulb or socket contact points. If the contacts are coated with a granular-looking film, sand lightly and spray with WD-40®, or a dielectric silicone grease. Silicone grease is sold in electronics supply stores, often in small syringes that make it easy to apply in tight spaces.

If the bulb is okay, and the switches are all on, then it's time to start eliminating causes. Is there any other accessory on the same circuit, and if so, is it working? If not, then the problem's with the source of power for the entire circuit. Recheck the circuit breaker or fuse. If they are functioning then the cause is confined to the light wiring.

Start at one end or the other of the entire circuit and use your VOM to find where there is current flow and where there isn't. Don't jump around, testing different parts of the system haphazardly. Start at one end, and methodically work your way to the other end, testing as you go. Take notes on the trickier problems—writing things down can force you to see the problem in a different context and often helps with logic problems.

If you find that there is power all along the conductor, and the bulb is good but still doesn't work, check your ground. Ground connections can fail or deteriorate, a source of problems that is often overlooked. We tend to think that current is all-important, and that ground connections are a kind of afterthought. But each side of the circuit is equally important, since a break anywhere causes the circuit to fail.

Troubleshooting can be frustrating and tedious, but if you approach each problem methodically and logically, eliminating possible causes one at a time, eventually you'll solve it. Take each instance as a learning experience, maintain a sense of humor, and, if necessary, take notes. Troubleshooting skills increase with use, and successfully tracking down and solving problems can actually be enjoyable.

AC THEORY

Alternating current, or AC, is the type of electricity used in homes. Generated in power plants and transmitted over high-tension wires for use in powering household appliances, it arrives in 120- and 240-volt increments. Light fixtures and outlets receive 120 volts, and the 240-volt lines are used for electric ranges, dryers, and other high-voltage appliances.

Basic 120-volt power is sometimes referred to as 115 or 110 volt, and 240 is sometimes called 220- or 230-volt power, as the actual voltage measured at the outlet tends to vary a bit. Most folks use 120 volts as the basic measurement, so that's what we'll use.

AC power comes aboard in a three-wire system, consisting of hot, ground, and neutral wires. The ground, or grounding, wire connects the system to the ground supplied by the power source, and the hot wire carries the 120 volts of alternating current. The neutral wire, sometimes confusingly referred to as the grounded (as opposed to grounding) conductor, is a wire that carries current, but not voltage.

Proper color coding of the system dictates that the ground wire is green, the neutral wire is white, and the hot wire is either red or black. (Some boats built in Asia use a system of green, white, and red.) If you're used to working on DC systems where the hot wire is red and the ground wire black, it's easy to forget that the black wire functions are completely different on AC and DC systems. Keep it in mind!

The distinctions among the functions of the three wires can be confusing, but a working knowledge of AC doesn't demand a full understanding of electrical theory. The main thing you need to know about conductor functions relates to polarity. If the hot wire, the ground wire, and the neutral wire are all connected to their proper on-board counterparts, everything works and nobody gets hurt. However, if for example the incoming hot wire is connected to the on-board neutral wire, we have a condition known as reversed polarity.

The wiring that goes from the on-board service panel to the AC accessories passes through a main breaker and through individual, branch circuit breakers on the panel. The main breaker is connected to both the hot and neutral conductors, so that when it is turned off, all power to the branch circuits is shut off. The breakers for the branch circuits, however, only break the hot conductor, the result being that in case of reversed polarity, the voltage travels through the neutral wire, straight to the appliance. When the shore power is connected, and the main breaker turned on, voltage bypasses the breakers by traveling through the neutral wire, and a safety hazard is present. In case of a problem, turning off the breaker will not turn off the electricity to the appliance. Only shutting off the main breaker or disconnecting the shore cord will render the system "cold."

SHORE POWER

Most midsize and large boats have provisions for connecting an on-board service panel to a 120-volt outlet at the dock. When 120-volt AC power is brought on board, it is referred to as shore power, and the waterproof extension cord made for such connections is the shore-power cord.

Some boats, most often from thirty feet in length in powerboats and forty feet or so in sailboats, have on-board generators, usually referred to as gen sets. These are gas- or diesel-powered engines that generate electricity for a boat's use, and their physical bulk usually confines their use to the larger boats. Another way to provide on-board AC power is with an inverter, as mentioned in the "Batteries" chapter.

Boats that have gen sets or inverters aboard also have provisions for shore power, since running a gen set in the marina is impractical, and inverter use shortens battery life. The standard shore-power service is a 30-amp connection, although some older marinas provide 15- or 20-amp services, and many provide 50-amp services for larger boats. If you're unsure about the amperage of a connection, inspect it carefully—there should be markings in the center of the twist-lock fitting indicating voltage and amperage. (See Figure 9.12.)

If you do a lot of marina hopping, sooner or later you'll encounter dock outlets that don't match your shore-power connector. If you've made no provisions for such an occasion, you're out of luck. However, if you plan ahead, problems can be avoided. Companies that manufacture shore-power cords also make adapters for them, so that you don't need to buy a new shore-power cord for every marina you visit. An assortment of types common to your cruising ground is a good investment.

If you plan on an extended cruise in unfamiliar waters, a few calls to marinas or friends in the area can prevent problems.

Be advised that even though your cord and fitting are 30-amp fittings, if you're plugged into a 15- or 20-amp service, 15 or 20 amps

E-8 (17)
8-5-85

STANDARD FEMALE CONVENIENCE RECEPTACLE CONFIGURATIONS

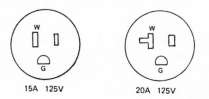

15A   125V   20A   125V

SHORE POWER CABLE CONFIGURATIONS

RECEPTACLE AND CONNECTOR – LOCKING AND GROUNDING

PLUG AND INLET – LOCKING AND GROUNDING

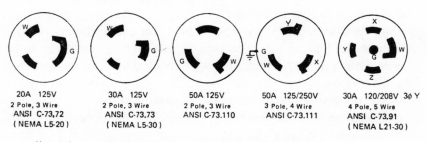

20A 125V	30A 125V	50A 125V	50A 125/250V	30A 120/208V 3φ Y
2 Pole, 3 Wire	2 Pole, 3 Wire	2 Pole, 3 Wire	3 Pole, 4 Wire	4 Pole, 5 Wire
ANSI C-73,72	ANSI C-73,73	ANSI C-73.110	ANSI C-73.111	ANSI C-73.91
(NEMA L5-20)	(NEMA L5-30)			(NEMA L21-30)

Unmarked – Black, G – Green, W – White, XYZ – Other Colors including Black

Fig. 9.12. *Drawing showing typical shore-power plug-in configurations.*
COURTESY ABYC.

is all you can use. The limiting factor is the output of the dockside connection.

The standard connector is a three-prong twist-lock type, with the male end plugged in on shore, and the female end connected to the boat. The connector on the boat is mounted on the outside, in a covered, weather-resistant fitting.

Whenever plugging into a shore-power connector, turn off the main breaker on your boat's panel, and connect the cord to the fitting on the boat. At the dockside connection, turn off the power if the switch is available to you, and line up the prongs on the cord with the proper slots at the box, using the offset tab on the ground terminal as an indicator.

Insert the connector firmly, and give it a clockwise twist to secure it. Turn on the juice, and you should be ready to go. Failure to make a firm and secure connection can result in arcing from the box to the cord, especially in damp weather.

Sooner or later, you'll find that you need to replace the end of your shore-power cord. If your home marina's connections don't match your cord, you may want to change, rather than deal with an adapter all the time. Or your cord terminals may wear to the point where they're loose when connected, increasing the danger of arcing.

When replacing connectors, use only marine-quality, weatherproof fittings. Cheaper connectors that will fit can be found in hardware stores, but their service life will be considerably shorter than marine items.

To remove the old fitting, unscrew the fasteners in the end and disassemble. You may need to go through a couple of layers of fasteners and plastic parts, but eventually you'll find the point where the conductors are connected. Make note of the color coding before disconnecting them. Standard practice calls for the green ground wire to be connected to a green terminal, the white neutral wire to be connected to a silver-colored terminal, and the black hot wire to be connected to a copper-colored terminal, but check to make sure.

Connect the wires to the proper terminals in the new fitting, and reassemble, making sure that all connections are firm and tight. Install weatherproof sealing collars when available, to keep the connection as dry as possible.

After you're done, connect the cord to the dock box and to your boat, and check your panel polarity indicator. If you've got one of the circuit testers mentioned above, and you should, plug it into an outlet as an additional check.

ADDING EQUIPMENT

The most common AC work is adding equipment and branch circuits to the existing system. Battery chargers and electric heaters are common items installed by boat owners.

Most AC panels supplied with new boats include at least a couple of spaces for adding branch circuits. To add a circuit, buy a marine-quality, trip-free circuit breaker of the appropriate amperage, and plug it into the panel. (First make sure that the shore-power cord is disconnected and the gen set turned off!)

Proper amperage determination is figured the same way as with DC circuits. Match the breaker or fuse size to the peak demand of the equipment to be installed. With most AC appliances, detailed installation instructions will tell you what size breaker should be used and if other appliances can be installed on the same circuit.

Run the three-conductor wire from the appliance to the back of the AC panel. The ground (green) and neutral (white) leads will connect to common terminals, usually a large stud securing a series of wires with ring connectors. Crimp the appropriate size ring terminal to each conductor and secure it to the proper common terminal. The hot (black) lead from the appliance is then secured to one of the connecting tabs on the breaker, and the other tab is hooked to the large common conductor linking the other breakers together. This common conductor is often referred to as a "hot bus."

Should you want to add more branch circuits than your panel can accommodate, you can purchase and install a subpanel. Typically, these panels have room for up to five branch circuits. If you find yourself adding numerous additional circuits, however, be sure to calculate the total current load of the accessories you're likely to be operating all at once. There's no free lunch here, and a 30-amp shore-power service will only provide 30 amps of power, no matter how many additional circuits are on the boat.

Because of the nature of alternating current, appropriate conductor size isn't as much a function of conductor length and amperage of the appliance as it is with direct current. Rather, as shown in Tables 9.8–9.11, the temperature rating of the insulation and the number of wires bundled together determine the allowable amperage for a particular wire size. (See Figures 9.13–9.16.)

The conductor must be rated for at least 600 volts, and should be double-insulated, triplex (three insulated wires encased in an additional layer of insulation) wire. When running wire from a panel to an appliance, it should be supported with noncorroding, insulated wire clips or ties spaced every eighteen inches along the length of the run. And it must be protected from chafing wherever it passes through a bulkhead.

Table 9.8 ALLOWABLE AMPERAGE OF CONDUCTORS WHEN 7 TO 24 CONDUCTORS ARE BUNDLED

TEMPERATURE RATING OF CONDUCTOR INSULATION

CONDUCTOR SIZE (AWG)	60°C (140°F) OUTSIDE ENGINE SPACES	60°C (140°F) INSIDE ENGINE SPACES	75°C (167°F) OUTSIDE ENGINE SPACES	75°C (167°F) INSIDE ENGINE SPACES	80°C (176°F) OUTSIDE ENGINE SPACES	80°C (176°F) INSIDE ENGINE SPACES	90°C (194°F) OUTSIDE ENGINE SPACES	90°C (194°F) INSIDE ENGINE SPACES	105°C (221°F) OUTSIDE ENGINE SPACES	105°C (221°F) INSIDE ENGINE SPACES	125°C (257°F) OUTSIDE ENGINE SPACES	125°C (257°F) INSIDE ENGINE SPACES	200°C (392°F) OUTSIDE OR INSIDE ENGINE SPACES
18	5.0	2.9	5.0	3.8	7.5	5.9	10.0	8.2	10.0	8.5	12.5	11.1	12.5
16	7.5	4.4	7.5	5.6	10.0	7.8	12.5	10.3	12.5	10.6	15.0	13.4	17.5
14	10.0	5.8	10.0	7.5	12.5	9.8	15.0	12.3	17.5	14.9	20.0	17.8	22.5
12	12.5	7.3	12.5	9.4	17.5	13.7	20.0	16.4	22.5	19.1	25.0	22.3	27.5
10	20.0	11.6	20.0	15.0	25.0	19.5	27.5	22.6	30.0	25.5	35.0	31.2	35.0
8	27.5	16.0	32.5	24.4	35.0	27.3	35.0	28.7	40.0	34.0	45.0	40.1	50.0
6	40.0	23.2	47.5	35.6	50.0	39.0	50.0	41.0	60.0	51.0	62.5	55.6	67.5
4	52.5	30.5	62.5	46.9	65.0	50.7	67.5	55.4	80.0	68.0	85.0	75.7	90.0
3	60.0	34.8	72.5	54.4	75.0	58.5	77.5	63.6	90.0	76.5	97.5	86.8	105.0
2	70.0	40.6	85.0	63.8	87.5	68.3	90.0	73.8	105.0	89.3	112.5	100.1	120.0
1	82.5	47.9	97.5	73.1	105.0	81.9	105.0	86.1	122.5	104.1	132.5	117.9	140.0
0	97.5	56.6	115.0	86.3	122.5	95.6	122.5	100.5	142.5	121.1	152.5	135.7	162.5
00	112.5	65.3	132.5	99.4	142.5	111.2	142.5	116.9	165.0	140.3	177.5	158.0	185.0
000	130.0	75.4	155.0	116.3	165.0	128.7	165.0	135.3	192.5	163.6	205.0	182.5	215.0
0000	150.0	87.0	180.0	135.0	192.5	150.2	192.5	157.9	222.5	189.1	237.5	211.4	255.0

Figs. 9.13–9.16. *Tables showing amperage, conductor size, and insulation temperature ratings for AC wire bundles.* COURTESY ABYC.

Table 9.9   ALLOWABLE AMPERAGE OF CONDUCTORS WHEN 4 TO 6 CONDUCTORS ARE BUNDLED

TEMPERATURE RATING OF CONDUCTOR INSULATION

CONDUCTOR SIZE (AWG)	60°C (140°F)		75°C (167°F)		80°C (176°F)		90°C (194°F)		105°C (221°F)		125°C (257°F)		200°C (392°F)
	OUTSIDE ENGINE SPACES	INSIDE ENGINE SPACES	OUTSIDE ENGINE SPACES	INSIDE ENGINE SPACES	OUTSIDE ENGINE SPACES	INSIDE ENGINE SPACES	OUTSIDE ENGINE SPACES	INSIDE ENGINE SPACES	OUTSIDE ENGINE SPACES	INSIDE ENGINE SPACES	OUTSIDE ENGINE SPACES	INSIDE ENGINE SPACES	OUTSIDE OR INSIDE ENGINE SPACES
18	6.0	3.5	6.0	4.5	9.0	7.0	12.0	9.8	12.0	10.2	15.0	13.4	15.0
16	9.0	5.2	9.0	6.8	12.0	9.4	15.0	12.3	15.0	12.8	18.0	16.0	21.0
14	12.0	7.0	12.0	9.0	15.0	11.7	18.0	14.8	21.0	17.9	24.0	21.4	27.0
12	15.0	8.7	15.0	11.3	21.0	16.4	24.0	19.7	27.0	23.0	30.0	26.7	33.0
10	24.0	13.9	24.0	18.0	30.0	23.4	33.0	27.1	36.0	30.6	42.0	37.4	42.0
8	33.0	19.1	39.0	29.3	42.0	32.8	42.0	34.4	48.0	40.8	54.0	48.1	60.0
6	48.0	27.8	57.0	42.8	60.0	46.8	60.0	49.2	72.0	61.2	75.0	66.8	81.0
4	63.0	36.5	75.0	56.3	78.0	60.8	81.0	66.4	96.0	81.6	102.0	90.8	108.0
3	72.0	41.8	87.0	65.3	90.0	70.2	93.0	76.3	108.0	91.8	117.0	104.1	126.0
2	84.0	48.7	102.0	76.5	105.0	81.9	108.0	88.6	126.0	107.1	135.0	120.2	144.0
1	99.0	57.4	117.0	87.8	126.0	98.3	126.0	103.3	147.0	125.0	159.0	141.5	168.0
0	117.0	67.9	138.0	103.5	147.0	114.7	147.0	120.5	171.0	145.4	183.0	162.9	195.0
00	135.0	78.3	159.0	119.3	171.0	133.4	171.0	140.2	198.0	168.3	213.0	189.6	222.0
000	156.0	90.5	186.0	139.5	198.0	154.4	198.0	162.4	231.0	196.4	246.0	218.9	258.0
0000	180.0	104.4	216.0	162.0	231.0	180.2	231.0	189.4	267.0	227.0	285.0	253.7	306.0

Table 9.10 ALLOWABLE AMPERAGE OF CONDUCTORS WHEN 3 CONDUCTORS ARE BUNDLED*

TEMPERATURE RATING OF CONDUCTOR INSULATION

CONDUCTOR SIZE (AWG)	60°C (140°F) OUTSIDE ENGINE SPACES	60°C (140°F) INSIDE ENGINE SPACES	75°C (167°F) OUTSIDE ENGINE SPACES	75°C (167°F) INSIDE ENGINE SPACES	80°C (176°F) OUTSIDE ENGINE SPACES	80°C (176°F) INSIDE ENGINE SPACES	90°C (194°F) OUTSIDE ENGINE SPACES	90°C (194°F) INSIDE ENGINE SPACES	105°C (221°F) OUTSIDE ENGINE SPACES	105°C (221°F) INSIDE ENGINE SPACES	125°C (257°F) OUTSIDE ENGINE SPACES	125°C (257°F) INSIDE ENGINE SPACES	200°C (392°F) OUTSIDE OR INSIDE ENGINE SPACES
18	7.0	4.1	7.0	5.3	10.5	8.2	14.0	11.5	14.0	11.9	17.5	15.6	17.5
16	10.5	6.1	10.5	7.9	14.0	10.9	17.5	14.4	17.5	14.9	21.0	18.7	24.5
14	14.0	8.1	14.0	10.5	17.5	13.7	21.0	17.2	24.5	20.8	28.0	24.9	31.5
12	17.5	10.2	17.5	13.1	24.5	19.1	28.0	23.0	31.5	26.8	35.0	31.2	38.5
10	28.0	16.2	28.0	21.0	35.0	27.3	38.5	31.6	42.0	35.7	49.0	43.6	49.0
8	38.5	22.3	45.5	34.1	49.0	38.2	49.0	40.2	56.0	47.6	63.0	56.1	70.0
6	56.0	32.5	66.5	49.9	70.0	54.6	70.0	57.4	84.0	71.4	87.5	77.9	94.5
4	73.5	42.6	87.5	65.6	91.0	71.0	94.5	77.5	112.0	95.2	119.0	105.9	126.0
3	84.0	48.7	101.5	76.1	105.0	81.9	108.5	89.0	126.0	107.1	136.5	121.5	147.0
2	98.0	56.8	119.0	89.3	122.5	95.6	126.0	103.3	147.0	125.0	157.5	140.2	168.0
1	115.5	67.0	136.5	102.4	147.0	114.7	147.0	120.5	171.5	145.8	185.5	165.1	196.0
0	136.5	79.2	161.0	120.8	171.5	133.8	171.5	140.6	199.5	169.6	213.5	190.0	227.5
00	157.5	91.4	185.5	139.1	199.5	155.6	199.5	163.6	231.0	196.4	248.5	221.2	259.0
000	182.0	105.6	217.0	162.8	231.0	180.2	231.0	189.4	269.5	229.1	287.0	255.4	301.0
0000	210.0	121.8	252.0	189.0	269.5	210.2	269.5	221.0	311.5	264.8	332.5	295.9	357.0

*—There is NO LIMIT on conductors in a bundle for under 50 volts.

Table 9.11 ALLOWABLE AMPERAGE OF CONDUCTORS WHEN NO MORE THAN 2 CONDUCTORS ARE BUNDLED*

TEMPERATURE RATING OF CONDUCTOR INSULATION

CONDUCTOR SIZE (AWG)	60°C (140°F)		75°C (167°F)		80°C (176°F)		90°C (194°F)		105°C (221°F)		125°C (257°F)		200°C (392°F)
	OUTSIDE ENGINE SPACES	INSIDE ENGINE SPACES	OUTSIDE ENGINE SPACES	INSIDE ENGINE SPACES	OUTSIDE ENGINE SPACES	INSIDE ENGINE SPACES	OUTSIDE ENGINE SPACES	INSIDE ENGINE SPACES	OUTSIDE ENGINE SPACES	INSIDE ENGINE SPACES	OUTSIDE ENGINE SPACES	INSIDE ENGINE SPACES	OUTSIDE OR INSIDE ENGINE SPACES
18	10	5.8	10	7.5	15	11.7	20	16.4	20	17.0	25	22.3	25
16	15	8.7	15	11.3	20	15.6	25	20.5	25	21.3	30	26.7	35
14	20	11.6	20	15.0	25	19.5	30	24.6	35	29.8	40	35.6	45
12	25	14.5	25	18.8	35	27.3	40	32.8	45	38.3	50	44.5	55
10	40	23.2	40	30.0	50	39.0	55	45.1	60	51.0	70	62.3	70
8	55	31.9	65	48.8	70	54.6	70	57.4	80	68.0	90	80.1	100
6	80	46.4	95	71.3	100	78.0	100	82.0	120	102.0	125	111.3	135
4	105	60.9	125	93.8	130	101.4	135	110.7	160	136.0	170	151.3	180
3	120	69.6	145	108.8	150	117.0	155	127.1	180	153.0	195	173.6	210
2	140	81.2	170	127.5	175	136.5	180	147.6	210	178.5	225	200.3	240
1	165	95.7	195	146.3	210	163.8	210	172.2	245	208.3	265	235.9	280
0	195	113.1	230	172.5	245	191.1	245	200.9	285	242.3	305	271.5	325
00	225	130.5	265	198.8	285	222.3	285	233.7	330	280.5	355	316.0	370
000	260	150.8	310	232.5	330	257.4	330	270.6	385	327.3	410	364.9	430
0000	300	174.0	360	270.0	385	300.3	385	315.7	445	378.3	475	422.8	510

*—There is NO LIMIT on conductors in a bundle for under 50 volts.

The crimp connectors used in DC wiring are acceptable for AC work, and the same strengths of connections apply. (See Table 9.3, page 135 above.)

When adding outlets to your system or upgrading the ones already on board, you should always provide covered outlets in areas such as heads and in the cockpit where moisture is likely to be a problem. You should also install ground fault circuit interrupters (GFCIs) in these locations. These outlets provide exceptional protection for areas where moisture and standing water are likely to be problems. They contain sensing circuits that detect ground faults and shut down the power in a fraction of a second, preventing electrocution—definitely a worthwhile investment.

When installing AC equipment, don't mix AC and DC grounds together. The systems must be kept completely separate both for safety's sake and to reduce galvanic corrosion.

AC TROUBLESHOOTING

When troubleshooting AC accessories, remember to pay careful attention to what you're doing, and follow safety precautions.

If an AC item fails, start at your main panel and work toward the item. Check all of the simple, easy things first. First, is there power to the panel? Check the voltmeter on the panel. Is the main breaker turned on? Is the shore-power cord plugged in, and is the breaker on the dock turned on? Is the breaker to the circuit being checked turned on?

When circuit breakers trip because of overload, the switch handle usually snaps into a position halfway between "On" and "Off." To reset it, turn it off, and then back to on. If it stays on, you're okay. It may have been just a temporary surge that tripped it. If it snaps back to the tripped position, you've got a problem, probably a short circuit.

A short circuit can occur when there is an internal fault in the appliance, or when wiring is broken or frayed. The appliance is the first thing to check, since that's generally where the moving parts are located. You can take it out and either take it apart yourself, if you feel comfortable doing so, or take it to a shop for inspection and repair.

To inspect the wiring, disconnect the shore-power cord from the boat. Then, disconnect both ends of all three wires to the appliance.

With your ohmmeter, test each conductor for continuity and for connection to ground.

Set your meter to its most sensitive range (usually RX1K), and zero the gauge with the "Ohms Adjust" dial. Connect one probe to the end of one of the wires, and the other probe to ground. Repeat for all three. The needle should stay on ∞ ohms, indicating infinite resistance, no continuity. If the needle jumps when you touch a wire, you've found a short, an unintended path to ground. Visually inspect the wire from end to end, looking for the break or abrasion in the insulation.

If nothing develops with this test, you'll need to check each conductor's continuity. To check, go to one end of the wire and connect two of the three ends together, either with a short jumper wire or by twisting them together. Just make sure that there's a good connection between the two conductors.

Go to the other end and touch one ohmmeter probe to one of the two joined wires, and the other probe to the other wire. If both wires are intact, you'll get a reading of 0—or very low—resistance. If one or both wires are broken, the reading will be infinite resistance.

If both are good, go back to the other end, disconnect the two conductors, and connect either one of them with the third wire. Repeat the test procedure at the opposite end. Again, if both are intact, you should read zero resistance.

By using the three possible combinations (white and black, white and green, black and green) you can isolate the faulty conductor.

When performing these tests, make sure that the conductors being tested don't touch other wires or other metal objects. You may have to wrap the connector with electrical tape to isolate it.

If you desire more information on electrical systems, consult the reference books listed in the Sources of Information. You should have a copy of the federal standards on board, and copies of the ABYC and NFPA standards can be very helpful.

10

FILTERS

DIESEL FUEL FILTERS

The single most important maintenance task for diesel engines is the regular, timely replacement of fuel filters. Diesel injection pumps are built to incredibly fine tolerances, and will perform flawlessly for years if they are supplied with clean, well-filtered fuel.

Most diesel engines include a filter installed on the motor. This filter alone, called the secondary filter, does not provide enough protection for an engine operated in the hostile marine environment. There should be a larger, water-separating primary filter installed in the fuel line between the tank and the engine.

There are several brands and types of add-on filters available, but the brand that we prefer is Racor. The combination of availability of accessories and filter elements, ease of use, and long-term reputation is unbeatable. They can be equipped with water sensors, fuel heaters, and pressure gauges, creating as sophisticated a filtering system as you're willing to pay for. (See Figure 10.1.

Follow the installation instructions that come with the filter and you can't go far wrong. There are a few details to keep in mind, however.

160

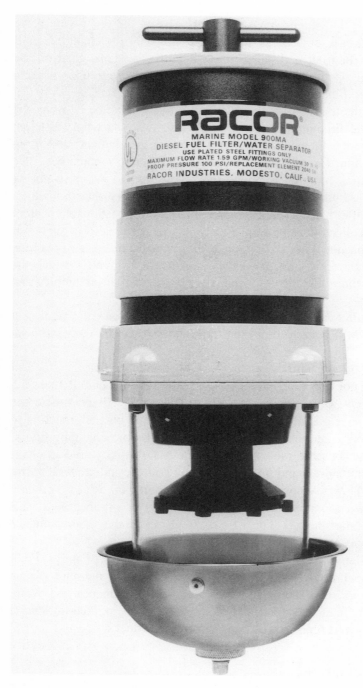

Fig. 10.1. *Racor diesel fuel filter.* PHOTO COURTESY OF RACOR CORP.

Your fuel line should have a shutoff valve at the tank. This valve is useful in case of a break in the fuel line, and for changing filter elements if the filter is installed lower than the fuel tank. Shut off the valve before opening the top of the filter, and be sure to open it again when you're finished.

Choose the location for the filter carefully. It must be between the tank and the lift pump. Keep in mind also that you need sufficient room above the filter to allow you to remove the element, and room below the filter for draining accumulated water into a container.

Most filters have clear bowls that allow you to see if water or sediment has collected. Check the filter visually every once in a while, especially after buying fuel from an unfamiliar or questionable source. Drain any collected water immediately. If you can see dirt in the bowl, it means that the filter element is saturated and you're way overdue for a change. Changing elements frequently will greatly reduce the number of times that the unit needs to be completely disassembled and cleaned.

If your filter can't be checked visually for water content or sediment buildup, you'll have to drain the filter and replace the elements *regularly!*

When working with diesel fuel, you'll soon learn that the smell of the fuel is not only unpleasant, it's also semipermanent. If there's a soap, solvent, or magic substance available that will neutralize the smell of diesel oil, it's certainly news to us. The best approach is to avoid getting it on yourself in the first place. Before changing filters, buy some disposable rubber gloves. These are usually sold in chandleries, paint stores, and fiberglass supply houses, and are well worth their cost. They also come in handy when changing oil. It's also prudent to put down a couple layers of paper towels or oil-absorbent pads before you start the job. This catches spills before they have a chance to run down into and contaminate the bilges.

As with any petroleum products, dispose of wastes properly. Fuel-soaked paper towels and filter elements should be put into plastic garbage bags, tied securely, and placed in trash receptacles. Water mixed with fuel that's drained from filters should be poured into waste oil containers, found at most marinas and fuel docks.

GASOLINE FILTERS

When changing gas filters, you must be extremely safety-conscious. Failure to observe all safety precautions can have severe consequences, such as fires or explosions. The safest way to approach any work on a gasoline fuel system is to treat the situation like refueling. This means extinguishing all open flames, such as pilot lights. Disconnect your shore-power cord and shut off your battery switch. See the "Gasoline Engines" chapter (page 108) for more details.

You'll probably have to use a flashlight to see what you're doing, and there are special flashlights made for use in hazardous environments. They have plastic or rubber-coated bodies to minimize stray sparks and are sealed in such a way that a broken bulb won't provide an ignition source.

Drain the fuel into a plastic container, preferably one with a tight-fitting lid. Don't try using Styrofoam cups, since Styrofoam dissolves in gasoline, and a dissolving container is one that doesn't contain for very long. Also, avoid metal coffee cans. They might be available and convenient, but we know of at least one individual who dropped a coffee can filled with gas onto his exposed battery terminals, and caused an explosion. As soon as you're finished changing the filter, get the container off the boat. No sense pushing your luck by leaving the thing around, just waiting to be kicked over.

Before taking anything apart, be sure to shut off the fuel line at the tank. Most gas systems have antisiphon valves installed at the tank fitting to prevent leaks, but it's best not to bet your life on them. Turn off the fuel valve to be sure that no gasoline can flow.

There are a variety of types of gas filters installed on marine engines. The most common are the spin-on type, similar to oil filters, and paper element types, encased in metal housings. There are also some that are located in the carburetors, as well as large, canister-type primary filters. (See Figure 10.2.)

The ideal filter system would be similar to that found on a diesel engine—a water-separating primary filter backed up by a secondary filter mounted on the motor. Some systems will even have a tertiary filter installed at the fuel line inlet of the carburetor.

Since the filters installed on marine engines are usually a part of the marinizing process, the filter elements are not always available from auto parts stores. The one possible exception to this is the carburetor filter.

Fig. 10.2. *Racor gasoline filter.* PHOTO COURTESY OF RACOR CORP.

Whenever you replace filter elements, check the package and the filter housing for O-rings. These are commonly used to seal filter housings, and should be replaced with the element.

After replacing gasoline filters, clean up any drips and spills thoroughly and leave the boat for a while. When you're exposed to gasoline fumes, it's easy to get so used to the smell that you can no longer detect potentially dangerous levels of fumes. If you get out of the environment for a while and give your nose a chance to clear, you'll be better able to detect telltale odors.

OIL FILTERS

Refer to your owner's manual for the recommended weight and grade of lube oil for your motor. Be advised that all oil of a given weight (such as 10W-40) is not the same—the American Petroleum Institute (API) has a grading system for lube oils, classifying them by engine fuel and intended service. These ratings are prominently listed on the oil container, and your engine manual will recommend the proper grade for your motor.

For instance, an API rating of SS-SF is for regular and heavy-duty use, gas engines, while lube oils for diesel engines are classified CC-CD for regular and heavy-duty. Some oils can be used in both gas and diesel engines, but don't make the assumption—check the ratings against your engine's requirements.

Also be aware that some engine builders advise against the use of multiviscosity oils, such as 10W-40 or 5W-30. These builders advise that you use only single-weight oils, such as 30W (30 weight), in their motors. If that's what the builder recommends, then that's what you should use, especially in an engine that's under warranty.

You can save a significant amount of money by buying name-brand aftermarket oil filters such as Fram, Baldwin, or AC by the case in discount houses or auto parts stores. Store a spare filter or two on the boat, but put the rest of them in a cool, dry place, where the elements will not absorb moisture.

Buy your oil by the case as well. You don't need oil that has your engine builder's name on it, which is probably just repackaged and marked-up automotive oil. Again, check viscosity and API ratings first.

An added benefit of buying oil and filters in quantity is that if you haven't paid an arm and a leg for the stuff, you'll be more likely to change your oil and filters regularly.

If you have a nonautomotive diesel engine, there are often alternative sources for filters. Get the model number and manufacturer's name from the filter and check with an auto parts store for equivalent filters from aftermarket manufacturers. This also works for some gas and diesel fuel filters. As with other filters, stick with name brands.

OIL AND FILTER CHANGING

Removing oil filters from boat engines is frequently a pain. Just because the engine builder placed the filter in a spot that's easy to reach when the motor is sitting on the shop floor doesn't mean that it's going to be easy to reach when it's installed in the boat. Cramped engine rooms, added accessories, and a lack of foresight by the designer or builder can combine to put filters in some extremely awkward places.

Chances are that you'll need a special tool to remove your oil filter. Auto parts stores have a great variety of types of filter wrenches, and it may take some experimenting and even some modifying of an existing wrench until you come up with the one that works best for your engine. (See Figure 10.3.)

If you've got twin engines, you may even need a different wrench for each engine. An engine that has the oil filter installed on the side will usually mean that one engine has an accessible filter, and the other engine has a filter that's buried. Too few twin-engine installations afford enough working room on both sides of both motors.

If your filter is in an especially awkward location, there are after-market remote oil-filter relocation kits that can be installed. Check with your engine dealer or marine engine parts store for possible options for your motor.

When you remove the used filter, oil *will* spill out, so be prepared. Before you start, put some oil-absorbent pads (available from most chandleries) or paper towels under the filter. Also, use a small plastic bucket or heavy plastic bag to catch the filter. The less oil you spill, the less you'll have to clean up.

Once the old filter is off, coat the gasket of the new filter with a thin film of clean oil and install it. *Don't* use the filter wrench to tighten it. Spin the filter on until you can feel the gasket make contact, and then tighten another one half to three quarters of a turn *by hand*. Filters tend to tighten themselves a bit as they age, and a filter that's been overtightened can be almost impossible to remove.

Drain as much oil as possible out of the used filter into the bucket you have set aside for your used oil. Wrap the filter in a plastic bag, tie off the end, and dispose of it.

The next problem that presents itself is actually getting the oil out of the crankcase. In cars and trucks, you just put a bucket underneath, unscrew the drain plug, and let the oil flow out. No such luck when it comes to boats. Since engines are mounted as low in the boat as

Fig. 10.3. *Different types of oil filter wrenches.*

possible to maintain a low center of gravity, there is seldom enough room underneath to allow access to the drain plug. The oil must be pumped out, usually through the dipstick hole. There are a number of devices on the market for this purpose, each with its advantages and disadvantages.

First there's the manual pump. These are inexpensive, and a wonderful way to build up your grip strength and stamina. Even a two-cylinder diesel with a four-quart crankcase can be an ordeal with one of these, but they are cheap, and there isn't much that can go wrong with them.

There are also little pumps driven by drill motors. These too are inexpensive, and are fine if you don't mind having oil splattered on your face, your clothes, and your engine room.

One of the more convenient (and less messy) units available is a 12-volt pump mounted on top of a plastic bucket. It has a pour spout, a reversible motor, and alligator clips to attach it to a battery. These are very nice outfits, but pricey.

You can save money by assembling your own pump system from available parts, but be sure that the pump you use is designed and approved for use with flammable liquids, and that the impeller is compatible with petroleum products.

There are some pumps on the market that are permanently attached to the motor for draining oil. These are especially handy on larger engines, and usually employ a manifold valving system to draw the oil from each motor and direct it into a bucket. A pair of eight-cylinder diesels can hold five to six *gallons* of oil each, and using a small pump can take an eternity.

Another option is a device that uses a hand pump to create a vacuum in a metal receptacle, drawing the oil out through the dipstick hole without using an electric pump or having to manually pump it out. Reports on this unit's effectiveness vary, so try to talk to someone who's actually used one before investing.

Some fuel docks have octopus-rig oil pumps or oil-changing services that can be cost-effective, depending on the size of your motor and the difficulty of access.

Remember to always dispose of your waste oil properly. Putting your oil into a plastic jug and throwing it into a dumpster is *not* the proper way to do it. This contaminates landfills and is environmentally irresponsible. Marinas, fuel docks, and many municipal landfills have facilities for receiving used motor oil—use them!

Engine oil analysis is a valuable engine diagnostic service performed specially by equipped laboratories—for a charge of twenty to thirty dollars they will analyze your oil for metal content, viscosity break-down, contamination with water and coolant, and other warning signs. Having the analysis performed regularly will help you to spot trends in the presence of certain metals that can indicate potential problems. This will help you to plan your major maintenance work, and can also help you to determine the optimum oil change intervals for your boat. Take a sample when you change oil, usually in a container supplied by the lab, and have it checked. It can definitely be a cost-effective procedure.

AIR FILTERS

There isn't a lot to be said about changing air filters. Check your owner's manual for details and recommended intervals, and just do it.

Aftermarket air filters usually aren't found in discount stores, since automotive air cleaners aren't used. However, it never hurts to check, and you might save some cash. Some diesels use cleanable filters that need to be washed in solvent and replaced. Do this at the recommended intervals, and at least once a year.

Also be aware that many turbochargers have their own filters, which must be changed as needed. Follow the manufacturer's recommendations for solvents and service intervals.

Filter changing and maintenance is an important part of your engine care regimen. Considering the low cost of filters and the high cost of neglect, it should be very high on your boat care priority list.

11
STEERING

STEERING SYSTEMS in pleasure boats are either mechanical or hydraulic. Each type of system demands care and attention, and each has idiosyncrasies that must be considered.

Mechanical steering is pretty much what the name implies. A system of cables, or cables and chains, is employed to transmit movement from the steering wheel to the rudder or rudders. Advantages are its simplicity, and the occasional possibility of making jury-rig repairs in case of a component failure. Disadvantages are the considerable wear factors inherent in a series of moving parts, and the friction loads present, making mechanical steering very difficult if not impossible on large boats.

Hydraulic steering consists of a closed system of noncompressible hydraulic fluid, enclosed in copper lines, connected to a hydraulic pump at each helm station, and a hydraulic cylinder at the rudder. As the wheel turns, the helm pump compresses one end of the fluid column, forcing the cylinder at the rudder end to push the rudder in the appropriate direction. Advantages to hydraulic steering are ease of use and relatively low maintenance. Moving parts are confined to the highly

170

reliable helm pumps, and the sturdy, easily inspected and maintained rudder arm and cylinder connections. Disadvantages are higher cost than a comparable mechanical system, and the potential for leaks and failure of the entire system, leaving the boat with no steering system and virtually no possibility of performing emergency on-board repairs.

MECHANICAL STEERING

Most mechanical steering in use today is found on older powerboats and on some sailboats with wheel steering in place of a tiller. The older powerboats used a system of chain and cable, run over a series of sprockets, pulleys, and turning blocks.

Maintenance consists of frequent inspection and lubrication, as well as keeping all the parts tightened down securely and properly aligned. Check all of the turning blocks (pulleys) for grease fittings and lubricate them regularly with a grease gun filled with a good grade of waterproof grease. Don't grease the cables, since it will attract and hold abrasive matter and accelerate wear. Instead, use a rag soaked in a light lubricating oil, rubbed over the length of the cable. While doing this, inspect the cable for burrs, especially near wear points such as pulleys and blocks. Presence of burrs indicates that the cable is wearing, and will need to be replaced before too long.

As a mechanical system ages, the cables gradually elongate, eventually loosening to the point where excessive play can cause the cables to jump off the pulley sheaves. To compensate for stretch, turnbuckles are usually installed at the rudder end of the system.

Turnbuckles can take up slack in the system, and must be inspected and lubricated regularly. When tightening, take up an equal amount of slack on each side. Tighten until the cable is snug, with no sag in the line. Excessive tension will accelerate wear, and can cause fasteners to work loose and result in misalignment. When the turnbuckles are adjusted to the maximum, the cable will have to be shortened or replaced. If you're considering shortening, first inspect the cable carefully to see if it's not nearing the end of its useful life. Give careful consideration to the relative costs of repair versus replacement—a cable that has stretched that much is probably a pretty old cable.

Check the fasteners that hold the pulleys and turning blocks in place, and tighten as needed. Inspect pulleys and blocks for proper alignment by sighting down the cable where it contacts the pulley sheave, and eyeballing the alignment as best you can. If misalignment is noticeable, loosen the fasteners at the base of the pulley assembly and realign. There is usually an adjusting bolt that passes through an elongated hole, and a tightening bolt through a round hole, similar to the bolt holes on engine mounts.

Sailboats with mechanical systems and wheel steering have additional items to tighten and align. The steering quadrant, the device below the cockpit sole that moves back and forth, transmitting movement from the wheel to the rudder cables, must be properly secured and aligned. Check the fasteners for tightness, and inspect the entire assembly to be sure that the leads to the pulley sheaves are true.

Wheel steering pedestals are secured to the cockpit sole and contain mechanical components, such as sprockets and chain. Access is usually obtained through removable cover plates on the pedestal, and by removing the compass from the binnacle mount on top. Check the chain occasionally for proper tension, and lubricate as needed.

If chain or cable replacement ever becomes necessary, make sure that any metal installed near compasses or autopilots is stainless steel and nonmagnetic.

The main problems with mechanical steering involve wear and misalignment of the moving parts. Regular inspection can keep these problems to a minimum by making sure that everything is maintained at the proper tension, and is well aligned and lubricated.

HYDRAULIC STEERING

Hydraulic steering is both more and less complicated than mechanical steering. It's more complicated in that very few of us have much of a handle on hydraulic system dynamics and engineering principles. It's less complicated because use and maintenance are very simple and relatively trouble-free.

Hydraulic steering systems fall into two categories—pressurized and nonpressurized. Pressurized systems are closed, and air pressure is applied through a valve, usually located on the hydraulic fluid reservoir, and monitored with an air pressure gauge. With nonpressurized steering, atmospheric pressure is maintained by a vent, usually at the upper helm station.

With either kind of system, *always* use the fluid recommended by the manufacturer, no matter how weird or hard to find. Inappropriate hydraulic fluid can foam, separate, or freeze, and given the high cost of repair and replacement of precision hydraulic parts, the smart move is to follow the manufacturer's recommendations to the letter. You can always contact the manufacturer for the names of suppliers in your area, or order it directly from the manufacturer.

If the proper fluid for your boat is hard to find, store some reserve stock for routine maintenance and the occasional leak that develops.

If you find that you have to add fluid regularly, you've got a leak somewhere. These systems are not subject to fluid evaporation or loss, so a careful inspection is in order. It's common to get into the habit of adding "just a little bit" occasionally, and before you realize it, you've got a sizable puddle forming somewhere.

Splits in tubing or hose are rare, so leaks are usually found at the connection points at the back of the helm stations, at the cylinder in the stern, and at any valving locations in between. Nine times out of ten, the problem is a loose tubing nut, and a quick snugging down with a wrench will cure the problem. Be advised that you're dealing with fairly soft metals, so don't go overboard on the tightening. (See the "Stoves and Heaters" chapter, page 237, for suggestions on tightening and replacing copper tubing fittings.)

Sometimes the leak can be very small and hard to trace. Even large leaks can be hard to locate, since the fluid can travel along the tubing for quite a distance before dripping off and forming a noticeable pool.

If that's the case, clean every connecting point thoroughly with a good household grease-dissolving cleaner, such as Formula 409, and operate the helm stations through several lock-to-lock turns. Then go back and feel around each connection for the unmistakable oiliness of hydraulic fluid.

If there's been a leak somewhere along the line, the system will have to be bled. Hydraulic action demands a solid column of fluid, and air bubbles give the steering a spongy feel.

Other indications of air in the system are unusual clicking noises when turning the wheel, an increased number of turns lock-to-lock, and a loose feel to the stops when the wheel reaches the locks.

These systems tend to be very individualized in their approach, and bleeding procedures vary from type to type, so your owner's manual is the best guide.

Don't try to fill and bleed large quantities all at once. If your helm pump is very low on fluid, add a little bit, certainly not more than a quarter of a cup or so, and bleed the system. Keep repeating with small quantities until the system is full. If you try to replace too much fluid at once, you may generate a large air bubble that hangs midway in the lines, temporarily blocked by the large quantity of fluid above it. The upper pump will appear to be full, but that bubble will wait until you're gone before working its way to the top, spraying fluid all over the place.

If a fluid leak continues unnoticed, generally the upper station on a nonpressurized system will fail first as the fluid level drops. The loss of fluid and steering ''feel'' is more gradual with nonpressurized steering, while pressurized hydraulics tend to fail all at once and without notice.

The upper station is the usual fill point, but before opening the system, be sure you first relieve the pressure from pressurized systems, according to the manufacturer's instructions.

Some nonpressurized systems are shipped from the factory with nonvented fill caps installed at both helm stations. On dual-station boats, the cap at the upper station should have a small vent hole drilled in the center to maintain the system at atmospheric pressure. This is supposed to be done by the dealer as part of the new boat-commissioning procedure, but is frequently overlooked.

If a vent is not provided, air bubbles can accumulate and, especially in hot weather, build internal pressure. Steering will begin to deteriorate, and the poor sap who unscrews the cap at the helm pump to check the fluid level will be greeted with a hydraulic fluid geyser.

Steering system maintenance consists of checking pressure and fluid levels, and periodic inspection of the moving parts at the stern. Occasionally, inspect the copper lines along their entire lengths for the telltale green of corrosion.

If significant corrosion is found, look around for the source. Water leaks from the exterior are common problems, and salt spray thrown from leaky packing glands is another one.

After the corrosion source is eliminated, clean off the tubing with Scotch-Brite® and cleanser, and inspect the area frequently, until you're sure that the problem is fixed. If the source can't be eliminated, try spraying the vulnerable section with WD-40® or LPS® lubricant, to provide some protection.

Should you ever be forced to replace a section of steering line, replace the damaged section with identical material. Copper, nylon, and reinforced flexible hose are all commonly used, but it's not a good idea to mix the materials. Some systems have working pressures in the neighborhood of 1,000 psi, and matching the proper material to your system is essential. Also, flex hose installed in a system not designed for it can give the steering a spongy feel that can't be eliminated by bleeding.

At the rudder end of things, the hydraulic cylinder, the drag link, the rudder shaft logs, and the connecting points all require occasional inspection and maintenance.

The cylinder should be free of surrounding obstructions—don't use the rudder area for storage of items that can foul the mechanisms. Check the fasteners securing the cylinder for tightness, and look around for signs of fluid leakage.

The ram that moves in and out of the cylinder must be clean and smooth, free of any scoring or nicks. The ram passes through seals in the cylinder, and a burr or scratch on the ram can damage the seals, causing fluid loss. Wipe the ram down with a rag soaked in light oil, but don't use grease, as it attracts and holds abrasives and small bits of foreign matter.

Inspect the fasteners holding the steering assembly to the rudder posts. Tighten and lubricate as needed. (See Figure 11.1.)

With twin-rudder boats, a solid bar called a drag link connects the rudder arms. There are pins located at the points where the drag link meets each arm, and they must be inspected regularly for excessive wear. (See Figure 11.2.)

When a twin-screw boat is hauled out, center the wheel by counting the number of turns lock-to-lock, and then turn the wheel halfway between locks.

Then visually check rudder alignment. Most boats with twin rudders employ a toe-in of the rudders' trailing edges, usually in the area of 5 to 8 degrees. This results in less steering effort, and reduces rudder chatter and the resultant wear by maintaining a steady pressure on the rudders when the boat is moving. Check with the boat builder for the proper amount of toe-in for your boat. If your boat was designed to operate without rudder toe-in, don't apply any.

An occasional exception to this rule can be made with the installation of an autopilot that just won't track correctly. Frequently, the addition of a few degrees of toe-in will help.

Fig. 11.1. *Typical method of securing rudder arm to rudder post.*

Should adjustment be necessary, the drag link ends are removed from the rudder arms, and the terminal fittings screwed in or out as needed. (See Figure 11.2.)

Most rudder stocks employ shaft logs and packing glands similar to the units found on prop shafts. These are adjusted and maintained in the same way, although rudder post glands can be tightened more securely. Since the rudder stocks don't revolve at high speed like prop shafts, there isn't the danger of generating excessive heat. However, don't make them so tight that increased steering effort becomes a problem. Lubricate occasionally and inspect for leaks.

Should you ever need to remove a rudder, such as after striking a submerged object, there are a few tips to keep in mind. For the most part, the procedure is a simple matter of removing the rudder arm, the rudder post collar, if present, and the key from the keyway. Loosen the packing gland, and it should slide right out. If you're doing this job alone, build a platform or pile of wood blocks that is just a couple

Fig. 11.2. *Photo shows drag link pivot pin and terminal fitting adjusting method.*

of inches below the bottom of the rudder. You want to avoid dropping the rudder onto the ground without any protection, and if you leave a bit of a gap between rudder and platform, you can tell from the inside of the boat when everything is loose enough and starts to move.

To replace the rudder, lubricate the rudder post slightly, slide it in place, and block it up or have someone hold it in place while you reverse everything you did to remove it.

SAILBOAT STEERING

Sailboat rudders present a few unique situations not found on powerboats. For outboard- and skeg-mounted rudders, check the hardware on the transom and rudder for wear. Excessive wear affects alignment, and you'll find steering effort gradually increasing as these parts age.

Spade rudders hang straight down from the hull, and are supported from inside by a pin-and-collar arrangement. They don't have pintles and gudgeons to wear, but are more susceptible to damage. When removing a spade rudder, a solid external support before beginning is very important. They're quite heavy, and can sustain considerable damage if allowed to drop to the ground.

Since spade rudders have no external support or reinforcement, they tend to move back and forth inside the hull as the boat moves through the water, and the rudder stock wears at the through-hull fitting. If the builder installed a replaceable bearing there, similar to the stern bearings found in prop shaft struts, the rudder should be removed and the bearing replaced when wear becomes evident.

If no bearing is present, brass shim stock (thin sheets of brass) should be cut and installed to take up the slack. This is a job best left to the boatyard.

Some sailboats equipped with wheel steering are supplied with emergency tillers. If you own such a system, *don't* wait until you've got an emergency before you see if the thing fits and works. Check fit and function ahead of time, and if an access port key is needed to fit the tiller, store a spare one with the tiller. A stormy night with thirty-foot seas and pouring rain isn't a good time to be rummaging through silverware drawers looking for a key.

AUTOPILOTS

With sophisticated electronics becoming more commonplace aboard boats, more and more people are opting for autopilots. Newer systems, which can interface with Loran, satellite navigation, and video chart monitors, are so effective that you can just about send your boat off on vacation by itself. You can stay home, make the boat payments, and program the thing to send you postcards.

The autopilots on the market today are a far cry from the old mechanical jobs. They employed systems of chains, belts, sprockets, and pulleys that looked, and in many cases operated, like Rube Goldberg contraptions. If you own one of these, and it works for you, hang on to it. Because of the nature of the system, regular maintenance is required, including lubrication at the appropriate wear points, and inspection and maintenance of the motors and shafts.

The newer autopilots are installed in hydraulic steering systems, and the pilot is maintained as an additional helm station. All the maintenance and inspection procedures for the rest of the steering system apply to the autopilot.

Be advised, though, that the presence of an autopilot will add to maintenance time and cost, and while their convenience factor is high, so is the increase in complexity and wear. The number of electrical devices and connections is high, and the combination of electrical complexity and sea air creates, as we've noted time and again, a constant battle against corrosion.

If you're accepting of the trade-offs between complexities and conveniences, an autopilot can be a tremendous aid to navigation, especially on long, offshore passages. However, a cheap, poorly maintained system will drive you nuts, and you'll never feel like you can really trust the thing. If you decide to take the plunge, do it right, and don't settle for second best.

12
RUNNING GEAR

THE CONGLOMERATION of items that lie between the propeller and the transmission is probably the least understood and the least likely to receive maintenance attention on pleasure boats. Packing gland adjustment, engine alignment, struts, and stern bearings aren't very much fun to deal with, and frequently aren't dealt with at all until something breaks. The prospect of trying to work in a cramped, dark area with limited access is often enough to deter all but the most motivated do-it-yourself boat owners. To avoid repeat trips, it is a good idea to lubricate the fasteners and fittings you encounter when you or someone you have hired is working in these areas.

Even if you don't want to routinely deal with these things yourself, however, there could come a time when you're forced by circumstances beyond your control to do so. If you're far from help and your packing gland starts dripping, you really should know how to deal with this relatively minor emergency.

Finally, it's helpful to be familiar with the jobs and some of the complexities involved when the yard manager or mechanic is explaining an estimate or bill. You'll understand each other better if you know the terminology and can ask intelligent questions about the work.

PACKING GLANDS

The packing gland, also referred to as the stuffing box, packing box, or stern gland, is the device that allows the prop shaft to pass through the hull below the waterline and to turn at high speed without leaking. The spud-type gland found on most boats consists of a body, a packing nut, and a lock nut. The nuts are threaded onto the forward end of the body, and the after end is connected to the shaft log by a length of reinforced rubber hose, secured with hose clamps. The prop shaft passes through the shaft log and the packing gland and is attached to the transmission with a pair of mated couplings. (See Figure 12.1b.)

The gland uses a packing material of wax-impregnated flax to form a seal around the prop shaft. The material is square in section, and varies in size depending on the sizes of the packing nut and shaft. It's cut to length and arranged in a series of stacked rings inside the packing nut so that the shaft passes through their inside diameters. The nut is threaded onto the gland, tightened until snug, and secured with the locking nut.

Tightening the packing nut compresses the material around the shaft to form a seal. As the packing wears, the nut has to be tightened to maintain the seal. Proper tightening is essential. A loose fit leaks, while overtightening generates excessive heat when running. Heat can cause the shaft to seize inside the gland, or it can melt the wax out of the packing material, resulting in loss of the seal and leakage.

There is a common dockside myth that says that your packing gland is *supposed* to leak when the boat's at rest, or when it's under way, or when the prop is reversed, in order to indicate that it's working properly. Nonsense. The thing is designed to keep water *out*, not let it in, and a gland that's perfectly adjusted won't leak and won't run hot.

This being an imperfect world, however, you won't always be able to achieve or maintain packing-gland perfection. If that's the case, an occasional drip from the shaft log won't hurt anything, and is preferable to a too-tight adjustment. If you find that your installation is consistently a bit wet, you can rig a spray shield over the shaft log, to prevent

Fig. 12.1a.   *Typical shaft log and packing gland installation.*

the entire engine room from being constantly doused with salt water. (See Figure 12.2.)

When adjustment is necessary, the job will be much less of a chore if you've been lubricating the gland periodically. Stern glands live in a very corrosive environment, and without regular lubrication become extremely difficult to adjust. If you have to adjust a gland that hasn't been lubricated regularly, a thorough soaking with WD-40® a day or so ahead of time will help.

Adjustment will require a packing nut wrench or pair of water-pump pliers (Channellocks®), a ¼-inch or larger punch, and a hammer. A wrench or pliers usually won't work on a corroded packing nut, since leverage alone will usually just twist the entire unit around the shaft log. You'll need the hammer and punch to knock things loose.

You need to separate the nuts by running the lock nut aft and the packing nut forward. Looking aft, place the punch near the 3 o'clock position on the lock nut, and strike smartly with the hammer. Then, place the punch near the 9 o'clock position on the packing nut and

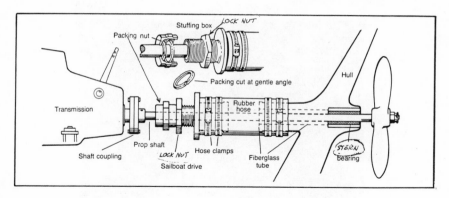

Fig. 12.1b.   *Diagram of shaft log and packing gland installation.* DRAWING
BY PETER HUNT.

strike. Repeat until the nuts separate. (After you've gone through this
drill once, you'll realize the importance of keeping these parts lubricated.)

Once the nuts have broken free, run the lock nut back several turns
and lubricate the uncovered threads. Then tighten the packing nut by
hand just until the leak stops, but don't overtighten it. An extra quarter-
turn after the leak stops is usually all that can be taken without risking
overheating. Back the lock nut up to the packing nut and secure it by
placing the punch near the nine o'clock position on the lock nut and
rapping firmly. If the lock nut isn't properly secured, the packing nut
can work loose and back itself off when the engine is reversed.

Spray everything with lubricant once more for good measure, and
check the nut for excessive heat when the boat has been run at cruising
speed. If it's too hot to touch after a twenty-minute run, it's too tight
and will have to be loosened.

Occasionally, proper adjustment is impossible, and tightening the
nut just enough to stop the leak causes it to run too hot. This probably
means the packing material is not forming a good seal around the shaft.

To re-form the packing, back the packing nut off the gland body
and slide it up the prop shaft. If water pours in around the shaft, tie
rags around it to slow down the flow. Then, while slowly rotating the
packing nut around the prop shaft, tap it gently with the hammer, using
the shaft to form the packing into an even circle to form a better seal.
Reinstall, lock, and recheck.

When no amount of tightening and re-forming will stop the leak,
the packing material is worn out and needs to be replaced. Replacement

Fig. 12.2. *Movable spray shield fitted over a flange-type packing gland.*

intervals are highly variable, with some frequently used powerboats requiring annual attention, while many sailboats can get by for three or four years. The packing should be checked at haul-out time, and if there's any doubt about its ability to last the year, replace it. Some boats have to be hauled out to replace packing, and paying for a haul-out just to replace two dollars' worth of flax makes no sense at all.

Replacing packing is a simple procedure, once you know how it's done, but botching the job could have dire consequences. The best approach is to pay to have it done once, and have the mechanic show you the procedure. This is one of those jobs that's easier to do than it is to describe. Nevertheless, here is a description of the procedure, should you decide to undertake it:

First, remove the old packing from the nut. Back the nut off the gland and slide it up the shaft. Right away, some boats present a problem. You need to be able to push the packing nut up the shaft far enough to allow room to reach up inside it with a tool. If the shaft length between packing gland and coupling is too short, you'll have to pull the coupling to change the packing. This procedure is detailed on page 186 below.

A pair of needle-nosed pliers or an O-ring tool can be used to remove the old packing, or a long sheet-metal screw can be used as an extractor. Simply screw it into the material and pull it out.

Once you've got the old material out, you need to determine its size. Take the old stuff to your chandlery, and match it with new stuff. Buy more than you think you'll need. You'll be making three rings of material for each shaft, and you'll be making some mistakes, so it's a good idea to have spare material on board.

To cut the packing to fit, wrap a length around the shaft, running the ends past each other. Cut with a *sharp* knife (razor knives and carpet knives work well) at about a 45-degree angle to the shaft centerline, so that the ends of the ring match. The ring should be just long enough to reach around the shaft, and should look like this:

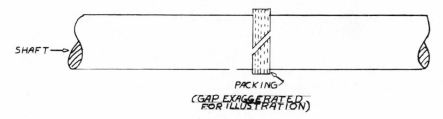

SHAFT→

PACKING
(GAP EXAGGERATED
FOR ILLUSTRATION)

Most packing nuts will hold three rings arranged inside the packing nut with the cuts staggered at 120-degree intervals.

The fit will be pretty snug at first, and it may be hard to push the packing into the nut. One way around the problem is to cut the first ring, wrap it around the shaft, and push it into the packing nut far enough to expose some threads. Slide the packing nut down, and thread it onto the gland.

Tighten firmly, moving the packing up inside the nut just far enough to install the next ring, and then back it off. Mark the packing gland with a scratch or with a marking pen to indicate the location of the seam. Repeat with the rest of the rings, staggering the cuts.

Snug the packing nut firmly by hand, secure the lock nut, and check as soon as the boat's in the water, preferably while still in the slings. If it doesn't leak, it should be safe to remove the slings. Check it again after running at speed for twenty to thirty minutes, and readjust if necessary. Lubricate the unit occasionally, and check for leaks from time to time.

Some boats use a stuffing box consisting of a collar-and-flange arrangement rather than the standard threaded packing and lock nuts. (See Figure 12.2, page 184.) Adjustment of one of these is accomplished by tightening the two or three fasteners that force the collar aft, compressing the packing material. Some use a pair of nuts on each stud, the aft one used for adjusting, and the forward one serving as a lock nut. Whichever system is used, make sure to tighten the fasteners in small, equal increments until the leak stops.

SHAFT COUPLING REMOVAL

The prop shaft coupling has to be removed in order to pull the shaft, to replace the shaft log hose, or occasionally to remove the packing nut. The coupling is fitted onto the shaft and located in place either with a pair of set screws that fit into dimples drilled in the shaft, or with a roll pin. A keyway is machined into the coupling and shaft, and a key inserted to allow the coupling to turn the shaft.

Larger boats sometimes use a split coupling that is clamped onto the shaft with large bolts passing through flanges on either side. This arrangement makes removal and replacement of large couplings easier.

Couplings are secured to each other with four or more bolts spaced around the coupling flanges. The bolts are run forward through the shaft coupling, and then either run through the transmission coupling and secured with lock washers and nuts, or threaded directly into the transmission coupling.

To unbolt, find a comfortable working position behind the engine (good luck!). With the engine off and transmission in neutral, rotate the shaft until you can reach one of the bolts.

If the bolt is threaded into the transmission coupling, you should be able to break the bolts free by putting the engine in gear and backing out the bolts. (If the shaft turns freely with the transmission in forward, try putting it in reverse.) This trick doesn't work with hydraulic transmissions and with some mechanical gearboxes. In that case, see the description below.

If the bolts run through both couplings, you'll need to get a wrench onto the nuts on the front of the transmission coupling, and another wrench (preferably a socket wrench) on the bolt head. Engage the transmission and go to it. If the force needed to separate the bolts is greater than the resistance afforded by your engine's compression, or if access is so limited that you can't get a good grip on both wrenches, you'll have to get creative.

With the transmission in neutral, put your wrench (a box-end works best here) on the nut, and turn the shaft counterclockwise until the free end of the wrench hits the hull. Snug it up to hold it in place, and put your socket wrench on the bolt head. Unbolt it, and repeat the process for the rest of the fasteners.

If your wrench is too short to make contact with the hull, use a wood block to take up the space. This is also a good idea if the fasteners are severely corroded, since you'll probably be hitting the wrench with enough force to damage the hull.

Soak any badly corroded fasteners with penetrating oil, WD-40®, or a lubricating oil before getting started. When you're trying to break things loose, a sharp rap on the wrench with the hammer will usually work better than steady, even pressure.

If your bolts thread directly into the transmission coupling, and if your engine compression isn't strong enough to resist the necessary unbolting force, you'll need other tricks.

Sometimes, you can wedge a wood block between the hull and the set-screw heads. This will keep the shaft from turning, and you can then unbolt the fasteners. (Reverse the procedure when it comes time to tighten things back up.) If that doesn't work, try putting a strap wrench around the shaft or around part of the transmission coupling to immobilize the shaft.

Once the couplings are unbolted, slide the prop shaft aft, separating the two couplings. (If they don't separate easily, put the transmission in gear and twist the prop shaft. Or, for really stubborn cases, start the engine and *briefly* put it in gear.) Cut the safety wire joining the coupling set screws, and back the set screws out.

Once the set screws are out, get your flashlight and look through the holes at the shaft. There should be shallow dimples drilled into the shaft to afford the set screws some purchase. Check for the presence of dimples, and that they are centered in the set-screw holes. If they are not, have the misalignment taken care of at the machine shop when you take the shaft in.

To remove the shaft coupling, you can try tapping it off using a wood block and hammer. Sometimes this actually works, but the other 99 times out of 100, more complicated measures are called for. The coupling is a pressed fit on the shaft, and usually has to be eased off. Most yards have a slide hammer arrangement that accomplishes this task easily enough and is well worth borrowing or renting. If you don't have access to one of these tools, the next best way to remove the coupling is with a combination of spacers, nuts, washers, and long bolts.

If your couplings use through-bolts and nuts, you'll need a couple of bolts at least two inches longer than the originals, nuts to fit, a handful of washers, and a set of pipe nipples smaller in diameter than the shaft to be used as spacers of various lengths.

Slide the prop shaft back far enough to slip a pipe nipple into the space between the couplings. Place it lengthwise over the end of the shaft, and push the shaft forward firmly to hold it in place. Then, put washers on the bolts, run them through coupling holes 180 degrees apart, and tighten up alternately on the nuts. This will eventually slide the shaft coupling off the end.

If your transmission coupling is threaded, you'll need bolts with the same thread as the originals. With through-bolts, any size that fits through the holes will do, as long as they're stout enough to stand up to the strain. Juggling washers, spacers, and bolt lengths can get tricky. It helps to have lots of everything on hand before you start, rather than get started and have to stop and run out for more material.

As you tighten up on the bolts, alternating back and forth, the shaft coupling slides forward, eventually meeting the transmission coupling. When this happens, slide the shaft back, remove the spacer you're using, and substitute one slightly longer.

When you change spacers, you'll also have to either use longer bolts, or remove some washers to make up for the difference.

As you're tightening, make sure that the spacer is centered on the shaft. If it slips down to overlap the inside diameter of the coupling, you can tighten bolts until the cows come home, and all you'll get is exercise.

Occasionally, because of positioning details and bolt and spacer lengths, you'll find yourself changing spacers frequently. This is where having a variety of lengths of pipe nipples comes in handy.

If you're taking the shaft in for servicing, such as straightening, machining, or to be inspected, take the coupling in as well, and have it fitted and trued. Check to be sure that the shaft is dimpled for set screws. When replacing a shaft, replace the coupling as well. All 1-inch shafts aren't exactly 1 inch in diameter, and the coupling has to be precisely fitted and trued according to each shaft's exact dimensions.

Replacing the shaft coupling goes much quicker with two people. You'll need a block of wood to place between the two couplings, another block to use as a cushion on the end of the shaft, and a good-sized hammer.

Apply a thin coat of grease to the forward end of the shaft. Push the shaft through the strut and into the hull. It helps to remove the packing nut before pushing the shaft through the shaft log. This prevents the shaft end from tearing the packing as the shaft is forced through. After the shaft is through the log, work the packing nut over the end and tighten it down.

When the shaft is inside the hull, put the key in the shaft keyway and slide the coupling on. If it's correctly fitted, it will be tight and have to be pressed or tapped in place. This is where the wood blocks and helper come into the picture. Place a block between the couplings and slide the shaft forward to hold it in place. Then, with one person watching closely from inside, the person outside places the other block over the tail end of the shaft and pounds just hard enough to move the shaft forward inside the coupling.

Be sure that the person doing the hammer work on the outside uses a block on the shaft end, and make sure that he can hear the person inside. He'll usually have to start out hitting firmly, and then back off as the coupling nears its destination. Sometimes the shaft key will ride up on the after end of the coupling and jam. Tap it forward with a hammer and punch, and continue.

When the inside person can see the shaft dimples centered in the set-screw holes, stop. Also, check the position of the key at the forward end. It should not protrude beyond the end of the shaft. If it does, tap it back with hammer and punch. Replace and tighten the set screws, and install stainless-steel safety wire.

Cut a length of wire approximately two and a half times the distance between the set screws. Run one end through one of the heads, centering it on the length of wire. Then, twist the length of wire in a tight braid, and pass the doubled end through the other set screw. Pull it tight and wrap it back and around itself. Push the couplings together, and bolt them up. (See Figure 12.3.)

Fig. 12.3. *Shaft coupling with safety-wired set screws.*

ENGINE ALIGNMENT

In order for an engine and prop shaft to work together as a unit, they have to be very closely aligned. Picture a line running through the transmission tail shaft and the prop shaft. The shafts meet and are joined together at their couplings. By aligning the engine, the center-lines running through the shafts are aligned, and the coupling faces are parallel.

Since the location of the propeller shaft is fixed, alignment is the process of moving the engine/transmission around on it's mounts. This is a precise adjustment, with the margin for error measured in thousandths of an inch. The engine should be aligned when a new boat is launched and once a year after that. For the procedure to be accurate, it must be done with the boat in the water, and with the sailing rig stepped and tuned.

If the boat is new, or has been hauled out for several months, allow the boat to sit in the water for a few days so that it takes its permanent shape.

Most engines have four motor mounts, two front and two rear, that sit on longitudinal hull members called stringers. A motor mount consists of a metal base surrounding a rubber piece into which a vertical threaded rod is embedded. There are nuts above and below an L-shaped piece bolted to the motor. The engine is raised and lowered by turning the lower nut on which the engine rests, and the upper nut is tightened to hold everything in place. (See Figure 12.4.)

There are two types of misalignment to be checked, and two planes of adjustment. The type and plane to be adjusted determines which mounts are adjusted, and in which direction.

Bore misalignment indicates that the rear mounts need to be adjusted. In the side view, the front and rear mounts would both need to be dropped, while in the top view, the whole engine would have to be moved to starboard, adjusting front and rear mounts. (See Figure 12.5.)

Face misalignment occurs when the bores of the prop and transmission shaft are in line, but the coupling faces don't meet evenly all the way around their circumferences when they're pushed together. This type of misalignment is more common, and indicates that the front mounts need adjustment. (See Figure 12.6.)

Generally speaking, it's less confusing to deal with as few variables as possible, so the best approach is to first try to align the engine using only the front mounts. If this proves impossible, and if it becomes apparent that bore misalignment is the problem, then and only then should you tinker with the rear mounts.

The size of the allowable gap depends on coupling diameter, and is usually figured to be $5/10,000$ inch (0.0005 inch) for each inch of

Fig. 12.4. *Motor mount, showing upper and lower adjusting nuts.* PHOTO
COURTESY OF W. H. DEN OUDEN (U.S.A), INC.

coupling diameter. Thus, a 4-inch coupling would allow $\frac{2}{1,000}$ inch of
slop. ($0.0005'' \times 4'' = 0.002''$)

Unbolt the couplings (see page 186) and separate them completely
to make sure that any tension or friction forces aren't sticking them
together. Push them back together, noting the ease with which they
mesh. If there's a long span between the shaft log and the transmission,
the weight of the shaft and coupling will cause the end to sag. Raise
the end approximately half the distance of the sag, slide the shaft
forward, and the couplings should match.

Feeler or thickness gauges are used to measure the coupling gaps.

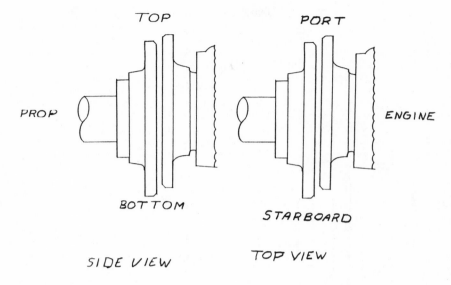

Fig. 12.5 *Drawing illustrates bore misalignment.*

A set of gauges consists of a series of metal leafs of precise thicknesses. Some of the less expensive sets don't contain the smaller sizes, so before buying, you need to know the diameter of your coupling and the size of the smallest gauge you'll be using.

Measuring alignment with a feeler gauge demands a bit of technique. If the engine and shaft were perfectly aligned, the couplings would mate effortlessly, and you wouldn't be able to insert a feeler gauge anywhere around their circumferences. If you were to move the shaft back 0.002 inch, a 0.002-inch feeler gauge would fit into the gap all the way around, but a 0.003-inch gauge would not.

If the front of the motor is dropped slightly, the couplings will be forced together at the bottoms, opening a gap at the top. So, if the couplings are flush at the bottom, but have a gap greater than 0.002 inch at the top (between the three o'clock and the nine o'clock positions), you know that the front of the engine has to be raised. Similarly, a gap on the right side of the couplings indicates that the front of the engine needs to move to the right.

To accurately measure the gap, slide the gauge between the couplings, holding it parallel to the coupling face. Then, move the gauge around the circumferences. When you come to a spot where the gauge stops, you've found a place where the gap is smaller than the size of

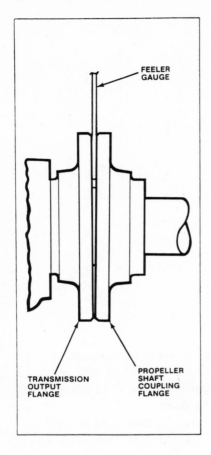

Fig. 12.6. *Drawing illustrates coupling face misalignment, feeler gauge placement.* DRAWING COURTESY OF BORG-WARNER CORP.

the gauge. Obviously, wherever the gauge will fit, the gap is equal to or greater than the gauge size.

So far, things sound straightforward enough, but complications set in quickly. If the motor has to move both horizontally and vertically, or if the coupling faces aren't perfectly matched, or if the rear mounts need adjustment, the time involved increases dramatically.

There's also the problem of actually moving the engine. Vertical adjustment is usually accomplished with adjusting nuts on the motor mounts. Moving horizontally, however, is a different matter. The lag screws securing the motor mount bases must be loosened, and the engine shifted from side to side. With small sailboat auxiliaries, you can usually use a lever or pry bar to ease the motor over. With six- and eight-cylinder engines, however, things get a bit tougher.

Here the tool of choice is a hydraulic jack. You can use a standard bottle-type jack, but access and convenient working locations are usually a problem. Your best bet is to borrow or rent a remote-control hydraulic jack. These tools have a hydraulic ram connected to a flexible hose that attaches to different end fittings, the most convenient of which is a set of clamshell jaws. These can easily be positioned between the stringers and the motor, and can adjust the engine in very small increments.

When using a jack to move an engine, you need a place to rest the jack base or jaws, and a place on the motor that will take the stress involved. Stringers provide a good base, but be careful where you place the jack against the engine. Trying to move a V-8 engine by pushing on the oil pan could cause expensive damage.

Generally, if the motor has to be moved in both planes, for instance down and to the right, it's best to solve one problem at a time. If your feeler gauge is blocked from the five to the ten o'clock positions (looking forward), for example, the right front motor mount needs to be raised. Once this is done, rechecking might show the problem to be solved, or it might show that now the tight spot lies between the eight and ten o'clock positions. Now, the front of the engine has to be moved to the right. You need to separate, remate, and recheck the couplings with the feeler gauge after each adjustment to attain accurate readings.

The ideal tool for motor mount nuts is a combination wrench. You'll need the box end for the upper nuts, and the open end for the lowers. Another possible combination is a socket wrench for the uppers and a large adjustable wrench for the lowers, *if* there's room enough. If an adjustable wrench won't fit on the lowers, try a crowfoot wrench.

To adjust the motor vertically, loosen the upper nuts on both mounts. This will allow the motor to move up and down without binding or catching.

The amount of adjusting you'll need to do is directly related to the size of the gap at the coupling. For instance, if the couplings are tight at the bottom (from three to nine o'clock), and there's a 0.002-inch gap at the top, the front of the engine will only have to be raised slightly. If the upper gap is 0.008 inch, you're obviously going to have to bring the front up a bit farther. Exact distances will differ, since the span between couplings and engine mounts will vary greatly from motor to motor, but you'll get a feel for your own equipment as you go along.

For your first attempt, adjust the lower nuts one sixth of a turn (one "flat" on the nut) at a time, tighten the lock nut, and recheck the fit as you go. Remember, the couplings have to be separated and refitted for each adjustment check.

Once you have things adjusted within tolerances, and you think you're almost done, guess again. For a final check, separate the couplings and remate them. Tighten all your motor mount screws and nuts, and recheck alignment. Then, separate the couplings again, and rotate the shaft coupling 180 degrees relative to the transmission coupling. Remate the couplings and check alignment again.

If your alignment is off after this check, your coupling faces aren't parallel. If it's only a thousandth of an inch or so, you can usually split the difference and adjust accordingly.

If it's off much more than that, however, and you can't align the engine within the allowable tolerances, you'll have to pull the shaft and coupling and take them to a machine shop for refitting. The usual problem is that the coupling face isn't perpendicular to the shaft centerline, or the shaft is bent. A machine shop can check and refit the coupling, and check and true the shaft.

STERN BEARINGS

Except for full-keeled sailboats, most boats use a strut suspended from the hull to support the prop shaft just forward of the propeller. The strut is bolted and fiberglassed to the hull, and contains the stern bearing. (On full-keeled sailboats, the bearing is inside the deadwood.)

The bearing holds the shaft in place, and allows it to turn freely. It is composed of a brass cylinder surrounding rubber-bearing material that comes in contact with the shaft. Eventually, the rubber wears out and has to be replaced. Unfortunately, this is another one of those jobs that can cost hundreds of dollars in labor to replace a twenty-dollar part.

To determine if the bearing needs to be replaced, try wiggling the prop shaft inside the bearing. If everything's snug, and little or no slop is detected, fine. However, if there's noticeable movement of the shaft inside the bearing, it'll have to come out.

First, the prop and shaft must be removed. Depending on how long it's been since these jobs were performed, how corroded things are, what the access to the shaft coupling is like, whether the rudder has to be removed, etc., this can take either an hour or the better part of a week.

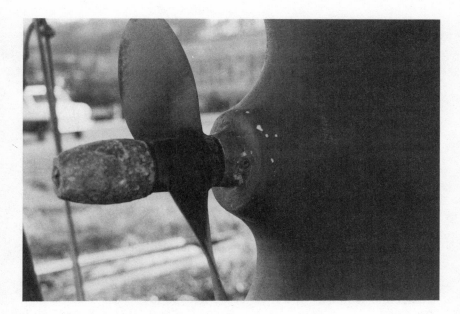

Fig. 12.7. *Photo shows nearly hidden stern bearing set-screw head.*

Once the prop and shaft are out of the way, it's time to remove the old bearing. If the old bearing was greased before it was installed, if it's held in by easily removed set screws, and if it decides to exit gracefully, your task is much simpler. The old one slides out, the new one is greased and slides in, the set screws are tightened, and you're done. Replace the prop and shaft and you're ready to go.

In the real world, however, things seldom go that smoothly. The more likely course of events includes a prop jammed onto the shaft, coupling bolts that haven't seen any lubrication since the Truman administration, and a coupling that's welded itself to the shaft. Then, either the stern bearing set-screw heads get rounded off and have to be drilled out, or there are no set screws, and the bearing is pressed in so tight it has to be cut out.

If the bearing has to come out, check for set screws. They're usually Allen-head screws set into the side of the strut, the heads flush with the surface. If the strut's surface is painted or fouled, it will have to be cleaned off for inspection. If you find set screws, spray them with penetrating oil or WD-40® before trying to back them out. (See Figure 12.7.)

Once the set screws are removed, or it's been determined that there are no screws, the bearing can be tapped out. The best way to accomplish this is with a section of pipe or tubing of just slightly smaller diameter than the bearing. Place the pipe over the end of the bearing and tap (or pound, depending on circumstances) it out. A punch or piece of wood dowel will sometimes work in this situation, if you can catch enough of the bearing's metal edge with the punch without damaging the strut.

Once you've got an inch or so of bearing protruding from the strut, a pipe wrench can be used to twist it and slowly work it out. Be careful not to score or gouge the internal diameter of the strut. Flailing away with punches, screwdrivers, and pieces of pipe can do just that.

If none of the above methods work, you'll have to cut. Surgery is no fun, and should only be used as a last resort, but extreme situations demand extreme measures.

If you can pry out the rubber bearing insert with a screwdriver or chisel and hammer, you'll be better able to see what you're doing. Then if you don't have a close-quarters hacksaw, the best approach is to run your saw blade through the inside of the bearing, and then attach it to a standard hacksaw frame around the outside of the strut.

Start your cut anywhere you can get a good angle on the saw frame, stopping frequently to make sure that your cut is parallel to the length of the bearing. As soon as you're through the bearing material, stop. Or at least stop sometime before you saw into the strut itself.

In some cases, a single cut will relieve enough compression to enable you to tap the bearing out. Usually, though, you'll find that you need to make a second cut, ½ inch or so from the first one. Then, peel out the strip of material between the cuts. What's left of the old bearing should then be easily removed.

When you buy a new bearing, if the old one has been multilated beyond recognition, you'll need to know three dimensions. The shaft diameter, the inside diameter of the strut, and the length. A set of calipers is ideal for measuring diameters, but a tape measure is acceptable, as long as you're very careful. Trying to hammer a 2¼-inch-diameter bearing into a 2-inch hole makes for a long day.

Grease the new bearing's exterior before installing. This makes installation easier, and should help when replacement time rolls around again. If your installation uses set screws, lubricate them before replacement as well.

If your boat uses a fiberglass strut, it's possible for the bronze tube on a standard bearing to succumb to galvanic corrosion. With a bronze strut that's bonded, the bearing is protected by the underwater zincs. A bearing in a fiberglass strut is isolated from that protection. In that case, you need to use one of the bearings made with a reinforced plastic tube rather than a bronze one, such as those made by Johnson Duramax® Products.

ZINCS

Zinc anodes are attached to a boat's underwater metal gear to protect against corrosion. The chemical, metallurgical, and physical processes involved are beyond the scope of this book and are well detailed in Miller and Maloney's *Your Boat's Electrical Systems* should you want to read up on the subject in depth. From a practical standpoint, though, here's what happens.

Zinc is a metal that corrodes readily, and when in contact with other metals under water, protects those other metals by sacrificing itself. Zinc is cheap, so we attach zinc anodes to our underwater gear, and replace them regularly, rather than replacing all the other underwater metal parts from time to time.

Keep in mind that your zincs are *supposed* to corrode and disintegrate. We've heard boat owners bragging that they've got great zincs that have lasted for years. A zinc that's not corroding is not working. If it's not your zincs corroding, then it's something that's a lot more expensive, like props, shafts, or rudders.

The amount of zinc that you'll need to protect your boat depends on quite a few variables, such as water temperature and salinity, amount and kinds of underwater metal present, hull material, whether or not you're plugged into shore power, and how galvanically "hot" your harbor and slip are.

When installing shaft zincs, first sand the area to be covered by the zinc. This removes any surface corrosion or oxidation. Clamp the zinc over the shaft, install and tighten the screws. Then, rap the zinc sharply on both sides 90 degrees from the seam—this will seat the zinc more firmly. Retighten the screws, and repeat until no more slack remains. For rudder zincs, sand the area to be covered. Install zincs and tighten.

Hull zincs are large zinc plates, drilled to fit over bolts protruding from the transom. If you need to drill your own hull zincs, be very careful. Zinc is a soft metal that tends to clog and bind drill bits. Use

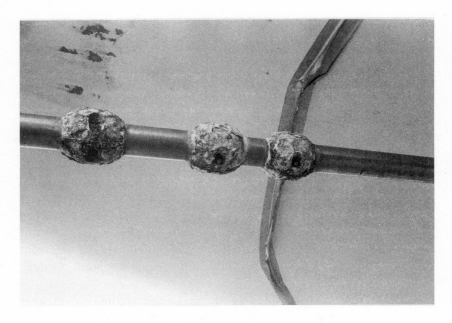

Fig. 12.8. *Prop shaft zincs that have done their job, and are due for replacement.*

a piece of wood for backing, clamp the zinc securely, and use a variable-speed drill and plenty of cutting fluid, turning the bit just fast enough to get through the metal.

In evaluating your zinc protection, be aware that a zinc anode's useful life is pretty much over when half of its mass is gone. Ideally, then, if your boat is hauled annually, all of your zincs should be one half of their original size. If they're completely gone, or nearly so, you need more or bigger zincs. If they look as good as new, they're not working. (See Figure 12.8.)

Don't paint your zincs. Paint will keep them from working, to the detriment of your underwater gear.

PROPS

Removing and replacing propellers isn't usually complicated, but there are a few things that will help. Unless you plan on spending a lot of time in very remote areas, you won't need to buy a prop puller. They can be rented or borrowed from most boatyards. The same goes for the oversize wrench you'll need for the prop nuts. The only wrench that most people have that's big enough for the job is a pipe wrench, and pipe wrenches present a problem. They tend to bind up when under strain, and the binding squeezes the nut at the same time that you're trying to loosen it. So, if possible, use a combination or adjustable wrench.

First, remove the cotter pin from the end of the shaft. Then turn the shaft counterclockwise, wedging a block of wood between the hull and a prop blade. (This is assuming that the shaft and nuts are a right-hand thread. We know of at least one Taiwan-built boat that uses a left-hand thread on its starboard prop shaft. The vast majority of shafts are right-handed, but if you're not sure, check before you start by rotating the shaft and observing the thread direction.)

There will be two nuts on the shaft, a prop nut and a lock nut. The aftermost one is the lock nut, so obviously you remove that one first. Then loosen the prop nut, but don't remove it. Back it off so that its after end is flush with the end of the shaft. This will keep the prop from falling off onto the ground, or your foot, when pulled.

Attach the prop puller (see Figure 12.9), and tighten the nuts alternately to apply pressure to the propeller. When everything's good and tight, smack the puller on the face directly behind the shaft. Tighten

Fig. 12.9. *Prop puller.* PHOTO COURTESY OF MICHIGAN WHEEL CORP.

some more and smack again until the prop springs free. When this happens, you'll see why you left the prop nut on the shaft.

Take your prop to your friendly neighborhood prop shop, and have it trued, pitched, and balanced. If you have any questions about prop materials, proper pitch and diameter, or cupping, this is the place to ask them.

When replacing props on a twin-screw boat, make sure that the correct prop is installed on each shaft. Most twin-screw boats use a left-hand prop on the port side and a right-hand prop on starboard. The letters "RH" and "LH" will be stamped on the hub, along with the prop's pitch and diameter.

Before replacing the prop, grease the shaft and threads with a good grade of waterproof grease. Place the key in the keyway, and slide the prop forward. Thread the prop nut on, and hand tighten.

Put your block of wood between the hull and the prop blade, and tighten the prop nut. Make sure that the key doesn't ride up in the shaft keyway on the forward side of the prop. If it does, and you tighten the prop nut with the key jammed like that, you'll be putting a strain on the hub that can split it if the prop strikes an object in the water.

Replace the lock nut, tighten, and replace the cotter pin, and you're ready to head out and chew up some more floating debris.

13

PUMPS

A TYPICAL midsize boat with a diesel engine can easily have a dozen different pumps on board. While all pumps are designed to move liquids, there are a variety of specialized kinds of pumps. A diesel engine alone usually has four different pumps installed on it—fuel-lift, injection, raw-water, and coolant-circulation pumps.

In addition, a typical boat can have both electric and manual bilge pumps, a shower sump pump, a freshwater-pressure pump, a head, and a holding-tank pump. Optional pumps include saltwater-wash-down, bait-well, fuel-transfer, and oil-change.

PUMP TYPES

There are several types of pumps used aboard boats to take care of a variety of functions. Each class has its advantages and drawbacks, and no one kind will perform all the necessary functions equally well.

Diaphragm pumps use flexible diaphragms to provide water pressure and are used as bilge and shower sump pumps. They are usually self-priming, and can run dry for extended periods of time.

Disadvantages include the diaphragms' tendency to develop holes and leaks, and that bits of debris can get caught in the valves, reducing the pump's effectiveness. They're also larger and more expensive than impeller pumps of similar capacity, and can be more difficult to repair. When used as bilge pumps, an effective strainer is essential. When used to provide water pressure, an accumulator tank is usually necessary to provide a steady water flow and to reduce "hammering" in the pipes.

Flexible impeller pumps, using vane-type impellers to create the necessary vacuum, are used for bilge and pressure water pumps, as engine raw-water pumps, for washdown systems, and—with the proper impellers installed—to pump oil. They are usually self-priming, and can pass fairly large solids without clogging. They're smaller and less expensive than diaphragm pumps, and don't produce pulses and hammering in pressure water systems.

The main disadvantage of these units is that when they're allowed to run dry, friction generates excessive heat, destroying the impeller. When the impeller breaks up, stray pieces usually travel downstream, sometimes making recovery difficult.

Fortunately, they are usually very easy to repair, requiring only the removal of a cover plate to allow access to the impeller for replacement.

When used for pumping motor oil or other petroleum products, it's essential to have an impeller designed for that use. Neoprene impellers will absorb oil and swell, eventually seizing in the housing.

Many impeller pumps are also reversible, making them ideal for use in oil-changing systems on larger engines. Old oil can be pumped out and, with a flick of a switch, fresh oil pumped back in. With engines requiring large quantities of oil, or where access to the fill hole is difficult, this is an especially nice feature.

While we're on the subject of pumping petroleum, *never* pump gasoline or other flammable liquids with a pump not specifically designated for such use. Specially shielded pumps made for use with flammables will be clearly marked, and if there's any doubt, don't use it.

Also, if a pump is located in an area where gasoline fumes are a possibility, it must be ignition protected. Remember, just because a pump is ignition protected doesn't mean it's approved as a flammable liquids pump, and vice versa. Pumps that run off 120-volt AC power are seldom ignition protected, and must be mounted far from any flammable vapors.

Centrifugal pumps are similar to impeller pumps, except that they use metal vanes. They are usually used for circulating engine coolant and in bait wells. They are not self-priming, but they run very quietly.

Submersible pumps are used for bilge pumping and in bait wells. The motors are sealed, allowing the entire unit to be submerged without harm. They are usually not self-priming, but can run dry without damage.

Hand pumps are used as oil-change pumps for small motors, as dinghy bailers, and to supply drinking water on boats not equipped with pressure water systems. They are especially handy for pumping oil, fuel, and spilled coolant from the pan underneath the engine. They're inexpensive and reliable, but depending on the job at hand, can be inconvenient and exhausting.

Foot pumps are frequently employed for potable water systems on boats without pressure water, the advantage over hand pumps being ease of use and free use of hands. Trying to wash and rinse your hands and face with a hand-operated pump can be hilarious entertainment for your shipmates, but not terribly efficient or graceful.

A *check valve* is a device placed in some water systems that allows water to flow in one direction only. They're frequently installed to keep hot water from backflowing into the cold-water lines, and in bilge pump exhaust lines.

BILGE PUMPS

Bilge pumps are used to remove water from a boat's nether regions. Usually, the process involves only the pumping out of accumulated dew, packing gland drippings, and the occasional spilled beer. However, when you're faced with a *lot* of bilge water, whether from a burst hose, a wave taken aboard, or a hole in the hull, bilge pumping becomes a critical function. While the majority of boaters will never be faced with a real bilge-pumping emergency, every boater who ventures into water too deep to wade home in should be prepared for the worst.

Stock boats come from the factories equipped with electric bilge pumps of wildly varying abilities and quality. A pump rated to move

500 gallons per hour (GPH) might sound like a pretty hefty little item, until you consider that a one-inch hole a foot below the waterline will admit up to 1,200 GPH.

Some boats use pumps driven by the engine as primary or secondary bilge pumps, as well as for bait-well circulation and washdown. These pumps are usually equipped with clutches to engage and disengage them, and have the ability to move lots of water, in some cases up to 5,000 GPH. They are usually of the flexible impeller type, so it's important that the clutch be disengaged when the pump isn't needed.

Bilge pumping is not a good area for scrimping. The safety of your boat and the lives of your passengers may one day be at the mercy of this system. Reliability, efficiency, and redundancy can be vital.

For starters, if your boat came equipped with one of those tiny 400–500 GPH items, either get rid of it in favor of a real pump, or keep it in place and install a larger pump for backup and emergency use. At least one good manual pump is essential. If the situation is such that the electric pump is not of sufficient capacity, if it clogs with debris or blows its fuse or circuit breaker, or if the batteries become submerged or discharged, having a manual pump aboard becomes crucial. Manual bilge pumps are usually diaphragm pumps, and they are standard equipment on most sailboats but seldom found on powerboats. The so-called logic behind this practice apparently reasons that a holed powerboat can just run for shore, while a sailboat can't. Obviously, this isn't always the case, and a prudent powerboat skipper will have a manual bilge pump installed to back up the electric pumps.

The pump should be sturdily mounted in a location allowing a comfortable seating or standing position when using it, and easy access for cleanout and repair. If it's mounted in the cockpit, use of the pump shouldn't require leaving a hatch or lazarette open. Heavy rains or waves breaking over the cockpit will only make an already difficult job worse.

For all nonsubmersible pumps that extend a hose into the bilges, a strainer on the end is needed to keep trash from being inhaled. Some forms of strainers employ a simple bronze casting consisting of a screen over the intake end, and a tab with a screw hole allowing it to be secured in place.

Other strainers incorporate a check valve to keep water from draining out of the hose and back into the bilge. This is an especially handy feature for shortening pickup time when the hose run is a long one. Inspect them occasionally, though, since some of them tend to deteriorate when they come in contact with petroleum products, and can be fouled by debris.

Strainers and hose ends should be secured in place, while at the same time allowing easy removal for cleanout. Also, the hose should be matched in size to the pump fittings, and be of a noncollapsible, smooth-walled design.

Submersible pumps are usually secured in the bilge, and incorporate strainers into their bases. With submersible pumps, as with remote strainers, easy access for cleaning and repair is important.

With any pump, but especially with bilge pumps, flow rates given by manufacturers should be taken with at least a grain of salt. Be advised that these figures are given for pumps tested under ideal lab conditions, and the probability of your boat matching those conditions and flow rates is slim, at best.

The numbers are useful in making comparisons, however, so you can safely assume that a pump rated at 2,000 GPH will probably pump approximately four times as much water as one rated at 500 GPH.

Automatic bilge pumps use any one of several devices to detect rising water levels in the bilge and automatically activate the pump, cutting it off when the water is gone. These devices include float switches, air pressure switches, and electronic sensing units.

There are two schools of thought concerning automatic pumps. One group reasons that with pleasure boats spending so much time unattended, an automatic pump is essential to ensure that, should the boat spring a leak, the system will keep the boat afloat until the owner returns.

The other group sees automatic pumps as devices that tend to mask problems rather than solve them. These folks reason that unless the boat's batteries are plugged into an automatic charger, the pump will only function until the batteries are discharged, merely postponing the inevitable.

If the boat does have an automatic charger and a reliable shore-power supply, however, it's too easy for the system to fool the inattentive owner. A sizable leak will keep the pump and charger working away faithfully, giving no notice of any problem. Sammy Sailor then comes down on the weekend, sails away, and anchors up somewhere, only to notice his pump cycling at an alarming rate. If he's lucky, he can locate and fix the problem there—otherwise it's back to the marina or risk sinking.

There are a couple of ways around the problems. If your boat will be left on its own for any length of time, an automatic pump and charger is probably your best solution. However, to avoid falling into the "zero maintenance" mind-set, try this:

In any installation, the float switch must be mounted higher than the pump intake. Otherwise, rising water will activate the switch before it reaches the pump, causing it to run dry. While most manufacturers recommend mounting the switch a few inches above the pickup, try mounting it a bit higher than recommended. Then, when you first board the boat, turn your three-way bilge pump switch to the "Manual" or "On" position, and note how much water is pumped overboard. Experience will show how much pump running time is normal for your boat, and deviations from this norm should be readily apparent. Another method is to mount a counting device or an hour meter in the hot lead to the pump, to tell you how many times the pump has cycled or how much running time has elapsed since your last inspection.

A valuable option is an indicator light incorporated into the pump switch panel. The light operates whenever the pump is running, alerting the skipper to possible problems belowdecks. The switch and light should be visible from the helm position, so that anything unusual occurring while under way will be immediately noticed.

It's also important that any float switches be protected from fouling. If a bit of stray debris gets caught under the float, it can jam in the up position, keeping the pump running away like crazy. While some pumps are advertised as "Can run dry without harm," there *are* limits. And in this situation, you'll find out what they are soon enough.

In order for bilge pumps to keep the bilges dry, all the compartments need to drain properly into the areas where the pumps are located. Most boats use transverse frames to stiffen the hull, which has the added effect of dividing the boat into compartments, especially in the bilge area.

Any compartment not having its own pump must drain into one that does through holes in the frame's lowest point, called limbers. In too many boats, the limbers are nothing more than small, easily clogged holes drilled in the framing. In order for the bilge pumps to work, the limbers must be kept free of debris.

Back in the old days, when men were made of iron and boats were made of wood, some boats used a length of chain or cable that ran through all the limbers. To clear them, the chain was yanked back and forth a few times, allowing bilge water to flow. If your boat doesn't have such a system, and chances are it doesn't, you'll have to inspect

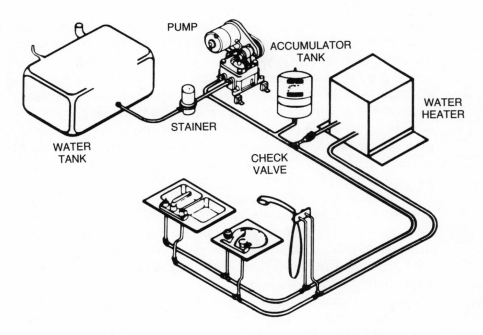

PUMP

ACCUMULATOR
TANK

WATER
HEATER

STAINER

WATER
TANK

CHECK
VALVE

Fig. 13.1. *Typical pressure water system.* DRAWING COURTESY OF ITT
JABSCO PRODUCTS.

and clear the limbers individually. This is a good reason not to have
your shower drain run into the bilge, since hair can accumulate and
clog the limbers.

The pan under your engine is *not* supposed to have a limber in it.
The purpose of the pan is to catch any stray oil, fuel, or coolant, and
contain it so that it doesn't get into the bilge, but can be picked up
and disposed of properly. Pumping oily bilge water overboard makes
you liable for a $5,000 fine, and is also rude and disgusting.

PRESSURE WATER SYSTEMS

Most boats over twenty-five feet and quite a few powerboats under
that length employ electric pumps to power on-board pressure water
systems, with many of them also providing both hot and cold water.
(See Figure 13.1.)

Sailboats equipped for long-distance cruising are less likely to use
electric pumps, relying instead on manual pumps, either hand or foot

operated. These systems are simpler, less likely to require much main-tenance, and, perhaps most important, force the users to conserve valuable water and battery power.

The pressure water systems most commonly used on boats are of the "demand" type. They use pressure switches to sense the demand created by an open tap. When the pump builds sufficient pressure, it is again sensed by the switch, turning off the pump at a predetermined point. These switches are usually mounted on the pump, and in some of the larger systems, allow the boater to vary the upper and lower pressure settings, to customize the system to his boat.

For boats equipped with electric pumps, there are several widely used systems available, each with its own peculiarities. Many boats, especially in the over-thirty-foot range, come equipped with PAR® diaphragm pump systems. These pumps are very reliable and long-lived, requiring little maintenance. When repair is required, parts and supplies are widely available.

Diaphragm pump systems usually include an accumulator or ex-pansion tank in the line. These are nothing more than an air tank acting as a buffer, smoothing out the pulses of pressure characteristic of diaphragm pumps. They also reduce hammering in the lines, which is heard as a thump in the line when water is suddenly shut off. Accu-mulator tanks are also sometimes used in systems employing impeller pumps to extend pump life by reducing pump cycling frequency.

PUMP TROUBLESHOOTING AND REPAIR

The most common problem in pressure water systems is a pump that cycles on and off when the system is not being used. This is almost always the result of a leak in the system on the pressure, or downstream, side of the pump, or bleed-back from a disk valve on a diaphragm pump. If your system is doing this, or if you want to test the integrity of the system, here's the drill:

First, make sure the tank has plenty of water. Run each of the taps for a few seconds to bleed off any air bubbles. Turn off the breaker supplying power to the pump or kill the power at the main battery switch. After several hours, turn the power back on. If it cycles on immediately, there's a leak in the system.

A tight system will maintain pressure for quite a while, but there are limits. If, after the boat sits idle for a week or two, your pump cycles on when you first turn on the power, it's probably not anything to worry about. A system that cycles on every couple of hours during the night, or that loses all of its pressure after a few hours, definitely needs attention.

The usual cause is a loose hose clamp. Go through the system, tightening all the clamps firmly, all the while looking for any other indications of a problem, such as dripping taps, leaks, or split hoses. Repair and retest.

When a diaphragm pump fails, it usually signals its demise by running at high speed without putting out any water. This is also how it acts when the water tank is empty, however, so if your pump exhibits this symptom, as always, check the easy things first.

The first thing to do is to remove the hose from the tank and lower it below the level of the water in the tank. If no water flows, you've found the problem. If there's water in the tank, but not coming out of the hose, there's a blockage in the tank or line.

If you've got water available to the pump, try hooking up the intake hose, disconnecting the exhaust hose, and turning on the pump momentarily. If water comes out, your problem is in the line between the pump and the fixtures. Find and repair.

If no water comes out, you've got a pump problem. Disconnect both hoses, mark and disconnect the wiring, and remove the pump to a good working location. This entails removing the hoses from the pump, plugging the hose that runs from the tank to the pump or securing the end in a position high enough that it won't drain the tank, cutting or unplugging the wires, unscrewing the mounting fasteners, disassembling the pump, checking or replacing the faulty diaphragm or repairing or replacing disk valves, then redoing everything you've undone.

If you're lucky, your pump will be in a relatively accessible location. If it's not, there are usually things to do that can improve access. See the "Access" chapter for help.

Carefully disassemble the pump, using the exploded view in the manual for guidance. Note the positions and orientations of the two disk-shaped valves—one is right side up, the other is upside-down. Make sure you replace them in the proper positions.

If debris is caught under one of the valves, or if it is damaged, you've found the problem. Clear or replace the valve, reassemble, and replace.

Most diaphragm pumps include a pulsation dampener, usually reached by removing the bottom cover plate. These sometimes fail and need replacement.

The same general troubleshooting procedure can be followed with impeller pumps. The main difference is that replacing an impeller is easier than inspecting and replacing disk valves and diaphragms, and can often be done with the pump in place, access permitting.

To inspect and replace an impeller, see the "Diesel Engines" chapter (page 66). If parts of the impeller have broken off and traveled downstream, the water hose will have to be cleared. This can usually be accomplished by backflushing the water line with another water source, such as a dockside garden hose.

Demand-type systems use a water-pressure-sensing switch to activate the pump when a tap is open. When these switches fail, the pump acts as if it's receiving no power. If your pump won't work, and you're sure it's getting proper voltage, replace the pressure switch. It's a fairly common failure point.

When removing and replacing water pumps, or any electric appliance that might require occasional service, it's usually easy to install spade connectors on the wiring, as mentioned in the "AC and DC Electrics" chapter. They make replacement simpler and save having to cut and reconnect the wiring every time.

On any connections made with spade connectors, crimp a male connector to the hot lead, and a female connector to the ground lead, minimizing the possibility of loose ends touching together and arcing. This also makes it impossible to connect the leads backward.

Water stored on boats that are used infrequently may get stale in the tanks. There are some additives that can be poured into the tank to eliminate the problem. Or you can empty and flush the tank occasionally, adding a box of baking soda to keep things fresh. Dissolve the baking soda in water first to keep it from forming clumps and blocking lines.

Another approach is the use of filters, but some precautions are in order here. Some pump manufacturers make filters specifically for their systems, while others warn against them. Their catalogs will detail which approach they recommend—follow their suggestions. Generally, they're installed on the intake side of the pump. (See Figure 13.2.)

A shower on a boat can present a problem, especially if the builder believed in cutting corners in "invisible" places. The ideal setup consists of a drain leading to its own self-contained sump, complete

Fig. 13.2.   *Water-line filter.*

with filter to remove hair before it reaches the sump pump. With this arrangement, the wastewater from the shower is drained into a small fiberglass holding tank. The sump contains a pump and overboard drain, activated by a float switch or by a manual switch in the shower compartment.

The cheap way to plumb a shower is to run the drain hose into the bilge, where the bilge pumps remove the wastewater. The disadvantage of this system is that all the dirt, soap, hair, and shampoo winds up in your bilge, where it leaves a residue and odor that are hard to remove.

If your boat has such a system and you'd like to upgrade it, use a bilge pump that can run dry without damage, and, if you've got the room, incorporate a float switch in the system. Be sure to install a filter, such as the one shown above, to keep hair and larger debris from clogging the system. And, as with any filter, check, clean, and/

or replace regularly. Some pump manufacturers, such as Rule and Lovett, sell preassembled sump kits for this purpose.

Most pump manufacturers also sell service kits for their pumps, including impellers or diaphragms, gaskets, and seals. Carrying one of these kits for each pump aboard is a good idea.

Water tanks come in two varieties—rigid and collapsible. The collapsible type are more common on sailboats, where they can be used in small, odd-shaped compartments. While collapsible tanks are advertised as not requiring vents for filling, their presence does speed things up.

When filling a tank, it's important that the vent be clear, and that the fill rate not exceed the vent's capacity. It's a fairly common practice for boaters to jam a dockside garden hose into the water tank fill fitting, crank the pressure up to full blast, and then leave it to take care of itself until it overflows. This works most of the time, but there are exceptions. If the hose is jammed tight into the fill fitting and doesn't allow any air to escape, and if the vent is clogged or too small to handle the considerable pressure being built up, something's got to give. If you're lucky, it'll be an inexpensive fitting in an easily accessible place, and you'll discover the problem before you've filled your bilges.

A more likely set of circumstances, however, will include a failed fitting, located in an impossible position, and possible water damage to the interior. To head off such a situation, fill your tanks slowly, monitoring conditions as you go, after checking to make sure that you're actually using the proper deck fitting. It's too easy, especially on an unfamiliar boat, to assume that since a fitting is located in the same place where you've found other water fill pipes, you're putting water into the proper fill pipe. It's also easy to glance quickly at a fitting marked "Waste" and see a fitting marked "Water." *Pay attention!* Filling your holding tank with water won't do you any good at all.

Go below and listen to the water flowing into the tank, to make sure that the water is going where it's supposed to, and not into the bilge. If possible, inspect the fill pipe and tank fittings while the tank is being filled. After it's topped off, check for loose clamps and leaking hoses.

As soon as the tank is full, indicated by water exiting the vent, the fill pipe, or one of the taps, remove the hose and let the tank settle for a minute. Sometimes a large air bubble can form, giving a false indication of a full tank. If it seems like your tank has gotten full much too quickly, stop filling and give the air bubble a chance to escape, then continue.

WATER HEATERS

Most pressure water systems include 120-volt water heaters, with many of them incorporating an auxiliary system that uses engine heat to warm the water while under way. (See Figure 13.3.) The heaters are equipped with relief valves designed to release excess pressure that can build up as a result of a faulty thermostat.

The most common repair to these heaters is the replacement of the heating element. The element is designed to operate when immersed, and operating it out of water destroys it in a matter of seconds. Before turning on the heater, run some water out of the hot-water tap first, to make sure there's something in there.

If your heater isn't functioning, test the element. Turn off the power, by turning off the appropriate breaker, by disconnecting the shore-power cord from the outlet at the dock, or by turning off the generator. Disconnect the wiring from the element, and, with your VOM set to "Ohms," touch the probes to the two terminals of the element. The meter should indicate infinite resistance, if not, the element's shot.

To replace the element, first drain the tank. Then, either unscrew the element itself or remove the bolts holding it in, and replace it with a new one. (This is one item that doesn't have to be marine-grade. A plumbing supply house should be able to furnish a new one. Take the old one in with you to be sure of a proper match.) Refill the tank, restore the power, and you're in business.

ADDING PUMPS

Before you add or replace pumps on board your boat, there are a few things to take into consideration. Is the type of pump chosen appropriate for its intended use? Check with the manufacturer's specifications for the pump's capacities, design qualities, and limitations, and the table on page 217.

If the pump will be installed above the level of the liquid to be pumped, is it a self-priming type? If so, the manufacturer will give a

Fig. 13.3. *Water heater.* PHOTO COURTESY OF ALLCRAFT CORP.

height in feet that the pump will lift in order to self-prime. Exceed these specs at your own risk.

Is the pump able to run dry without damage? Generally, diaphragm, submersible, and centrifugal pumps can, but flexible impeller pumps cannot. Check with the manufacturer to be sure.

What is the pump's maximum capacity? Some pumps designed for

Table 13.1   DIFFERENT TYPES OF PUMPS

PUMP TYPE	TYPICAL APPLICATIONS	ADVANTAGES	DISADVANTAGES
Diaphragm	Pressure water, bilge and shower sump	Self-priming, can run dry	Expensive, noisy
Impeller	Pressure water, bilge, engine raw water, oil change, fuel transfer	Self-priming, inexpensive, small, easy to repair	Can't run dry
Submersibles	Bilge pumps, bait well	Sealed, can run dry	Not self-priming
Centrifugal	Coolant circulating, bait well	Quiet	Not self-priming

pressure water systems are limited in the number of faucets or fixtures that they can supply.

If you're replacing an existing pump with a different type, are the uses compatible, and are the hoses, fixtures, and wiring the right sizes? Mixing pump outlet and hose sizes can result in inefficient or damaging results, and pumps too big for the existing wiring, fuses, and breakers are dangerous.

If the pump being replaced died before its time because of inadequately sized wiring, or if it had to work too hard against too-small fixtures, or was not adequate for your uses, installing an identical pump will result in the identical problem.

Too often, boaters assume that the items installed by the builder are there because they're the perfect units for the job. The more common situation, however, especially with price boats, is that the item supplied by the factory is the bare minimum in terms of quality and longevity.

Also, if the pump you're installing is used for washdown, bilge pumping, or bait-well circulation, is it designed for use with salt water (assuming, of course, that you're operating in salt water)? Most pumps are, but don't assume so—check it out first.

When repairing, replacing, and maintaining pumps, keep an eye on the entire system, not just the pump as an isolated unit. This will help you to get a feel for what the pump's job is, how well it's performing, and how to keep it functioning for as long a time as practical.

14
MARINE HEADS

THE SUBJECT of marine heads can be uncomfortable and mildly embarrassing to many people. For this reason, proper care and maintenance is too often given little or no attention. However, routine maintenance and care of your marine head and sewage disposal system is extremely important. While neglect of your engine, your fuel and electrical system, and accessories can result in mere loss of your boat or your life, a major problem with the boat's head can make an on-board explosion and fire seem like a day at the beach.

For most of us, sewage isn't a subject that we spend a lot of time thinking about. Our waste disposal facilities are usually located far from our residences, and any problems with the system are handled by municipal employees. On the rare occasions when we have problems in our homes, we call a plumber, pay for his services, gripe about the size of the bill, and that's about it.

Aboard our boats, however, things are a bit more complicated. There are a number of federal regulations that need to be considered when dealing with this subject, as well as some practical installation, maintenance, and repair tips. There are also state and local regulations that

218

may be applicable in your boating area that can be more restrictive than the federal regulations. Check with local boating groups or state department of natural resources for details.

Environmental Protection Agency regulations generally prohibit any overboard discharge of treated or untreated wastes in freshwater lakes and impoundments and in some rivers. Check with local authorities if you're unsure about regulations in your boating area.

There are also some differences in the law when applied to device requirements for boats over sixty-five feet in length, possibly requiring a Type II device on board. Refer to Title 33 of the Code of Federal Regulations, or your nearest Coast Guard office for details.

Marine sanitation device (MSD) is the Coast Guard term that covers marine heads and waste disposal systems. Federal law classifies MSDs into three categories. Type I and Type II devices are waste treatment units that use chemical, biological, or electrical means to treat sewage, and discharge it overboard.

Type II devices provide a more thorough treatment than do Type I devices. Type III devices are holding tanks that may only be emptied at approved pump-out facilities. Each type of MSD has advantages and disadvantages, and we'll outline and summarize them for you. In addition, we'll include some ideas on maintenance and repair.

The simplest solution is to have no facilities on board at all, which will most often be the case on a small day sailer or runabout. The next step up in the complexity of devices is the portable toilet. This is the modern equivalent of the old cedar bucket, with some convenience features added. After several uses, depending on the size of the unit, it is taken ashore and dumped into a toilet or pump-out facility.

The permanently installed Type III holding tank system is a bit more involved than the portable toilet, but the principle is the same. Waste is stored in a tank, and pumped out at a shoreside facility. The advantage over the portable toilet is that you don't have to lug it ashore to dump it, but you do need to find a properly equipped station for pump-out.

The on-board treatment plants, both Type I and II, are more expensive and complex than holding tanks, but no pumping out is required. Sewage is treated and discharged overboard without the need for a shoreside facility.

Some treatment systems can also be used as temporary holding tanks and emptied at pump-out stations when the boat is operated in a no-discharge area. If you anticipate using your boat in such areas, even for short periods of time, investigate the applicability of this option. This can be especially important if you're buying a used boat in a different part of the country from where you'll be cruising. A retrofit of an MSD system can be very expensive. Space and electrical requirements differ among the three different types, making some units more practical for powerboats than for sailboats.

The simplest system that you can use is generally the best. If a portable toilet serves your boating needs, stick with it. While larger boats that spend considerable time away from shore facilities might need on-board treatment systems, keep in mind that every mechanical, electrical, or chemical component in the system is just another potential failure waiting to happen.

When problems do arise, you've got two options. You can either fix it yourself, or pay someone else a lot of money to travel to your boat and fix it for you. If you think that plumbers who come to your home are expensive, wait until you pay for a qualified MSD service person. And, for our money, they're worth every cent. The combination of the access problems inherent with boats, and the nature of the work, makes the job a nasty one.

GENERAL GUIDELINES

As usual, we're going to first recommend that you read your owner's manual thoroughly, and follow the manufacturer's recommendations on use and maintenance. An MSD is not the nearly trouble-free device you're used to at home, and differences in use, care, and cleaning are very important. Marine heads are not at all tolerant of various nonstandard items. Cigarette butts, matches, and paper towels can cause serious problems.

Some treatment systems have specific recommendations concerning cleaning supplies, toilet paper, and other chemicals. Follow these instructions and warnings very carefully.

Speaking of toilet paper, it's best to use the special stuff made for marine and RV (recreational vehicle) systems. It's designed to reduce clogs, and to break down more rapidly than regular paper. It's more expensive, but will pay for itself in problems avoided. If you can't find special paper, use only white, single-ply toilet tissue. The dyes in colored paper can delay breakdown, and single-ply will clog less.

After using the head, keep flushing for a while after the bowl is clear. Too often, boaters try to extend the time between pump-outs by reducing flushing time. However, this can present problems by allowing material to stand for long periods of time in the exhaust hose, rather than in the holding tank where it belongs. Even the best waste hose isn't as odor-impermeable as the holding tank, and failure to keep it clear will result in unpleasant smells, as well as premature breakdown.

A well-maintained head system that's functioning properly should not have unpleasant odors present. If you find that the system is beginning to emit unusual smells, track down and find the problem immediately—don't just start pouring deodorant into the thing, hoping that that will cure your problem. A loose hose clamp or a leaky fitting won't be fixed by pouring chemicals into the head, and the longer you ignore the problem, the worse it's going to get.

Generally, if you think that you've got a problem, you do. You should know what's normal for your boat, and any sign that things aren't normal should be dealt with promptly.

Chemicals and deodorants are sometimes appropriate and desirable, but only if they're compatible with your system. Never use household drain cleaners to try to dissolve clogs—they're not compatible with MSDs and can sometimes kill a Type II system's bacteria, effectively destroying it. Again, follow the manufacturer's recommendations closely.

TOILETS

Marine toilets are similar to the familiar porcelain conveniences found in the home, but the flushing system is quite different, especially on the units installed in most yachts.

Manual flushing is the most common system. There's usually a lever or valve mounted on the side of the manual pump, marked "Flush," and "Pump Dry," or words to that effect. To flush, turn the lever or valve to the flush position, and pump until the bowl is clear. Keep pumping for an additional ten to fifteen strokes, to be sure that everything reaches the holding tank or treatment system. Flip the lever to the other position, and pump until the bowl is dry.

Failure to return the lever or valve to the closed "Pump Dry" position can be costly. Water can continue to flow through the inlet line at a slow but steady rate, overflowing the toilet and possibly sinking the boat.

A few models make use of a foot pedal rather than the two-position valve. The principle is the same: Depressing the pedal opens the valve, and returning to the normal position closes it. Some owners install an additional ball valve on the inlet line, which can be easily reached and shut off after the head is pumped dry. Of course, the line should also have a sea cock installed at the through-hull, but it isn't always easily accessible.

Most electric flush toilets are nothing more than manual models with a motor added to supply the muscle. Some variations in procedures for flushing and pumping the bowl dry might be necessary—check the manual. Some electric models are more sophisticated, and use vacuum pumps or water-pressure pumps to do their jobs. Flushing procedures for these units may be substantially different.

Electric toilets are easier to use than the manual ones, but they require a fairly heavy current draw. Adequate wiring and switching is a must, and the current draw usually precludes their use on cruising sailboats. Also, motor failure leaves you without any means to flush.

Maintenance of the toilet and pump is usually just a matter of proper use, and occasional repair to the pumping mechanism. The pumps themselves can wear out, as can washers and O-rings. Toilet manufacturers sell pump-rebuild kits, and you should have one on board as part of your spare parts kit.

Depending on your use of the boat and head, pump rebuilding should be done every year or two. Preventive maintenance is an excellent idea in this case, since waiting for a part to fail can prove to be a real inconvenience.

An indication that rebuild time is near is that the pump gradually gets harder and harder to work. Some builders recommend a lubricant to pump through the system to keep things pliable and working freely. Vegetable oil works well here. Just add a tablespoonful to the pump every once in a while. If after lubricating the system it still pumps hard, rebuild.

A common problem when operating in salt water, besides the abrasiveness that can cause rapid wear, is the buildup of hard deposits inside the pump and near the joker valve on the bowl. (The joker is a check valve on the discharge side of the bowl, sometimes called a duckbill valve or a backwater check valve.) These deposits can be dissolved with vinegar—trying to chip them away is time-consuming, and carries the risk of damaging the equipment.

Some cruising sailors keep an entire spare pump on board. If something breaks down at an inappropriate time, the new pump can be slapped on quickly, and the old one rebuilt when convenient.

To winterize the toilet, don't just pour antifreeze into the bowl. Close the sea cock for the inlet line, remove the line and drain it. Then place the hose in an open container of potable water system antifreeze and pump the toilet until antifreeze flows out the discharge side of the toilet.

If you have a Type I or Type II treatment system on board, check the manufacturer's recommendations for winterizing. Don't use incompatible chemicals in the toilet that can harm the treatment system without disconnecting the toilet from the system first.

A very important maintenance item that's frequently overlooked is the vented loop. On any toilet installed at or below the waterline, or in a position where it's likely to be below the waterline when the boat is heeled over, vented loops must be installed in the water inlet line, and in the discharge line between the head and the holding tank or treatment system, above the waterline. (See Figure 14.1.)

The loops prevent both backflow into the head and continuous inlet flow, by breaking any siphoning effect. However, the devices only work if the vents are clear. Some older systems used all-metal loops

Fig. 14.1. *Vented loop.*

and vents which could become clogged by corrosion. These days, though, all-plastic loops and vents, as well as bronze loops with plastic or nylon vents, are available.

To clear a clogged vent, disassemble the vent and clean the parts thoroughly. Some systems employ check balls, leather washers, rubber washers, and/or hoses, so proceed carefully. In some cases, replacement of the vent, or of the entire loop, might be simpler.

TYPE I TREATMENT SYSTEMS

Type I systems use chemicals or electricity to treat the sewage before discharging it over the side. Chemical treatments use formalin to kill harmful organisms, and an electric macerator pump to grind and mix the waste with the chemicals. The treated material is then discharged over the side with a separate pump.

The advantages to a system of this type are its compact size, allowing flexibility in mounting locations, and freedom from having to find a pump-out station. And, a single treatment unit can be connected to several heads. Disadvantages are complexity and the need to deal with dangerous chemicals. Current draw is relatively low, but still could be a consideration on a boat with a marginal electrical system.

Another Type I system uses electric current to break down and treat sewage before discharging it overboard. Advantages of this kind of system are its compact size and the absence of dangerous chemicals.

The main disadvantage is high current draw, meaning some fairly hefty wiring and electrical drain that can put a dent in a sailboat's batteries. There are a series of potentially vulnerable electrical components in the system, and each toilet has to be connected to its own treatment unit.

TYPE II SYSTEMS

Type II treatment systems treat waste material more thoroughly than do Type I systems. The requirements for bacteria counts and other physical characteristics of the treated material are more stringent, and some areas only allow Type II overboard discharge.

The most common Type II system uses fiber filtration and bacterial activity to decompose the wastes. Chlorine is used to provide final treatment before overboard discharge.

Advantages include no electrical parts, little if any maintenance, and, other than the toilet itself, no moving parts. Sewage is treated naturally, and, provided the unit is installed above the waterline, flows over the side unaided.

The primary disadvantages are size and cost, both of which are considerable. One of the smallest units takes up over 11 cubic feet and weighs a couple of hundred pounds. The system's cost is commensurate with its size.

TYPE III SYSTEMS

The least technologically complex kind of system is the Type III holding tank. The toilet discharges into a large tank, which is then pumped out at a shoreside facility. There are no chemicals, no high current demands (unless an electric flushing motor is installed), and few moving parts to fail. (See Figure 14.2.)

Disadvantages are size and the need to locate pump-out stations regularly. If you live in an area with a large boating population, pump-outs are usually no problem. More remote areas can be a different story, though.

It's very important that the system be properly installed, using only appropriate materials, and maintained to keep everything functioning. As in several other areas we've covered, even low-tech, low-maintenance items need proper attention.

If you need to replace any of the hoses in the system, especially the lines that carry sewage, use *only* hoses and fittings made for that purpose. There's a lot of different 1½-inch hose on the market, and most of it is cheaper than the stuff made and sold for MSD use. You'll rue the day you made the decision to try to save money by installing cheap hose. Head hose must be strong, smooth-walled inside, and impervious to odors. Many types of hose can meet one or two of those criteria, but in this case, two out of three will not do.

Likewise, the end fittings made for the hose must pass muster, or else you've added a very weak link to the chain. When you buy the hose and fittings, have the salesperson show you how to properly cut the hose to length and install the end fittings. And, as we've mentioned

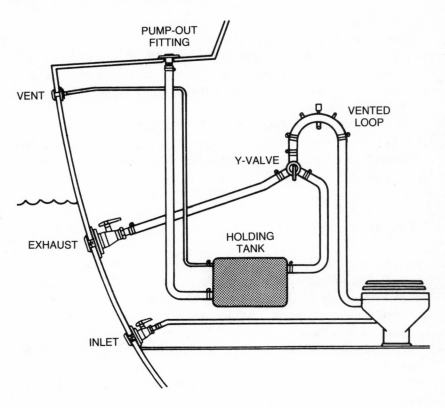

Fig. 14.2. *Typical Type III head and holding tank installation. Ideally, there would be a vented loop installed in the intake line also.* DRAWING COURTESY OF FORES MANUFACTURING CO.

elsewhere, use only marine, all-stainless hose clamps, properly sized and installed. The hose run should be as direct as possible, with no sharp turns or valleys.

The tank vent line should also present as straight a run as possible. If this line clogs, pressure from inside the tank can build up, a situation you definitely want to avoid. There are filters available to install in this line, should you have a problem with odor from the overboard vent fitting.

There are several devices available for indicating holding tank fill levels. Since head use is hard to monitor, these items can come in handy.

Boats that operate offshore and are equipped with holding tanks usually possess a method of pumping the contents of the tank overboard, or of bypassing the holding tank completely. The most common means of doing this is with a Y-valve. Y-valves provide a way to direct the material flow in either of two alternate directions by rotating a handle. If installed between the head and the holding tank, sewage can be flushed directly overboard.

A valve and pump, either an electric macerator pump or a manual diaphragm pump, can be installed in the pump-out side of the holding tank, allowing the tank to be emptied overboard.

Use of either of these types of setups is prohibited in United States inland waters and territorial seas, which include coastal waters within twelve miles of shore. Check the Code of Federal Regulations, Title 33, Part 159 for exact details. Be advised that using a Y-valve to discharge raw sewage overboard in inland waters or territorial seas makes you liable to a sizable fine.

The use and maintenance of your on-board toilet and waste system can be as simple as an oak bucket, or it can involve a system of toilets, motors, chemicals, and pumps. Whichever system you find yourself living with, a certain amount of attention and care is required. Preventive maintenance is by far the best approach, so to avoid unpleasant consequences and expensive repairs, make upkeep a part of your regular boat maintenance schedule.

15

STOVES AND HEATERS

Most boats over 25 feet in length and even some pocket cruisers in the 18- to 25-foot category have a stove of some sort on board. Whether you've got a little two-burner alcohol stove, or a four-burner electric range complete with oven, there are things you should know about advantages and disadvantages of different types of stoves and their fuels, and some safety ideas as well.

If you already own a boat equipped with a stove or heater, and you're unhappy with some aspect of its performance, this chapter can help you to evaluate upgrade options. If you're in the market for a boat, new or used, we can help you to match the unit you plan to buy with your expectations and demands.

Fuel expenses for stoves and heaters are relative, and, especially in the case of stoves, seldom much of a consideration, unless you live aboard and cook all your meals on the boat. Heating fuel costs, however, can be considerable on long cruises in cold, damp conditions.

Safety considerations demand that all stove tops be fitted with guardrails around the cooking surface, to prevent hot items from being emptied onto the cook in a seaway. Ranges on sailboats are usually hung from gimbals, free to swing and remain upright as the boat rolls. If a range is gimbaled, there must be sufficient slack in the flexible fuel hose to allow it to swing through its full range of motion. A hook or other locking device is necessary, so that the stove can be secured in place. A safety bar should be mounted in front of the stove to give the cook a solid handhold in a seaway, and also to protect the cook from pitching forward against the stove when things get rough.

All nonelectric stoves should be used with adequate ventilation, and stoves shouldn't be used to provide cabin heat. Since the burning process uses oxygen, a tightly closed cabin with open flames going is a potential problem.

Fuel tanks and lines should be matched to the fuel in use. One type does not suit all. They should also be inspected regularly, and checked for compliance with the appropriate ABYC and/or NFPA standards.

The ABYC applicable standards; are A-1, "Liquefied Petroleum Gas Systems"; A-3, "Galley Stoves"; A-7, "Boat Heating Systems"; and A-22, "Compressed Natural Gas Systems." NFPA Standard 302, Chapter 6, covers "Cooking, Heating, and Auxiliary Appliances." Information on obtaining these standards is in the Sources of Information.

STOVES

Alcohol

Alcohol stoves are frequently found on small boats with a limited amount of space available for a real galley. The stoves are compact and inexpensive, the fuel is readily available, burns clean, and as advocates are so fond of repeating, you can extinguish alcohol fires with water. That's about it as far as advantages.

On the down side, alcohol is a relatively expensive fuel; it's wet, in that burning alcohol promotes condensation inside the boat; and the BTU content is low, meaning that the flame isn't as hot as most fuels, and heating food or liquids takes considerably longer than with other fuels. Boiling water can be time-consuming, and you can starve while preparing a real meal. The burners need to be preheated by pouring fuel around the burner base and lighting it, a sometimes irritating process.

Kerosene

Kerosene stoves are also compact and relatively inexpensive, often found in two-burner, countertop models similar to alcohol stoves. The advantages of kerosene are its higher BTU content, meaning that boiling a quart of water isn't necessarily an all-day job. It's a drier fuel than alcohol, and spilled fuel is less volatile than alcohol. This can be both an advantage and a disadvantage, in that it's less likely to ignite if spilled, but it's also harder to clean up.

Disadvantages are the need for preheating and the dirty combustion by-products. Preheating necessitates carrying another kind of fuel, usually alcohol, and can be a chore. Soot from the burners is a problem, especially if they aren't thoroughly preheated.

Kerosene, being a thick fuel of low volatility, needs to be heated in order to vaporize and burn readily. This is done by filling a cup at the burner base with alcohol, and lighting it. Once the burner and fuel jet are hot enough, the kerosene vaporizes and burns cleanly. Problems arise when the burner is turned on before it's hot enough to vaporize the fuel sufficiently. Then, unburnt fuel particles are emitted as soot, which accumulates in the cabin. New users will learn through experience when it's time to turn on the burner.

When properly used, kerosene can be a relatively clean burning fuel, but there will always be some soot emitted, requiring a bit more interior care than most other fuels.

With alcohol and kerosene stoves, the fuel tanks, whether integral with the stove or mounted in remote locations, have to be filled and pressurized. Occasional spills are inevitable, and, depending on tank location, can be sloppy.

Propane (LPG)

Both propane and butane are classified as LPG, liquefied petroleum gas. Their use and safety precautions are identical, the fuels differing only slightly in their physical properties. The LP gas used on boats is almost always propane.

Propane is a common stove fuel on midsize boats, and has a number of advantages. It's inexpensive and widely available; no messy on-board filling is required; stoves, with ovens, are available in a variety of configurations and as easy to use as a home gas stove. The system maintains a steady, even pressure, and the burners are very controllable, even for long simmering times.

Disadvantages are that the fuel is fairly wet when burned, forming condensation in cool weather, and considerable extra hardware is required, all of which must meet certain standards for proper, safe operation. A separate storage locker for the tank is necessary, and it must be equipped with the proper ventilation, drains, etc., and isolated from the boat's interior. Regulators, shutoff valves, remote solenoids, and pressure gauges must all be properly installed and maintained.

The reason for all of this hardware and safety consideration is that the fuel is both explosive and heavier than air. It must be treated like gasoline in that fumes tend to collect in low places rather than dissipate into the air, and carelessness can be disastrous.

The fuel tank must meet U.S. Department of Transportation standards and be so marked. Propane dealers won't fill disposable cylinders intended for one-time use or tanks that don't comply with government standards.

The tank storage locker must be outside the boat's cabin, and isolated from all interior spaces. It must be equipped with an overboard drain, have a tight-fitting lid, allow easy access to the tank valves, and the pressure gauge must be easily seen.

Fuel delivery lines can be either copper tubing or flexible hose, marked and approved for use. If copper tubing is used for a gimbaled stove, a section of flexible hose must be attached at the stove end, allowing free range of motion for the stove. The tank end of the line is equipped with a threaded spud for attaching the fuel line to the tank, a regulator to reduce fuel tank pressure to safe levels before it enters the fuel line, and a pressure gauge for testing fuel line integrity. A remote solenoid should also be installed here, for additional safety. (See page 233 for details.)

The spud that screws into the fuel tank has a *left-hand thread,* to prevent the use of inappropriate fittings. Therefore, your normal tightening and loosening procedures are reversed.

The pressure gauge is not a fuel-level gauge. LPG fuel, whether propane or butane, is a gas at normal air pressure. When compressed, however, it turns into a liquid, allowing easy transportation and dispensing. It's injected into the fuel tank at high pressure, and the regulator and burner orifice combine to return it to atmospheric pressure for burning. There can still be air pressure left in the fuel tank when all the fuel is gone. Some tanks have liquid-level fuel gauges installed, but most don't. Determining fuel levels is frequently a case of guesswork and anticipation.

Serious cruising types usually carry two fuel tanks, and switch back and forth as they empty them. Be advised, however, that you can't just take your spare tank and throw it into a lazarette or hanging locker when not in use. Spare tank stowage requirements are the same as for tanks in use.

To use the pressure gauge for checking the system, turn off all burners and pilot lights, open the solenoid, if so equipped, and open the tank's main valve. The pressure gauge should shoot up, usually to around 100 psi, although this reading will vary between 30 and 100 psi, depending on ambient temperature.

Close the valve, and watch the gauge. If the pressure starts to fall, there's a leak in the line. The ABYC and NFPA standards require the reading to stay constant for ten to fifteen minutes.

If the pressure reading falls, it's time to go leak hunting. It seems too obvious even to mention, but human nature being what it is, it doesn't pay to take too much for granted. So here it is—*don't use flame to check for leaks!* Propane supply houses sell a special soap solution for this purpose, but any soapy water solution will work, as long as it makes bubbles, and doesn't contain ammonia, which can damage fittings. Kids' bubble soap is especially good, producing nice big bubbles when air is applied.

Start at one end of the system, with the valve and solenoid open, and go to each connection, pouring a dab of soap on each one and looking for bubbles. When you find a leak, tighten the connection snugly, and proceed. If all of your tank and tubing connections are intact, and you're still showing a pressure drop, remove the stove top and check all the pipe connections and the burners.

If a pipe fitting leaks, such as at the pipe nipples at either end of the regulator or where the pressure gauge screws into the T-fitting, Teflon® tape can usually fix it.

Plumber's pipe dope works also, but the tape does just as good a job and is less messy. Marine and plumbing supply houses stock Teflon® tape, and it's a worthy addition to your tool and supply collection. The tape must be properly applied to the fitting in order to form a seal. Wrap the tape around the threads in a clockwise direction as you're looking at the end to be inserted. Make two complete overlapping revolutions, wrapping tightly, and starting several threads from the end, to prevent any tape from getting into the inside diameter. After making two turns, pull tightly enough to tear the tape free.

Never use Teflon® tape or pipe sealant on a flare fitting—a damaged flare must be replaced. (See page 238.)

When the propane system is not in use, the fuel supply should be shut off at the tank. To avoid having to shuttle back and forth to a sometimes inconvenient propane locker, several companies sell remote solenoid kits. These devices consist of a control panel mounted near the stove, with an on-off switch and a red light that indicates when the switch is open. It connects to a solenoid that opens and closes the fuel line at the tank fitting.

Installation is simple, amounting to nothing more than running a couple of wires to the propane locker, hooking the switch to a power source, and attaching the solenoid to the regulator. Use of these switches is highly recommended, since they encourage safe propane use.

When leaving the boat for extended periods, turn off the gas at the tank valve as well. You can't be too safe.

Compressed Natural Gas (CNG)

A fairly recent addition to the cooking and heating fuels available to boaters is compressed natural gas. This gas is identical to the gas used in homes, it's just pressurized and stored in steel cylinders.

The main advantage that it has over LPG is that it's lighter than air. That makes it safer, since it dissipates into the atmosphere rather than collecting inside the hull, and requirements for tank storage are less restrictive than for propane.

Disadvantages include tanks that are larger and more cumbersome than propane tanks, and the fact that CNG tanks can't be owned by individuals. The fuel distributor owns them, and they are leased or loaned to users, and returned and exchanged when refilled. CNG is not as universally available as propane, and appliances and fuel lines must be specifically made for CNG use.

Diesel

Diesel fuel stoves are used on quite a few work and fish boats, but aren't common on yachts. If you've got a diesel engine, you don't need to make provisions for an additional fuel tank for cooking or heating, and condensation is reduced since the stoves are vented to the outside. They also provide considerable cabin heat, which can be an attribute or a drawback, depending on local climate.

Disadvantages include the size, weight, and expense of the stoves, and their need for a rigid stack between stove and cabin exterior that precludes gimbaling. Stove exhaust is dirty, requiring a constant effort to keep the boat's exterior clean. A pulse-type fuel pump or a day tank and pump are required, meaning increased maintenance.

Solid Fuel

Stoves using solid fuel such as wood, wood chip logs, charcoal, or coal are inexpensive and can also provide cabin heat. However, as with diesel stoves, whether or not cabin heat is an advantage varies with location and season.

Disadvantages include the need for a rigid stack to the outside, messiness of the fuel and its by-products, including ashes inside and soot outside the boat. Fuel storage can be a problem, as can the fuel's burning characteristics. The heat isn't easily controllable, and must be watched and tended constantly.

Electric

Electric ranges are identical in use and function to home units. The heat provided is dry, and the stoves require very little maintenance. However, to use them you need to be connected to shore power or a gen set. Installing a generator just to power a stove is very expensive, and gen sets are noisy and require regular maintenance.

Other

In an attempt to save money, some folks mount camping stoves in their boats, an unwise move. These stoves aren't made for the marine environment, and white gas such as Coleman fuel has the physical properties of gasoline, being very flammable and forming fumes that are heavier than air. Save your camping stove for camping trips.

CABIN HEATERS

Cabin heat is not much of a consideration in southern boating areas, but in the north, a good heater can extend your boating season considerably, even making year-round boating a pleasant and comfortable possibility. You can visit cruising grounds at times of the year when the crowds are gone, and see seasonal changes and events that most people miss.

Possibilities for providing cabin heat range from inexpensive, portable, and simple, to expensive, permanently installed, and complex. As with all things marine, complexity equals increased maintenance, so simpler is usually better, provided it meets your needs.

The type of heater you require depends on a number of factors, such as local climate, cabin configuration, boat size, engine fuel, and how much you're willing to spend. Fuel type is a determining factor for heater size and cost, so that's how we'll list them.

Kerosene

A popular and inexpensive means of providing cabin heat is the portable kerosene heater. These units are readily available, use easily obtained fuel, and are equipped with automatic shutoff devices in case they're knocked over. They're especially nice for boaters who only occasionally indulge in cold-weather boating, and also make good supplements to marginal heating systems when the weather is especially frigid.

However, they don't vent to the outside, and so must be used with caution in enclosed cabins. Odor is sometimes a problem, as is priming, and they can be a bit cumbersome and hard to stow in a secure position in small boats. Make sure the safety shutoff works before using it aboard your boat.

Permanently installed kerosene heaters are more convenient to use than portable models, since they're secured to a bulkhead and out of the way. Most use a Primus-type burner, identical to kerosene stove burners, and can sometimes use diesel fuel as well as kerosene. The heaters vent to the outside, so the heat provided is dry.

Disadvantages include having to provide a fuel supply system to the heater, usually requiring a tank-and-pump arrangement. Some odor is usually noticeable, priming is required, and exterior soot must be cleaned up.

Diesel

Diesel cabin heaters are divided into two categories—radiant and forced-air. Radiant heaters are simpler, relying on a central location and normal air movement to heat the required area. Forced-air heaters employ ducting and fans to distribute the heat to all parts of the interior.

The larger the area to be heated, the more likely you are to need forced air.

Radiant heaters are usually mounted on a bulkhead, with a vent stack leading outside. A pulse-type fuel pump is connected to a separate tank or to the boat's fuel lines, and an additional fuel filter should be included. Current draw and fuel usage are low, and, once installed, the system is easy to use and maintain. Adequate shielding of surrounding bulkheads is required, and proper installation of the vent stack and overhead heat shield is vital.

Forced-air furnaces are more versatile, in that they can be mounted out of the way, and the heat can be directed to several areas of the boat's interior. Thermostatic controls are available, enabling precise adjustment of temperature. Larger boats may require such a system for all-around comfort, especially for adequate heat levels in staterooms.

Disadvantages are high installation costs, since installing ducts can be time-consuming. More maintenance of the system is required, and noise and current draw are also considerations.

Systems that provide circulating hot-water heat to the boat are available for large boats, with all the attendant plumbing complexity and expense.

Propane

Catalytic propane heaters are available, and are relatively inexpensive. If vented to the outside, the heat is very dry, and some heaters include thermostatic controls.

Disadvantages include high current draw for starting on some models, and units not vented to the outside are very wet, promoting considerable interior condensation. Installation must be done with care, allowing for adequate clearance between the heater and combustible materials.

There are also some propane forced-air heaters on the market, their primary disadvantages being relatively high installation costs and fuel consumption, and the high current draw necessary for the fans.

Electric

Electric heaters are very reliable, and provide dry, thermostatically controlled heat. Portable and permanent types are available and portable units are inexpensive.

Disadvantages include the need for a shore-power connection or gen set, and of course, high current draw. Many portable heaters aren't made for continuous duty, and only one per circuit can usually be operated. If your shore-power plug-in is a standard 30-amp service, only a total of two 1,500-watt units can be used, and no other electric motors can be run simultaneously.

Engine Hot Water

Cabin heaters that run off engine heat are available, and are inexpensive to operate and easy to maintain. They run engine coolant to heater cores and electric fans in one or more cabin locations, and operate like the heater in your car.

The main disadvantage is that they only provide heat when the engine is running.

Solid Fuel Heaters

Heaters that burn solid fuel such as wood, charcoal, and chip logs are subject to the same attributes and drawbacks as solid fuel stoves. Their main advantages in providing cabin heat are that they're inexpensive and, in a tight spot, you can always break up the interior woodwork and burn it to keep warm.

The disadvantages are the mess of cleaning up ashes all the time, and the need to keep stoking the thing on cold nights.

Every type of stove and heater has advantages and drawbacks. Your job is to match each system's characteristics to your own situation. Consider cost, complexity, maintenance requirements, and your personal boating style. The challenge is to get your needs and wants to line up with a certain level of cost and complexity that assures that you're comfortable and happy with the system, without having acquired a white elephant in terms of cost and upkeep.

Copper Tubing Repairs

Most factory propane installations use copper tubing as the fuel line. Copper tube is inexpensive and strong, and as long as certain rules are followed, perfectly safe for such uses.

When handling copper tubing, be very careful not to bend it without using proper tools. Copper is very soft, and any attempt to bend it too sharply will result in a kink in the line, ruining it. If you do need to bend tubing, check with a plumbing supply house for the proper tools.

Copper line should be supported along its length with noncorroding hangers. Vibration and flexing will quickly fatigue copper tube to the point of failure. Connections should be kept to a minimum, and the line should be provided with chafing gear where it passes through bulkheads.

If you find a leak at a flare fitting, manufacturers suggest tightening the nut with a wrench until a solid feeling is encountered, and then turning an additional one sixth of a turn. If this doesn't stop the leak, there's probably a flaw in the tubing, and a new connection will have to be made.

For this job, you'll need a tubing cutter and a flaring tool. *Don't cut copper tubing with a hacksaw!* The resulting cut isn't clean and smooth enough, and bits of copper can get into the tubing, eventually clogging burner orifices. (See Figure 15.1.)

When buying flare fittings, make certain that you're getting 45-degree, SAE fittings. Some applications call for 37-degree JIC fittings, but they are few and far between.

To cut off the old flare, attach the cutter to the copper tube as close behind the flare as possible. You don't want to remove any more tube than necessary, since the stuff doesn't stretch worth a damn. Tighten

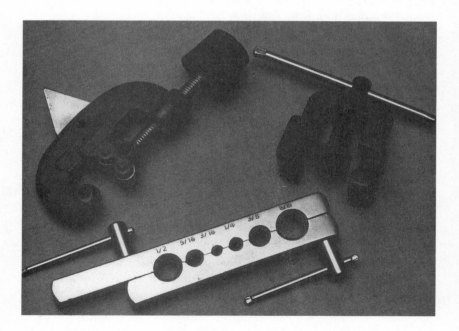

Fig. 15.1. *Copper tube flaring tools.*

the cutting wheel just enough to make contact and hold the cutter in place, and rotate it several turns. Tighten slightly, and repeat. Keep repeating the sequence until the cut is through. Clean the inside diameter with the reamer attached to the cutting tool. Don't try to hurry the job by tightening the cutter too firmly—you'll only crush the tubing and have to start over.

Before beginning, lubricate the threads on the flaring tool lightly, to provide a smooth turning action. Also, apply a very light coat of oil to the flaring cone itself, to reduce friction and the possibility of burrs.

After making sure that the flare nut is on the tube and out of the way, attach the yoke to the tube, matching the tubing size to the appropriate flaring fixture. Sizes are marked, and copper tube is measured on the outside diameter. Tighten the yoke snugly, leaving just enough tubing exposed inside the tool to form the flared end. Exactly how much to allow is a matter of judgment and experience, but if too much tubing is exposed, the flare will be too large, and the flaring nut won't seat properly.

Attach the flaring cone to the yoke, with the cone inside the tube, and tighten, flaring the tubing out as it goes. Stop when hard resistance is felt. Remove the tools, and inspect the flare. Cracks, scratches, and burrs will ruin a flare connection, so check closely for these kinds of flaws.

16
HOUSEKEEPING

O NE OF the most difficult problems of belowdecks maintenance is the constant battle against moisture and its effects. A boat that hasn't been kept dry will have mold and mildew problems, and will always smell like an old, neglected bath towel.

The most effective defenses against moisture are heat, ventilation, and the elimination of water sources—especially saltwater sources. Salt is hygroscopic, meaning that it attracts and holds moisture. Materials such as carpeting, rope, and upholstery that are soaked with salt water will never dry completely, but remain damp and clammy forever, exuding an unpleasant smell. Even fresh water will remain in fabric for quite a long time when there isn't sufficient heat and ventilation to dry it out.

Some boats have much more severe ventilation problems than others, owing mostly to design characteristics and climate. Factors such as deck ventilators, hull insulation, louvered locker doors, and hanging locker placement and design are all important for effective ventilation, but aren't the kinds of details that most people consider when buying a boat, especially a first boat. If your boat was designed with these things in mind, you're a step ahead of the game. If not, there are things that you can do to improve matters, but, as usual, they generally take time and cost money.

Local climate also plays a large part in the situation. Boats that spend all their time in southern California, Florida, New England, and the Pacific Northwest all have varying degrees of moisture difficulty, but even a well-designed boat in Mexico in the summertime will have problems if some basic rules are ignored.

Good ventilation is essential for keeping things dry. Heat alone won't do the job—if you seal your wet gear in a locker with no means for moisture to escape, you can heat it for months, and the moisture still won't have any place to go.

Elimination of salt is also vital. Hanging wet, salty rain gear in an unventilated locker and throwing wet, salty anchor lines, life jackets, and cushions into lazarettes are great ways to cultivate a mildew farm and all its attendant smells.

Hull insulation is another area for consideration, but it's not a problem that lends itself to easy solutions. If your boat has a liner separated from the hull exterior and is insulated, your problems with condensation forming on the inside of the boat will be considerably reduced. However, if no liner and insulation are in place, there's not a heck of a lot you can do about it. This is something that you need to consider before purchase, not afterward. If you'll be doing lots of cool-weather boating and operating a cabin heater, this feature bears serious consideration when making your boat-buying decision.

To keep belowdecks humidity to a minimum, dry things out as much as possible before bringing them below. If your gear is soaked with salt water, rinse it thoroughly in fresh water before storing it. If you're caught in a rainy period and forced to stow things when they're wet, don't forget about them when the weather breaks. When the sun shines, drag all that wet gear out on deck, rinse it with fresh water, and dry it as best you can before putting it away.

Keep your bilges as dry as possible. If your pump hose has a long run, and empties lots of water back into the bilge when it's shut off, install a check valve in the line to minimize the problem (see ''Pumps'' chapter, page 206).

Deck ventilators are an excellent way to direct moving air belowdecks. The solar-powered fans are excellent, and can sometimes be installed in existing deck cutouts.

Hanging lockers should have fully louvered doors. Surprisingly many high-priced boats are fitted with solid wood doors which inhibit ventilation. If you're unable to find and fit louvers onto existing doors, prop open or remove the door when wet gear is stored inside.

Lazarettes are frequent trouble spots. Even an insulated boat won't have insulated lazarettes, and the tendency to throw all sorts of wet stuff into them, such as sails, sheets, fishing tackle, and lunch hooks, compounds the problem. The only real solution is regular care, removing and rinsing salty stuff, and drying things in the sun as much as possible before stowing.

When laying the boat up for any length of time, whether for the winter or just between weekends, a little preventive care will reduce moisture problems considerably. Local conditions will dictate how much preventive care is needed, but some steps should be taken even in ideal conditions. Before leaving the boat, prop open or remove all locker doors and interior doors, especially the head door, to promote good air flow. (Some folks block their engine room vents to try to retain heat and to eliminate cold breezes. Any advantage you may gain from some heat retention will probably be offset by the reduction in air movement.)

Pump the bilge as dry as possible, and remove any standing water from sinks, shower, refrigerator or icebox, etc. A vacuum cleaner designed to pick up water can be a great help in drying out nooks and crannies that might hold puddles.

If you'll be leaving the boat unattended for a long time, and if moisture is a problem in your area, additional dehumidification may be needed. Options range from a few silica gel crystals to electric heaters. The crystals are pretty marginal in effectiveness—trying to keep the inside of a forty-foot boat dry with a six-dollar ashtray filled with crystals is really the height of optimism, especially in the Northwest. For the most part, more drastic measures are called for.

Electric appliances are necessary in most cases. Rod-type devices, consisting of a heating element encased in a metallic sheath, can sometimes be used in hard-to-ventilate areas, but don't do much to keep air moving.

Some boaters just leave a couple of 120-volt lights burning all the time. This can help in a marginal situation, but again, it doesn't move much air around, and the fixtures must be of high quality to allow twenty-four-hour-a-day use.

Other boaters place small, household-type electric heaters aboard to move and dehumidify the air. Problems arise because the units are being subjected to around-the-clock operation for which they weren't designed, such as leaving them in place and running for weeks or even months at a time. And what happens when the fan falls over unattended? It's best not to use these heaters. A bit of mildew is much less of a problem than a fire. They also draw quite a bit of current, frequently in the neighborhood of 12.5 amps. Do you really want to subject your electrical system to that kind of draw, for that long a time, unattended? And what happens when the fan fails, or a large wake in the anchorage knocks it over? Are there safety devices on the unit that will prevent catastrophe, and do you want to entrust your boat to them?

Dehumidifiers that move air through convection are ideal. Consisting of little more than a low-wattage heating element encased in a ventilated housing, they have no moving parts, draw little current, are inexpensive, and they work. We have found that the "Air Dryer," made by Idea Development Corporation, is a good unit.

Brooder lamps, such as the ones used in raising chickens, are also quite effective, operating on the same principle as the convection dehumidifiers. If you don't live in chicken country, you'll have a hard time finding them, but they are simple, effective units.

BILGES

For most boaters, keeping bilges clean and relatively dry is a constant battle. All that water outside your boat is working full-time trying to get inside your boat.

The best way to keep your bilges clean and inoffensive is to prevent contamination in the first place. The fewer things that drain into your bilge, the better. This goes for showers, iceboxes, engine pans, etc.

If your shower drains into the bilge, install a sump kit as mentioned in the "Pumps" chapter (page 213). If your icebox drain goes there as well, either redirect it into a sump or overboard, or attach a strainer to the end of the hose to keep loose organic matter from collecting in the bilge. Inspect and clean the strainer regularly.

As mentioned on page 209 of the "Pumps" chapter, the engine pan is supposed to contain fluid spillage before it reaches the bilge. That way, it can be isolated and pumped out separately, and disposed of properly.

If you do find petroleum products in your bilge water, oil-absorbent pads work very well, picking up oil but not water. However, if you have a chronic problem, don't just throw a few oil absorbers into the bilge and forget about it. Either correct the problem at the source, or, if that's not possible, change the absorbers frequently, before they become saturated.

If your bilges are especially dirty, you're going to have to get down in there and scrub them out. There are bilge soaps advertised as being able to thoroughly clean the bilges using only the rocking motion of the boat to do the work. Life should be so easy! The soap helps to remove some accumulation, but a really dirty bilge needs to be thoroughly scrubbed in order to maintain an acceptable level of cleanliness. As we said, it's much easier to keep dirt out in the first place than to have to get down there and clean it out by hand. Remember, the smell of a slimy bilge can permeate the entire boat.

A final hint about bilges—if you're going to be drilling, cutting, or grinding wood, fiberglass, or metal near the bilges, pump them as dry as possible beforehand, perhaps going so far as to sponge them completely dry, or by using a wet-or-dry shop-type vacuum cleaner *only!* Dust and shavings floating on bilge water are nearly impossible to clean up!

LEAKS

Rainwater leaks are an almost constant problem with some boats, and even the best of them will encounter the occasional drip through a window, exterior fastener, etc.

Considering the ways in which a boat's hull flexes when under way, the different materials involved, the stresses induced by hard rain and taking green water over the bow on offshore boats, and freezing and thawing cycles undergone by boats in northern latitudes, it's a wonder that they don't all leak like colanders. Add to those factors the shortcuts taken by builders in the name of price and economy, and the problem increases dramatically.

Finding the source can be more of a problem than actually making the repair. The task is complicated by the fact that it's rare for water to appear on the inside exactly opposite its source on the outside. It usually travels behind headliners, bulkheads, and cabinetwork before making its presence known.

Your job is to find the source and repair it *on the outside*. Stopping the flow on the inside alone doesn't stop the leak, it merely treats the symptom. The water will still enter from its source on the outside, and just find another place to appear on the inside. There are some shortcuts to finding and repairing leaks, but not many. It's normally a time-consuming, irritating exercise, characterized by plenty of guesswork and false starts.

There are lots of different types of sealants on the market, each kind having advantages and drawbacks. Silicone sealants are among the most popular, since lots of home-repair jobs use it. In boat use, however, you should evaluate the job to be done and match the proper sealant to the job, rather than just automatically reach for old faithful silicone.

If you use a silicone sealer, make sure you buy a marine grade. The stuff made for home use isn't adequate, not having the necessary resistance to some of the exotic growths that the marine environment can support. Silicone frequently fails to bond properly, either because of faulty preparation of the bonding surfaces, or because it just isn't suitable for the job.

For bedding plastic parts, such as antenna bases, access plates, and plastic porthole frames, silicone is probably your best bet. Some plastics used in these applications may deteriorate if exposed to polysulfide sealants, and silicone's lack of adhesive qualities is an advantage if you have to remove relatively fragile plastic parts.

When using silicone, or any sealant for that matter, be sure to remove *all* of the old bedding material. Scrape away as much as possible, and remove the rest with solvents. Some solvents such as acetone will attack certain types of plastic, so check first by touching a bit of the solvent to a small, hidden portion of the plastic.

After all the old material is removed, lightly rough up both bonding surfaces with sandpaper. A smooth, glossy finish, especially on fiberglass, will resist bonding.

Silicone is especially suited to the gasket-forming procedure outlined on page 247 below.

Other types of sealants include polysulfides, such as some of the bedding compounds sold by Boat Life®, and polyurethanes, such as 3M 5200® and Sikaflex®. Check the manufacturer's directions for each type's applicability for certain jobs, such as whether or not it's suitable for use below the waterline or on plastics.

Be sure to note whether your bedding material has adhesive properties or not. Usually, adhesive substances are labeled as such. Don't use adhesives on parts that are likely to be taken apart again—some of the stuff bonds so well it will pull gel coat off fiberglass if you try to remove it.

Quantity of sealant isn't nearly as important as placement. A huge gob in the wrong place is a waste of time, effort, and materials, while a small, strategically placed bead of the proper material will work wonders.

Marine sealants are sold in small tubes and in cartridges for caulking guns. You should match container size to the job. Cartridges are more economical than small tubes, but most packages don't have very good means of resealing, and once a tube or cartridge is opened, its shelf life is fairly short. Use a good caulking gun, and keep a supply of several types of sealants on board.

When tracking leaks from the outside, learn to check all the obvious suspects first. Hull-to-deck joints are notorious leakers, because of the difference in stiffness between hull and deck, and the way they work against each other. Some boats use easily accessible, easily sealed fasteners, while other builders make it absolutely impossible to reach the joint without completely disassembling the entire boat. Generalities are pretty useless here, since every builder has his own ideas about what constitutes a proper hull joint.

Some joints have the exterior fasteners hidden by a strip of rub rail, while others are hidden in less obvious ways, or covered completely. If in doubt, before tearing everything apart, give the builder a call and ask for suggestions. If it turns out to be truly inaccessible, complain! Enough customers calling about things like that can have a real effect on future designs.

Other obvious leak points are grab-rail and lifeline stanchion bases and deck-mounted sheet winches on sailboats. These items get a lot of use, and work back and forth under heavy loads quite a bit, so leaks are common.

Tracing leaks is a matter of running water from a hose over one part at a time, and watching the leak point on the inside for the telltale drip (or waterfall, depending on circumstances). One thing that you can almost always count on is gravity. Water seldom flows uphill, but there are circumstances where it can seem to, such as when it builds up in a hidden location and spills out when the boat rolls. For now, though, let's assume that it flows downhill.

Start at the closest suspected point, and secure the hose in position or have a helper hold it in place. Run the water over successive probable leak points, starting with the lowest one and working uphill one point at a time.

At each fastener or exterior fitting, give the leak a minute or two to appear inside, longer if the point is separated from the leak by more than a few feet. It's not at all uncommon for the entrance point and the interior leak to be ten or more feet apart.

If you suspect a stanchion or grab rail, don't just glob a bunch of sealant on the outside edge and call it a day. It looks terrible and doesn't stop the leak for long, if at all.

You need to remove the fasteners and clean off the old material. You can sometimes find the cause of the problem at this point, if it's a crack in the fitting or other obvious flaw. Remove each bolt, and spiral a bead of sealant around it, starting a short distance from the nut end and running it all the way to the head, making at least one full rotation with the spiral. Apply another bead under the bolt head, and another under the washer backing up the nut. Apply thin beads— you don't need huge gobs of sealant to stop leaks. Then apply sealant around the inside edge of the stanchion or grab-rail base, and bolt it tight.

Ideally, with all of these sealing jobs, you'll have twenty-four hours or so of good weather in which to work. If you do, check the cure time of your sealant. Most run about twenty-four hours. If so, apply the sealant, and tighten the fasteners until they're just barely snug. Wait twenty-four hours, and then tighten completely. This gives the sealant time to set up, and it then does double duty as sealant and gasket.

Leaks around window frames are often fairly easy to track and repair, depending on your boat's construction methods. Some window frames come out easily, and others are nearly impossible. One thing they all have in common, though, is leaks.

Water dripping down the inside of a window frame usually indicates that the entire frame has to be removed and rebedded with fresh sealant. Occasionally, you can get by with just applying a dab of sealant at a strategic location on the outside of the frame, but in most cases, such a fix is only temporary.

Aluminum frame windows are the easiest to remove and replace. Generally, fasteners on the inside and outside are removed, and the frame pops out in one piece. If you're lucky. If you're not so lucky, the window will have teak trim around it, meaning that plugs will have to be removed and replaced, and the corners precisely fitted. See the "Access" chapter (page 54) for teak-plug details.

If you can pop the window out in one piece, first remove all the old sealant or bedding around the inside edge of the outside of the frame. Clean the bedding surfaces with acetone, and sand lightly. Removing large window frames is usually a two-person job, since you normally have to push out against the frame, and someone should be there to catch it.

Silicone sealant is probably your best bet, since future removal is pretty much a given. If you don't like silicone, check with a local glass shop for possible alternatives. Run a large bead of sealant all the way around the frame, near the outer edge so that it contacts the deckhouse side.

Reposition the frame, secure it in place, tightening the fasteners just enough to spread the sealant, and wait to tighten completely, as mentioned above.

MISCELLANEOUS

Keeping your engine clean is much easier if you take care of small things regularly. If you wait until the engine really needs it, you'll probably take one look at it and decide that it's not worth the effort. Oil, grease, and rust can accumulate steadily, and before you know it, the engine looks so bad that you don't even want to go near it, much less try to keep it looking good. A clean engine not only encourages regular maintenance and adds to resale value, it also makes it easier to spot leaks as soon as they occur. Some motors we've seen are so bad you could pour a quart of oil over the top of them and never notice the difference.

Keep the engine clean by washing it down periodically with a good, nonflammable solvent. There are several kinds made for automotive use that do a pretty good job.

Buy some touch-up paint and primer from your engine dealer. When you first notice signs of rust, sand or wire-brush the area, wipe it with a solvent, and then prime and paint. Keep the drip pan under the engine clean and dry. Just because it's there doesn't mean it has to be full!

At least once a year, clean out your chain locker thoroughly. Take out the chain and anchor rode and wash them down with fresh water. Scrub the inside of the locker with a solution of warm water and bleach, and rinse. If you use your anchor very often, mud can accumulate there, and get really foul if left untended.

If you've got an icebox aboard, give it a good cleaning once in a while also. A solution of about ½ cup of bleach to a gallon of water works well, and you should run some of it through the drain. Leave the lid off when leaving the boat unused for any length of time.

When cleaning interior items, don't use abrasive cleaners on fiberglass. Keep metal items clean and bright, and keep a coat of wax on them. Interior teak doesn't demand the attention that exterior teak does, but if it starts to fade, lightly sand and reoil it. Check with the builder to see what kind of finish was applied at the factory, and match it as closely as possible.

Regular interior care and maintenance will encourage you to keep things looking (and smelling) nice. Once things get away from you, it can be awfully hard to muster the motivation to tackle what have become major projects. A regular series of small tasks is much easier to keep up with.

Besides making your boat a more pleasant place to spend time, you're also protecting your considerable investment.

WINTERIZING

When laying up a boat for the winter, there are several things to take care of that will make springtime commissioning easier. Gasoline and diesel fuel shouldn't be allowed to sit for long periods of time without treatment. A fuel stabilizer such as Sta-Bil® should be added to the tank, and the tank then filled to minimize condensation. Diesel fuel should also be treated with a biocide (see the ''Diesel Fuel Systems'' chapter, page 88). Make sure that the additive you choose is compatible with your fuel system and filters. If in doubt, check with your engine or filter dealer.

Add the stabilizer first, and then fill the tank to mix everything thoroughly. Run the engine for a while, to allow treated fuel to run through the system, and to reach the carburetors or injectors.

Winterizing the engine is critical. Just pulling the boat out of the water and hoping for the best can get expensive. Water left in the engine's cooling system can freeze and crack the engine block, which almost always means you'll be shelling out money for a new engine.

If your motor is freshwater-cooled, the freshwater side of the system should already be protected with a fifty-fifty mix of water and antifreeze. You can check the condition of the coolant with an inexpensive antifreeze tester, available from auto parts stores. Coolant wears out, and should be changed annually.

Don't just buy the cheapest antifreeze you can find. Some antifreeze contains additives that aren't compatible with aluminum, and if you've got an engine with aluminum parts, you could be creating problems. If in doubt, ask your dealer or builder for recommendations. Also, stay away from coolant that supposedly seals leaks, since small water-jacket passages might be sealed off, restricting coolant flow and effectiveness.

Here's the drill for winterizing raw-water-cooled motors, and the raw-water sides of freshwater-cooled motors:

After the boat is hauled out, or at season's end, close the engine seawater sea cock or valve, and remove the hose. Put a fifty-fifty mixture of water and antifreeze into a bucket, and place the intake hose in the mixture. Start the engine, and run until the antifreeze mixture comes out the exhaust pipe. Kill the engine. The raw-water side of your cooling system is now protected with antifreeze.

Leftover coolant can be poured down the sink and shower drains, to displace any standing water trapped there. Remember to flush the lines with fresh water in the spring before the boat is launched, so that you can catch the mixture in buckets and dispose of it properly. If your boat isn't going to be hauled out, use potable water system antifreeze in the drains, to avoid pouring poisonous antifreeze into the water.

If your boat uses small, automotive-sized batteries, remove them from the boat and take them home. Store them in a place where they won't freeze, and keep them charged. Don't store them on a concrete floor—the moisture in concrete will cause the batteries to discharge. Separate batteries from concrete with wood blocks.

If removing the batteries is impractical, charge them fully before laying the boat up, and disconnect the cables. A fully charged battery won't freeze until it gets to about −70 degrees Fahrenheit, so if properly stored, and assuming that you don't live in an area where such temperatures are common, you should be pretty safe.

See the "Batteries" chapter for more information on batteries.

This is a good time to look over your electrical system, especially the connections on the engine and in the engine room. Winter dampness accelerates corrosion, so look over and clean off the alternator and battery terminals. Also, pay attention to the ground contacts, especially on the engine. These tend to suffer from neglect, and are easily corroded.

Remove the spark plugs from gas engines, and squirt a couple of tablespoons of motor oil into each cylinder. Turn the engine over a couple of times to coat the cylinder walls. Replace the plugs and tighten.

Your pressure water system will also have to be winterized. Merely running the pump until no more water comes out is not sufficient—there's usually just enough water left in the tank, the water lines, and the pump to freeze and break things.

These precautions are especially important since access to water tanks, water lines, and plumbing fittings is almost always terrible. As mentioned in the "Access" chapter, it's entirely possible to spend several hundred dollars to replace a broken fifty-nine-cent fitting.

First pump the tanks as dry as you can. Then, pour a mixture of potable water system antifreeze into the tank, enough so that the pump can pick up the mixture and send it through the system. The container will probably list additional instructions, if necessary. *Don't* use engine antifreeze—it's poisonous! Water system antifreeze can be obtained from most marine and recreational vehicle supply houses.

After you've added the stuff to the tanks, run the pressure pump until antifreeze comes out of each of the faucets, on both the hot and cold sides if your boat is so equipped. Turn off the power to the pump, and where practical, disconnect the hoses from the pumps. When disconnecting hoses isn't possible, leave the faucets open. Even if freezing does occur, the open faucets serve as pressure relief, limiting or preventing damage.

See the "Marine Heads" chapter for details on winterizing marine toilets and waste systems.

This is also a good time to inspect and service the through-hull fittings and valves. If you've got ball valves or sea cocks, move the handles back and forth, to see if they're operating easily. Too often, boaters neglect the sea cocks until a hose bursts or some other catastrophe strikes, only to find that the handle on the cock or valve is permanently frozen in place. Bad idea!

If the valves have grease fittings, remove the plugs and pump a generous supply of waterproof grease into each one. Sea cocks should be disassembled once a year, and internal parts inspected and lubricated.

If you're one of the unfortunate folks whose boat came equipped with gate valves rather than sea cocks or ball valves, now's the time to change them. Gate valves have one positive trait that endears them to many builders—they're cheap. The disadvantage is that, while the valve body is made of bronze, the valve stem is made of brass. Bronze

Fig. 16.1.   *Ball valve and gate valve.*

is an excellent metal for below-the-waterline applications, and brass is a terrible one.

The problem with brass is that it's an alloy of copper and zinc. If you've seen what happens to zinc anodes installed on underwater metal parts, you can imagine what happens to the zinc component of brass in the same situation—it dissolves. When the zinc corrodes out of the valve stem, it loses strength, and the valve can no longer be closed. As soon as convenient, replace all underwater gate valves with proper sea cocks or ball valves. (See Figures 16.1 and 16.2.)

Each through-hull fitting should have a tapered wood plug tied to it, in the event of catastrophic failure of the hose and/or the valve. The plug should be sized so that it can be driven into the fitting, stopping the leak. (See Figure 16.3.)

If your boat is going to spend the winter afloat, close all through-hulls below the waterline, except for cockpit and deck drains. Tape notes to the helm stations as a reminder, so that no one operates engines or equipment with the sea cocks closed.

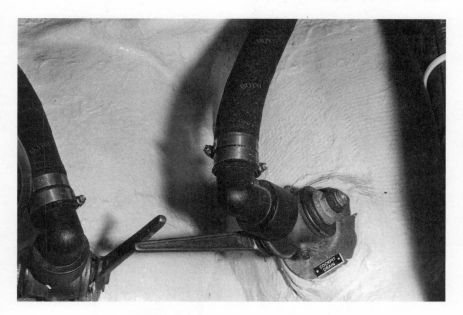

Fig. 16.2. *Sea cock.*

In the spring, remove the cover from the water-pump impeller, and check the impeller's condition. Replace it if it's showing signs of wear. Do this in the spring rather than in the fall, since a new impeller installed and left for the winter can take on a set, making the vanes more liable to break off when the motor is started up in the spring.

Fig. 16.3. *Wooden through-hull plug.*

SOURCES OF INFORMATION

FROM TIME to time, we've mentioned the standards prescribed and regulations enacted by various groups. We've also mentioned some other source works in passing, and it's important that you know how to obtain these materials so you can be as smart as we are.

The American Boat and Yacht Council is a private organization of representatives from the boating industry that formulates and publishes a set of standards for pleasure boats. The standards are very extensive, and contain quite a bit of material that's of interest only to builders. You can buy a complete set of the standards, or you can join the council and receive a set with your membership. You can also purchase copies of the individual standards, the price varying with each standard's size and complexity.

The ABYC has also compiled a complete set of the federal regulations applying to recreational boats, in a compact, easily referenced volume. Known as *Rules and Regulations for Recreational Boats,* it's a worthwhile addition to your library, especially if you plan on doing any work on your gasoline fuel system, the electrical system on a gas boat, or your marine head.

Their address is:

American Boat and Yacht Council, Inc.

P.O. Box 747

405 Headquarters Drive, Suite 3

Millersville, MD 21108

(301) 923-3932

The federal standards are also available in a volume entitled "Title 33 CFR, Parts 1–199" of the Code of Federal Regulations, available from:

Superintendent of Documents

U.S. Government Printing Office

Washington, DC 20402

These regulations are also available at public libraries.

The National Fire Protection Association publishes a volume of standards known as NFPA 302, *Pleasure and Commercial Motor Craft*. This volume doesn't cover nearly as much ground as does the ABYC book, but rather confines itself to the nuts and bolts of engine, fuel, electrical, cooking and heating, and fire protection equipment. The material is practical and easily understood by the layman, and costs a lot less than the complete set of ABYC material. NFPA's address is: National Fire Protection Association, Battery-march Park, Quincy, MA 02269.

You can order copies of this volume over the phone from NFPA's Customer Service Department, at (800) 344-3555. These standards are updated every few years, so if you've got an old volume lying around, give the association a call to see if there have been any recent updates.

Some excellent reference books are available for boat electrical systems. The ones we use most often are:

Your Boat's Electrical System, by Conrad Miller and E. S. Maloney, is published by Hearst Marine Books, 105 Madison Avenue, New York, NY 10016. The latest edition was updated in 1988. It contains over 500 pages of good, solid information on just about everything you need to know about electricity aboard your boat, covering theory and practice.

The 12 Volt Doctor's Practical Handbook, by Edgar J. Beyn, published by the Spa Creek Instruments Company, 616 Third Street, Annapolis, MD 21403, is another excellent source book. This volume is very practical, easy to understand, and contains lots of simple but very effective drawings, and a ton of practical tips. Spa Creek also publishes a book on alternator care and service.

The Bullet Proof Electrical System is sold by Cruising Equipment, 6315 Seaview Avenue NW, Seattle, WA 98107. It concentrates on 12-volt systems, and is more or less a long sales pitch for the battery and charging systems handled by Cruising Equipment. The book does contain quite a bit of useful information, and is well worth the seven or eight dollars they charge for it.

The *Battery Service Manual* is sold by the Battery Council International, 111 East Wacker Drive, Chicago, IL 60601. It's a 60-page technical manual covering battery care, service, charging, etc.

Boating Industry magazine publishes a *Marine Buyers' Guide* once a year. It contains names and addresses of boat and accessory manufacturers, listing everything by equipment type, manufacturer's name, and by brand name. This is a very useful volume, especially for that hard-to-find or oddball part that you inherited from parts unknown.

An annual subscription to *Boating Industry* includes a copy of the *Guide,* published in December, and costs about five dollars less than if you buy it alone. At any rate, write to:

Boating Industry
CCI
6255 Barfield Road
Atlanta, GA 30328
(404) 256-9800

International Marine Publishing Company distributes a mail-order newsletter listing a variety of books on boats, engines, and related subjects. The address is:

International Marine Publishing Co.
Division of Tab Books, Inc.
Blue Ridge Summit, PA 17294
(800) 822-8158

National Fisherman magazine is geared more toward commercial fishermen than toward recreational boaters, but it frequently has excellent technical articles on subjects of interest to pleasure boaters. The articles assume a basic knowledge of which end of the boat is which, and are usually more specific, and thus more helpful, than most of the very general information in the popular boating magazines.

National Fisherman is found on newsstands in most coastal areas, or you can get subscription information from:

National Fisherman
Subscription Service Department
P.O. Box 51014
Boulder, CO 80321-1014